In Defense of Disciplines

Interdisciplinarity and Specialization in the Research University

JERRY A. JACOBS

The University of Chicago Press
Chicago and London

Jerry A. Jacobs is professor of sociology at the University of Pennsylvania. He is co-author, with Ann Boulis, of *The Changing Face of Medicine: Women Doctors and the Evolution of Health Care in America* and, with Kathleen Gerson, *The Time Divide: Work, Family, and Gender Inequality*, among others.

The University of Chicago Press, Chicago 60637
The University of Chicago Press, Ltd., London
© 2013 by The University of Chicago
All rights reserved. Published 2013.
Printed in the United States of America

22 21 20 19 18 17 16 15 14 13   1 2 3 4 5

ISBN-13: 978-0-226-06929-6 (cloth)
ISBN-13: 978-0-226-06932-6 (paper)
ISBN-13: 978-0-226-06946-3 (e-book)
DOI: 10.7208/chicago/9780226069463.001.0001

Library of Congress Cataloging-in-Publication Data

Jacobs, Jerry A., 1955–
   In defense of disciplines : interdisciplinarity and specialization in the research university / Jerry A. Jacobs.
      pages ; cm
   Includes bibliographical references and index.
      ISBN 978-0-226-06929-6 (cloth : alkaline paper) — ISBN 978-0-226-06932-6 (paperback : alkaline paper) — ISBN 978-0-226-06946-3 (e-book)   1. Interdisciplinary research.   2. Interdisciplinary approach in education.   3. Communication in science.   I. Title.
      Q180.55.I48J23 2013
      001.4—dc23

                                                            2013011400

♾ This paper meets the requirements of ANSI/NISO z39.48-1992 (Permanence of Paper).

Contents

Figures

Tables

Preface

This project began innocently enough nearly a decade ago when I served a term as editor of the *American Sociological Review*. Because my tenure at *ASR* coincided with the centennial of the American Sociological Association, I was asked to publish some type of commemoration. I did so by writing about the most-cited papers published in the history of the journal, which appeared in a research note entitled "ASR's Greatest Hits."

I became curious about whether these articles were popular outside of sociology. They were. This curiosity led in turn to a grant from the Spencer Foundation to study the movement of ideas into and out of the field of education research. As this work proceeded, I began to recognize the tremendous number of initiatives designed to break down disciplinary "silos" in order to promote cross-disciplinary collaborations—at universities, grant foundations, and even the National Institutes of Health. I found this puzzling, since my research on education showed that ideas moved quite easily between fields under the prevailing arrangement of disciplines and research centers. I began to wonder if these reforms might make the university more like schools of education, which led me to the literature on interdisciplinarity and eventually to this book.

My skepticism about the promise of interdisciplinarity grew, yet I found myself presented with the opportunity to help establish an interdisciplinary scholarly association, the Work and Family Researchers Network (WFRN). I pursued this opportunity because I saw only benefits from promoting conversations and connections among work and family researchers from different disciplines and different countries if the goals of these efforts remain realistic. The concerns I express in this book are not to interdisciplinary conversations per se but instead represent objections to organizing the research university along interdisciplinary axes rather than around arts and science disciplines.

I have had many useful conversations about these topics over the course of this study, and I have not been able to keep track of every useful suggestion. Scott Frickel's collaboration on the *Annual Review of Sociology* paper helped to familiarize me with theoretical and empirical studies of interdisciplinarity. Indeed, his paper with Neil Gross (published in *ASR* when I was the editor) helped to rekindle my interest in the sociology of science, which had been dormant since my graduate school days. I thank Cynthia Fuchs Epstein, Susan Lindee, Eliza Pavalko, Daniel Raff, and Mitchell Stevens for giving me the opportunity to present portions of this research.

The greatest debts I owe are to Steven Brint, Andrew Abbott, Harvey Graff, Michèle Lamont, Paul DiMaggio, Randall Collins, Mitchell Stevens, Myra Strober, and Lowell Hargens. Richard Arum, Josipa Roksa, Steven Brint, and Kristopher Proctor graciously provided analyses of data from their own studies that are reported here and enrich the findings, especially in chapter 8. Richard Pitt shared useful data on dual majors, and Sarah Winslow tabulated the disciplinary backgrounds of education-school faculty. Howard White and Catherine McCain generously offered guidance on citation analyses. Rebecca Henderson's analysis of interdisciplinary journals made chapter 4 possible. Terry Labov, Sam Summers, Megan Kohler and Taylor Williams all provided excellent research assistance. The anonymous reviewers of the manuscript at the University of Chicago Press provided very detailed and helpful suggestions. Kathleen Gerson and Brian Powell generously offered unerring guidance and numerous editorial suggestions.

In addition to the Lyle M. Spencer Foundation, I am indebted to the Alfred P. Sloan Foundation for a grant to study cross-field connections in work and family research, and for a subsequent grant that facilitated the creation of WFRN. Kathleen Christensen, a senior program officer at Sloan, is the most helpful foundation grant officer I have had the opportunity to work with.

My family—Sharon, Elizabeth, and Madeleine—have always there for me, including the times when I most needed them. Their probing questions helped to clarify a number of issues examined here, and their love and support made the completion of this book possible.

Introduction

Higher education today faces a series of challenges: cash-strapped parents, declining support from state governments, questions about the future of research support, and increasing demands for accountability in terms of cost, graduation rates, and contributions to students' knowledge. While competition from foreign universities does not yet pose the threat to universities that it does to manufacturing, the question of how to position American universities in an increasingly global system of higher education preoccupies leading university presidents. Most recently, leaders in higher education have had to confront the question of how universities should position themselves relative to virtual courses and for-profit colleges. These tests may be largely external in origin, but they have produced serious internal debates about the future direction of higher education.

While all of these issues are important, an even more fundamental question centers on the very structure of the liberal arts. Are academic disciplines, such as biology, economics, and history, obsolete? The system of disciplines, departments, and majors, which became a standard feature of most American colleges and universities after the Second World War, is being questioned today in basic ways.[1] In part, this is due to financial pressures that have led many students to pursue applied fields of study. The shrinking share of enrollments naturally raises concerns about the place of the liberal arts. Despite the many successes the various disciplines have achieved as dynamic centers of intellectual activity, they face new scrutiny regarding their role in American higher education.

The case for interdisciplinarity, once advocated by a small number of critical writers, has become a popular idea in academia in the United States. Calls for closer connections and greater integration are increasingly common. Presidents, provosts, and deans espouse it in an effort to create a sense of excitement and novelty on their campuses while also seeking sizable contributions from foundations and prospective donors. For example, in her year-end message to members of the Harvard community, President Drew Faust mentioned multi- or interdisciplinary initiatives six times in just four paragraphs (2011). Julie Thompson Klein, the leading analyst in the field, suggests that interdisciplinarity has become ubiquitous, the "mantra du jour" in discussions of American higher education (2010a, 153).

Natural scientists also increasingly embrace interdisciplinarity. In 2004, a committee of the National Academy of Sciences, the National Academy of Engineering, and the Institute of Medicine published a report entitled *Facilitating Interdisciplinary Research*. A Massachusetts Institute of Technology "white paper" (2011) on the convergence of the life sciences, the physical sciences, and engineering pointed in the same direction. Perhaps even more significant is the fact that "interdisciplinarity" has become a special category of funding at the National Institutes of Health and the National Science Foundation. Some observers (Geiger and Sa 2009) see interdisciplinarity as a prominent feature of the twenty-first century university, whose role is to "tap the riches of science" and serve as an engine of economic growth. Interdisciplinarity has also become a touchstone in the humanities, although in different ways and for different reasons (Menand 2010a, 2001).

The concept of interdisciplinarity is not new but the frequency of conversations on this topic have become more frequent and concrete developments in this area have become commonplace (Braun and Schubert 2007). University presidents routinely announce multimillion dollar donations and grants for interdisciplinary activities, and cross-field initiatives of one form or another are popping up on campuses everywhere: well-funded research centers in the sciences; plans for cross-disciplinary or "cluster" hiring; seed money for new interdisciplinary research projects. Equally telling, the adjective "interdisciplinary" now generally has a positive valence.[2] Indeed, it sometimes seems that interdisciplinarity has become an end in itself. It was not always so. The negative connotations of the term, such as "undisciplined" and "flakey," remain sufficiently powerful that some promoters of interdisciplinarity still take pains to counter these images (e.g., Lattuca 2001, 3–4).

Interdisciplinarity can take on a wide range of meanings, from simply encouraging contact and communication among scholars in different fields to far-reaching proposals that involve restructuring doctoral training to efforts to dismantle the disciplinary system entirely. While some steps to facilitate communication across fields might raise few objections, the notion of a fundamental restructuring of the arrangement of disciplines poses serious questions about how the goal of interdisciplinarity should be advanced—in what ways, at what cost, and with what potential side effects?

Disciplines, as organized into departments, are the key units of social organization in higher education, although the role played by research centers at major research universities bridging structures is often overlooked. Publications, professional associations, and careers are shaped by the structure of disciplines. Disciplines, departments, and majors overlap to a considerable degree, although, as we will see, the correspondence is far from complete. The challenge to disciplines thus represents a potential revolution in the basic structure of academic life.

This book addresses the current wave of calls for more interdisciplinarity in academia. While any institution as large and complex as American higher education is vulnerable to criticism, critics of liberal arts disciplines have overstated their complaints and underappreciated the value of the interconnected system of academic disciplines. Discussions of interdisciplinarity have not always posed the hardest questions in a systematic way. While there are kernels of truth in some of the critiques, the sheer diversity of arguments on behalf of reform has made it more difficult to discern a clear alternative vision of the university. Suggestions for change point in many, often inconsistent, directions, and not all of these suggestions would necessarily improve the organization of the academy.

This book challenges the case for interdisciplinarity. I review the arguments on behalf of this perspective carefully and respectfully by concentrating on the main ideas of the some of the most thoughtful and influential analysts rather than considering every facet of every argument. The jungle of terminology in this field is just too thick and the arguments have more twists and turns than can be fully surveyed here. While this book delves into a wide range of topics, two sets of questions are central. The first concerns the extent of communication across fields of scholarly inquiry. While the criticism of disciplines as isolated silos has become commonplace, the evidence indicates that communication across fields is not only common but is remarkably rapid. The spread of techniques and ideas between fields is the rule and not the exception. The first half of the book takes on this set of concerns. Chapters 2–6 are concerned with these interdisciplinary exchanges.

The second half of this book approaches interdisciplinarity from the longer-term vantage point of the development of new fields of inquiry, rather than the eureka moment of scientific insight or the successful collaborative project. The principal question is whether successful interdisciplinary ventures over time come to emulate established disciplines, especially in terms of developing their own journals, professional associations, internal specialties, departments, and tendency to hire from within. The discussion explores what can be learned about the likely trajectory of new interdisciplinarity fields from prominent historical examples. Specifically, the prospects of interdisciplinarity for "integrating" knowledge are considered. Moreover, I examine whether interdisciplinarity is best viewed as a complement to existing fields of inquiry, a viable alternative, or simply a transitional phase traversed before a new field of inquiry. Chapters 7–10 examine the meaning and viability of an interdisciplinary university.

While my main focus is on scholarship conducted in research universities, undergraduate education is also an essential part of the disciplinary system. The analysis considers whether undergraduates are clamoring for greater integration in their educational experience, and, if so, in what sense. The promotion of integrative education for undergraduates turns out to be as complex and paradoxical as the quest of interdisciplinary research. In addition to the integration of knowledge across disciplinary lines, reformers have called for stronger connections between students' personal and intellectual development, between academics and real-life experiences, between theory and practice, and even between academic life and spiritual values. In intellectual terms, the challenges posed by the traditional liberal arts disciplines stem from their intellectual breadth, not their narrowness. Some aspects of integrative education may be best implemented in the context of the more circumscribed agendas of preprofessional education, but this comes at the cost of losing the scope and critical perspective offered by a liberal arts education.

A prominent theme of this work is the unavoidable fact of intellectual specialization in the face of the daunting volume of contemporary scholarship. Disciplines reflect a rough and admittedly imperfect response to the need to divide intellectual domains. With over twenty-eight thousand peer-refereed journals currently being published and hundreds of scholarly societies convening regular meetings, no new organizational arrangement for academia can hope to avoid some form of specialization. Indeed, it is quite easy to show that ostensibly interdisciplinarity fields are themselves elaborately divided into specialties, and that newly emerging interdisciplinarity projects quickly develop their own forms of segmentation. As we will see, interdisciplinary undertakings are likely to result in the proliferation of academic units rather than the consolidation of knowledge into a more unified whole.

While this study focuses on the development of disciplines in the United States, the issues raised here have implications for systems of higher education throughout the world. Universities everywhere are now indispensable for promoting economic development and broadening opportunities (Altbach 2011; Schofer and Meyer 2005). Countries around the world have been expanding their university systems, yet growing costs, exacerbated by the current economic crisis, lead policy makers to scrutinize educational investments ever more closely. In this context, global university rankings proliferate (Holmes 2011), and countries seek to identify the essential ingredients needed to build world-class universities. Claims that interdisciplinarity is vital to the successful twenty-first century university are heralded at a moment when "tectonic change" is not simply academic hyperbole but may well be upon us.[3]

In addition to asking hard questions, the book will present data that have played too small a role in earlier discussions. The research presented here draws on many data sources in order to shed light on the pivotal questions underlying the case for a more interdisciplinary form of higher education. Data are presented on cross-disciplinary communication patterns, including the timing of citations and the number of studies examining the important applied topics of the day. Counts of the number of research centers at the leading US research universities help to assess their potential to foster interdisciplinary communication. An examination of 789 peer-reviewed journals founded in 2008 was conducted to see how many were interdisciplinary in orientation. Dissertation abstracts in American studies along with a wide range of other materials offer insights into the trajectory of this interdisciplinary field over its sixty-year history.[4] These and many other types of data are described in the appendix in order to provide sufficient detail about these investigations without unduly distracting from the flow of the text.

The book is organized as follows. Chapter 2 examines the main criticisms leveled at disciplines that radiate from the assumption that they have become "silos." This view holds that excessive compartmentalization inhibits communication between fields and stifles innovation. Disciplines are viewed as the wrong units to tackle the vexing social problems of the day, most of which are multifaceted and require insights from diverse areas of expertise. Increasingly, the case is being made for the university as an engine of economic growth; again, disciplines are seen as limiting rather than maximizing this potential. Finally, disciplines are criticized for impeding a more holistic and integrated undergraduate educational experience.

Chapter 3 presents an institutional theory of academic disciplines. This approach emphasizes the vibrant forces for innovation at work within disciplinary contexts. Discussions of interdisciplinarity generally ignore or downplay competition over status and resources among scholars within a field, competition among specialty areas within disciplines as well as competition among disciplines. In other words, disciplines are dynamic, with both internal and external forces propelling scholarship forward. Disciplines thrive because they create effective research communities. While research specialties can run the risk of becoming insular and stagnant, over time this problem tends to self-correct because such groups have increasing difficulty in recruiting new generations of students, maintaining the allegiance of mid-career researchers, and garnering the resources needed to pursue new agendas.

The keys to this institutional approach are the breadth of individual fields and the fuzzy boundaries between them. A review of the number of degree-granting disciplines and departments suggests that the number of liberal arts disciplines is quite small. Evidence on the rise of academic specialization shows that the modern academic department was common during the 1930s but generally had very few faculty members. The expansion of the liberal arts disciplines into intellectually vital units is only two-thirds of a century old.

Chapter 4 emphasizes the unavoidable need for specialization by examining the size and rapid growth of new research and scholarship. It also considers the issue of scholarly communication from the point of view of research journals with an analysis of 789 academic journals founded in the year 2008. A typology of six different approaches to interdisciplinary publishing is presented, including a paradoxical category, specialized interdisciplinarity. These are journals that cut across traditional disciplinary lines, but they do so in a focused and relatively narrow manner. The chapter concludes with a discussion of the forces that mitigate the push toward specialization by pulling in the direction of intellectual synthesis.

Chapters 5 and 6 address issues of scholarly communication. Chapter 5 asks whether disciplines can indeed be viewed as isolated silos. The evidence indicates that all fields are connected to one another to varying degrees, as is evident in maps of science derived from the Web of Knowledge database. The flow of particular ideas across disciplinary boundaries is tracked. Evidence is presented on the prevalence of research directed at important social problems, as are data on the ubiquity of research centers. I also consider why the "silo" idea remains so appealing despite the considerable evidence against it.

Chapter 6 builds on the ideas developed in chapter 5 by considering the timing of intellectual exchanges. If "isolated silos" is not a tenable model of communication patterns among disciplines, it may nonetheless be the case that some fields are slow to pick up on the latest research techniques and the most promising conceptual advances. The idea of an intellectual delay is specified by mapping out "receptivity curves" that trace the timing of attention to research in particular disciplines. This concept is put into action by considering the case of research and scholarship moving into and out of the field of education. While critics of educational scholarship abound, especially in schools of education, this analysis suggests that excessive delay in responding to the latest developments in the liberal arts disciplines is not characteristic of education scholarship.

Chapters 7 through 10 consider the practicality and viability of interdisciplinarity as an alternative to the current system of disciplines. This part of the book shifts attention from the communication of individual ideas to the longer-term trajectory of interdisciplinary units. Chapter 7 considers the question of whether successful interdisciplinary lines of inquiry will congeal into new research fields or disciplinary subspecialties. It revisits some of the themes developed in chapters 2 and 3 and includes a discussion of the multiple meanings of the term "integration." The theme of antidisciplinarity that weaves through much of the thinking of reformers is considered here.[5] Despite the appeal to some of breaking down institutional structures, successful academic fields require social organization that serves as the functional equivalent of a discipline. The enduring success of any interdisciplinary arrangement will thus require the recreation of discipline-like units that function as intellectual, social, career, and political systems. The discussion emphasizes the importance of research communities to the vitality of the current disciplinary system. Chapter 7 also includes a brief review of extant interdisciplinary doctoral degree programs.

American studies, one of the first academic fields to embrace the principle of interdisciplinarity, is the topic of chapter 8. I summarize its main intellectual currents and organizational evolution since the late 1940s. In interdisciplinary terms, American studies can be viewed as having achieved the "transdisciplinary" intellectual synthesis that is sometimes held up as the holy grail of interdisciplinary knowledge, only to lose that synthesis at a later date as new political and intellectual developments took the field in very different directions. American studies has contributed to a substantial expansion of the domain of cultural and material studies, and in this respect it is a good case of "subject matter expansion" along the lines outlined by Walter Metzger (1987).

In other respects, however, the example of American studies represents a mixed model at best, as it has by no means unified the study of American society and culture. Instead, it helped to foster a climate that was receptive to the creation of additional interdisciplinary fields of inquiry, including African American studies and women's studies. As a result, in this case, interdisciplinarity did not foster the consolidation of academic units in the humanities and social sciences but instead furthered the proliferation of new academic units. The point of this analysis is not to criticize the many fine scholars who have contributed to American studies over the years, but rather to assesses the long-term trajectory of a prominent interdisciplinary field and its relationships to its intellectual neighbors.

In chapter 9, which considers interdisciplinarity in the context of undergraduate education, many unexpected conclusions emerge. Connections between diverse subjects are surprisingly common, as is evident from the prevalence of cross-listed courses, team-taught classes, and dual majors. Trend data since the 1970s indicate how small many of the interdisciplinary majors are. This finding, among others, questions the notion that undergraduate demand is responsible for the expansion of interdisciplinary programs.

The chapter reviews the meaning of the concept of "integrated knowledge" in the context of teaching undergraduates. Integrative education is paradoxically more feasible and more likely the narrower the student's specialty. In terms of enrollments, interdisciplinarity does not represent the principal competitive challenge to the traditional liberal arts disciplines, but instead it is applied fields, including business, criminal justice, and communications, that have seen considerable expansion in the number of majors. Ironically, the traditional disciplines have created the intellectual underpinnings of many of the applied fields that now draw substantial undergraduate enrollments.

In chapter 10, a number specific proposals designed to promote interdisciplinarity are considered. The most elaborate proposals for the interdisciplinary university necessarily involve the creation of new forms of scholarly communities. If they succeed, they will do so by reproducing many of the elements of the disciplinary structures they seek to replace. There is also a risk that they would contribute to a decline in the power of academic departments and a concomitant rise in the centralization and consolidation of decision making. Ironically, an interdisciplinary university is less likely than present arrangements to protect the very academic independence that reformers seek to promote.

Chapter 10 also considers a number of specific proposals that have been advanced, including cross-disciplinary faculty appointments, "cluster hiring," eliminating departments and disciplinary degrees, more extensive interdisciplinary training of graduate students. These reforms are assessed in terms of their likely consequences, along with the implications they have for the autonomy and viability of existing disciplines. Many of the proposals advanced thus far would do little over the long term to consolidate knowledge into broader themes, since specialization will remain a powerful force. Some of the reforms designed to integrate knowledge would instead contribute to the proliferation of specialized interdisciplinary niches. Academic departments in particular and faculty members in general are likely to find their position in university affairs weakened as a result. Rather than promoting interdisciplinarity as an objective, I consider better ways to strengthen the liberal arts and sciences.

In short, this book challenges many of the premises of the case made for interdisciplinarity. While it surely has its place in the modern university, interdisciplinarity should not be viewed as an end in itself. In organizing research, advancing knowledge is the goal, and reforms should be undertaken when they represents the best means of achieving that objective. Proposals for a transdisciplinary university remain vague and based on sketchy premises.

Disciplines as currently constituted are central to the creativity and dynamism of the modern research university. The arts and sciences are specialized in many ways, but they are also fundamentally broad and dynamic. Discipline-like organizational arrangements in one form or another are needed and will continue to be needed. Proposals for reform of the research university should place the disciplines at the center, and strive to protect and enhance their central role.

Reinforcing the liberal arts ethos throughout the academy is vital to the future of American higher education. Despites its many weaknesses, idiosyncrasies, and internal contradictions, the arrangement of the liberal arts into disciplines, departments, and majors has produced remarkable intellectual advances in a short period of time and has provided the conditions for relatively unfettered critical inquiry. While these arrangements must evolve and adapt to changing circumstances via experimentation and reform, a wholesale reorganization of this system is unlikely to improve on the current system. Scholarly communities are pivotal to the success of the research enterprise and the preservation of academic independence. In the end, this book is a defense of the liberal arts disciplines and the research universities in which they have thrived for the last sixty years. I hope that a reexamination of the strengths of these institutions helps them to thrive for at least another sixty years.

PART ONE

Academic Disciplines, Specialization, and Scholarly Communication

The Critique of Disciplinary Silos

Proponents of interdisciplinarity have offered diverse objections to existing scholarly disciplines. The large literature on interdisciplinarity, however, can be distilled into five main criticisms. Disciplines, it is charged, inhibit communication, stifle innovation, thwart the search for integrated solutions to social problems, inhibit the economic contributions of universities, and provide a fragmented education for undergraduates. Amidst these varied lines of criticism, the central complaint is that disciplines have become isolated "silos." This fundamental weakness is a premise that undergirds the other main charges levied against disciplines.

While the current reform movement is significantly more vigorous than earlier ones, the case for interdisciplinarity is not new. A detailed review of an edited volume from the 1960s raises many of the themes that continue to echo today. This will be our point of entry. The balance of the chapter examines the five themes just outlined.[1]

Donald Campbell: Voids versus Overlaps

Donald Campbell, a prominent social psychologist, defined the problem of disciplines as one of sets of important social topics that receive little or no attention because of the inward orientation of disciplines. This essay appears in a collection edited in 1969 by Muzafer and Carolyn Sherif, along with a number of other interesting contributions. The issue with the American organization of academia, as Campbell saw it, was "'the ethnocentrism of disciplines,'

Portions of this chapter draw on and further develop themes addressed by the author and Scott Frickel in their 2009 essay in the *Annual Review of Sociology* (Jacobs and Frickel 2009).

i.e. the symptoms of tribalism or nationalism or ingroup partisanship in the internal and external relations of university departments, national scientific organizations, and academic disciplines" (1969, 328).

Disciplines not only act like tribes or ethnic groups in advancing their group interests, but the principal tendency is to direct intellectual focus toward the center of the field. Each discipline defines a hierarchy of topics, and enterprising scholars seeking to have a successful career understand they need to address the issues defined as significant in their area. Disciplinary pressure thus acts as a centripetal force that pulls scholars toward issues defined as central and away from topics that are considered marginal to the field. So powerful are these inward-directed forces that topics at the margins or peripheries of fields lie fallow and are neglected.

Campbell effectively captures his view of the state of academia with a diagram (see figure 2.1). Each discipline is seen as a tightly knit configuration of people and ideas, with overlapping strands of research taking the shape of a ball. Between these tightly knit units are voids, domains neglected by science. In Campbell's view, academic fields are scattered like galaxies across large stretches of empty space. A more effective organization of science would devise a way to cover the entire span of social experience and remove the gaps between fields, which he labels "the fish-scale" model of "omniscience."

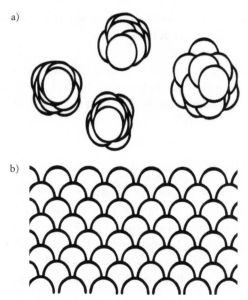

FIGURE 2.1. Donald Campbell's fish-scale model of omniscience. a. Present situation: Disciplines as clusters of specialties, leaving interdisciplinary gaps. b. Ideal situation: Fish-scale model of omniscience. Source: Adapted from Campbell 1969.

Campbell's wonderful diagram captures the idea of academic silos quite effectively, although he does not use this term. As soon as he presents the diagram, however, Campbell hedges: maybe these empty voids are not ignored but relatively neglected; perhaps there is attention to these interstitial issues but this attention is not as useful as it could be because the practitioners in different fields ignore one another's contributions. In other words, perhaps the problem is that disciplines are operating on different planes rather than truly intersecting. In the end, Campbell never tries to label the void. In other words, he does not offer a list of the important topics that he thought were neglected by scholars at that time.

The notion of fields being isolated is a common argument for interdisciplinarity, but it is by no means the only one. Campbell's diagnosis of the problem was quite different from that offered by Stanley Milgram, who argued that all interesting problems touch on a variety of disciplines. In his essay discussing the "small world" experiment that attempted to ascertain the number of links needed to connect two disparate individuals, Milgram wrote, "The small world problem is a relatively new topic of investigation, and thus has not yet been 'claimed' as the exclusive property of any one discipline. Communications specialists, city planners, social psychologists, mathematical sociologists, political scientists, and historians have felt free to talk about the problem. Let us hope that it does not become the 'private property' claimed by any single discipline, which then posts 'no trespassing' notices on it, and thereby denies it the benefit of new insights from a variety of sources" (1969, 119). In Milgram's view, then, the typical pattern is not huge chasms separating disciplines but rather intellectual overlap and potential turf wars.

In their own essay, Muzafer and Carolyn Sherif also emphasize the *overlap* between fields, rather than the gaps between them, as the central problem: "man does not arrange his problems or divide them up neatly along lines laid down by academic disciplines. On the contrary, there is a great deal of overlap in the subject matter of topics considered by the social science disciplines" (1969, 7). The objective of interdisciplinary research, for the Sherifs, is not the solution to particular practical problems, such as how best to allocate police to reduce crime. Rather, the fundamental goal of interdisciplinarity should be to check the validity of findings across fields.

> We propose that each discipline needs the findings from others as a check on the validity of its own generalizations. For example, formulations about intergroup relations, or leader-follower relations, or power relations cannot be one thing when taught in a department of psychology and another thing when taught in a sociology department, and still another in a political science

department, if any of the disciplines in question claims validity for its formu-
lations. (1969, 5)

Campbell does not consider the possibility that disciplines might compete
with each other for resources by claiming the latest, sexiest, and best-funded
topics as their own. One might expect disciplines to venture forth into unchar-
tered territories that abound in Campbell's map of the intellectual universe.
Enterprising scholars would seek to build their own reputations by claiming
some of this void for themselves and in turn for their discipline. After all,
tribes and nations pursue expansionist strategies: why not disciplines?[2]

In addition to territorial conquest, another, more prosaic, motivation for
academic entrepreneurship is offered by Raymond W. Mack, another con-
tributor to the Sherif and Sherif collection. He notes the role of money in
shaping the intellectual terrain. Mack is clearly uncomfortable with the subject of financial support for research, which he seems to think pulls scholars
away from their most fundamental and most important ideas: "research em-
phases in social science tend to go where the money is. Because this a somewhat embarrassing point, let us be brief about it" (1969, 55). He proceeds to
cite examples from medical sociology and the study of poverty: when funding
became available, sociologists were drawn to these fields. What neither Mack
nor Campbell considers explicitly is that the lure of research funds might
serve as a countervailing force to what Campbell sees as the "ethnocentrism"
of disciplines. If topics such as educational disparities, global warming, or international terrorism are interdisciplinary by nature and become well funded
because they become seen as urgent social problems, researchers from different fields may well feel inclined to explore them.

Campbell does not consider the possibility that disciplines might be dynamic entities because of competition between scholars, or even competition
between specialty areas within a field. Nor does he offer any evidence regarding the ostensible failures of disciplines. But there is an even more basic
flaw in Campbell's argument. His suggestion that powerful, inward-directed
forces make disciplinary scholars narrow and limited assumes a rather neat,
structured internal hierarchy of problems. But disciplines, according to
Campbell himself, are more like a "hodgepodge" of disparate areas of inquiry
and groups that are only affiliated in the loosest of ways. The "hodgepodge"
terminology would seem to undermine the argument that disciplines narrow
the vision of researchers. If one can affiliate with any number of subareas
within one's field, and if the configuration of the hodgepodge evolves over
time (not a possibility Campbell specifically explores), then it would be hard
to see how disciplines force scholars into rigid boxes.

In trying to distinguish between overlaps and voids, I believe the facts point more in the direction of the Milgram/Sherif side of this debate. The educational challenges facing our society may serve as an example. Many believe that national and individual success in a global economy requires academic achievement, and much public discussion has been centered on how to improve our educational system. Academics have not shied away from this problem. Psychologists have delved into educational issues, as have sociologists, anthropologists, political scientists, economists—all have had much to say about educational issues, as have faculty members in schools of education. The case of education, which is examined in detail in chapter 5, suggests that the overlap model is more applicable than the void model. Researchers and scholars from various fields do not avoid but instead actively seek out social issues when they believe that insights from their discipline may be informative. Many academics want their discipline to be relevant, and by conquering widely recognized problems, their personal prestige, along with that of their discipline, is enhanced. Moreover, research funding not infrequently accompanies attention to social issues.

This review of Campbell's essay and its companions suggests that the case against disciplines is not a single argument but a set of related and sometimes contradictory positions. The literature on interdisciplinarity has expanded considerably since the late 1960s, yet many of the lines of reasoning developed then continue to inform the current debates.

The writings of today's reformers echo the concerns raised in the Sherif volume. In his introduction to the *Oxford Handbook on Interdisciplinarity*, Robert Frodeman (2010) includes among the criticisms of disciplines "excessive specialization, the lack of societal relevance and the loss of the sense of the larger purpose of things are tokens of these concerns" (xxxii). He warns against the dangers of "disciplinary capture, where new questions become just one more regional study or specialist's nook" (xxxiii) in terms that closely resemble Stanley Milgram's in the late 1960s.[3]

Disciplines as Silos

One of the central claims of advocates of interdisciplinarity is that disciplines become inwardly focused, and actively block attention to developments occurring in other fields. As we have seen, criticism of disciplines is not new, but the use and popularity of the term "silo" is a departure. Neither Campbell (1969) nor Klein (1990) used the term, although both anticipated this idea.

The association between academic disciplines and this terminology has become commonplace, especially since 2000. A Google search of the terms "disciplinary silos" and "academic silos" yielded 6,000 and 4,000 hits, respectively (conducted January 1, 2011). A search in Google Scholar found these terms were rarely used before 2000 (20 instances), 55 times between 2000 and 2005, and 450 since 2006.

There is reason to believe that the term spilled over from the business world to academia. An Ngrams (a Google search of terms in English-language books) analysis reveals that the term "organizational silo" increased in use between 1995 and 2000, to a greater extent and well before the term "disciplinary silo" came into use. The critique of disciplines thus may have landed in a cultural setting receptive to this line or criticism.

The term as applied to academia sometimes emphasizes ignorance of developments in other fields, and sometimes points to the importance of informing the public of a scholar's findings. The suggestion that silos stifle innovation is often wrapped together with the idea that real-world problems are bigger than any one discipline can handle. Sometimes the term refers to the distance between university life and "the real world."

For example, writing in the *Chronicle of Higher Education* in 2008, Juan Gilbert emphasizes the way silos make it more difficult to follow developments in related fields.

> It is clear that diversity research and programs take place within specific academic disciplines, or "silos." We don't reach beyond our own silos enough to know that colleagues in other silos are wrestling with similar issues and ideas. (Gilbert 2008)

The need for academics to try to reach a broader audience is another way in which the term silo is employed. For example, an NSF graduate fellowship recipient (Neal 2011) offered this advice online to other NSF candidates:

> "Tie it [your research] to a real-world problem. No one wants an academic that just hides in his/her cubicle, only working in an academic silo, with no desire to make an impact in the real world. How can *you* or *your own work* be disseminated to society? (Neal 2011)

Silos, it is often suggested, inhibit innovation. Thus, Alan Saltiel, the director of the University of Michigan Institute for Life Sciences, explains:

> We have so far brought to the Institute 20 talented researchers and their groups, spanning disciplines and bridging interests to flex a more powerful scientific muscle than might be found in a single academic silo. We hope that collaboration among these hundreds of capable and diverse researchers will help us solve problems faster and with more ingenuity. (Saltiel 2011)

Mark Taylor conveys two facets of this notion of remoteness when he bemoans the separation of academia from society: "Colleges and universities are more isolated from the world and inwardly fragmented today than ever before" (2010, 47).

The associations of the term "silo" are not in keeping with the self-image most universities have as open and lively centers of research and learning. The term is probably most often associated with grain storage but may sometimes conjure up missile shelters as well. In both cases, silos are remote, lonely, and quiet places with high walls; they are designed for insulation; they protect their contents from the external environment.

Jamming Communication

At its core, the silo thesis emphasizes the inadequacy of communication across fields. This ostensible problem might have a variety of contributing causes. For example, it might be difficult to keep abreast of technical advances in diverse fields because of insufficient training. The unending tide of new information could compound this problem. As we will see, there are some twenty-eight thousand peer-reviewed scholarly journals currently being published, and the number continues to grow. A further obstacle to communication might be genuine disagreements over intellectual frameworks. Thus, cultural anthropologists have an elaborate approach to culture that does not comport easily with economists' assumptions regarding the utility maximization of self-interested individuals.

However, each of these explanations would raise questions for interdisciplinarity. Thus, if communication requires intensive training and specialized knowledge, then any serious interdisciplinary alternative would have to figure out a way to effectively train scholars in a variety of specialties. If the problem is too much information, no simple solution presents itself. If intellectual differences, what Karin Knorr-Cetina (1999) calls diverse "epistemic cultures," are at the heart of the matter, then again this would pose serious challenges for any attempt at transdisciplinary synthesis.

Thus, several prominent explanations for gaps in communication are problematic from the perspective of interdisciplinarity, and consequently these explanations tend to be de-emphasized or ignored. The root cause of silo-ism leveled by critics is willful ignorance—the collective, coordinated, and deliberate effort to make one's own knowledge esoteric and thus inaccessible to outsiders and the related strategy of keeping the ideas of other specialists at bay. This claim can be belittled as mere "turf wars," or it can be elevated to a contest for intellectual authority, autonomy, and legitimacy.

Either way, what is at stake is the ability of specialists in a field to "own" their intellectual domains, to be seen as legitimate and ideally exclusive authorities. The sins of disciplines are thus essentially viewed as political and perhaps cultural rather than intellectual. If scholars could just be persuaded to set aside the self-interested and self-directed concerns of their disciplines, then the hard work of making true synthetic scholarly advances could begin. Reformers have generated a lengthy list of critical epithets along these lines. Klein's compilation includes "feudal fiefdoms" and "warring fortresses" policed by "no trespassing notices" (1990, 77).

From time to time, advocates of interdisciplinarity acknowledge that communication between fields does occur. For example, Allen Repko suggests that "disciplines are fluid and their boundaries porous" (2008, xiii). Klein's own empirical work (1996) is even more explicit regarding the openness in the humanities.[4] Focusing on the humanities in the UK, Joe Moran (2010) reaches a similar conclusion. Lisa Lattuca (2001, 243–45) suggests that disciplinary boundaries have softened in recent years. Repko suggests that "disciplines are fluid and their boundaries porous" (2008, xiii). Yet the emphasis on silos still dominates, and it does so for a good reason: the openness and fluidity of current academic fields undermines the main critique of the disciplinary system.

Stifling Innovation

The failure of disciplines to communicate with each other slows down the advancement of knowledge because researchers in one field are not poised to take advantage of insights and breakthroughs developed in other disciplines. Thus, the premise that disciplines are isolated silos is fundamental to the claim that they fail to innovate. If disciplines were open or porous, then they would not stifle innovation.

But the charge goes deeper. Disciplines become self-referential, small communities of performers enchanted with the sound of their own voices, concerned more with their position in the field's status hierarchy than with advancing knowledge. While this uncharitable description certainly applies to some professors who unfortunately have more ego than insight, the question is whether this is a general pattern, and whether it inheres in the organization of disciplines.

At its extreme, the suggestion is that graduate students simply reproduce their adviser's work. For example, Mark Taylor, writing in the *New York Times*, warned that "the emphasis on narrow scholarship also encourages an educational system that has become a process of cloning. Faculty members cultivate those students whose futures they envision as identical to their own pasts" (2009, A-23). This charge is leveled more frequently at the humanities than it is at the obviously more dynamic fields such as the biomedical sciences. The review of the field of American studies presented in chapter 8 shows that this claim is not fair even for the humanities, which have undergone noteworthy theoretical and empirical transformations in each decade since the 1950s. But rather than focusing on the specific issues pertaining to the humanities, the tendency is to elevate this problem as being characteristic of disciplines in general.

Diversity of ideas is held up as the source of innovation, and any set of social constraints is seen as impeding the exchange of ideas. For example, Myra Strober draws on noted historical figures, academic administrators, and cognitive psychologists in making the case that "diversity fosters creativity" (2011, 22).

While there is much to be said for the possibility of intellectual synergy bringing diverse sources together, there are also strengths deriving from the deep training in a subject matter that disciplines can provide. In fact some ideas are too distant from others to serve as useful points of connection. Some points of cross-disciplinary dialogue are ripe for development while others are not. In short, while complementary skills and insights can be valuable, not all interdisciplinary conversations are successful. Also lost in the clamor for interdisciplinarity is the simple fact that many advances require digging deeper within a field rather than borrowing from other places. The virtues of disciplines as centers of intellectual creativity are developed in chapter 3.

Thwarting Solutions to the World's Problems

The litany of the world's challenges—poverty, hunger, disease, water shortages, and climate change among them—is prominently featured in discussions of interdisciplinarity. As we have seen, this line of reasoning dates to Donald Campbell and no doubt even earlier.

The logic here seems inescapable: the social problems confronting society are numerous and serious; all require insights from disparate fields; many of these challenges are new and thus the disciplines that are rooted in divisions that emerged in the nineteenth century may seem increasingly out of sync with the society's needs.

Taylor cites the case of diabetes:

> The causes of this epidemic are not only medical but social, political, economic, environmental and psychological as well. The only way we can begin

to meet the challenges this epidemic poses is by bringing together experts and professionals from all fields to share their knowledge and develop productive strategies. (2010, 151–52)

One could substitute AIDS or any number of other social issues and most of Taylor's words would remain applicable.

Yet a closer examination reveals the issue is far more complex. One way to reframe the debate is to recognize that many social issues are multifaceted. This way of putting the matter suggests that there may be specialized knowledge from disparate fields that needs to be brought to bear on the issue at hand. The question is how closely these different facets need to be in contact for research to advance.

For example, the challenges of the AIDS epidemic require medical investigators who have the skills and training needed to develop drug cocktails that suppress the virus. The fight against AIDS is also aided by epidemiologists who can map out the likely trajectory of the epidemic based on an understanding of social networks. The question is whether the laboratory scientists need extensive training in epidemiology and vice versa. Awareness of each other's work is certainly important, but this might be promoted by conferences, review articles, and research centers. It is not at all clear that a department or school of AIDS studies is the best solution to this problem. This topic is considered more systematically in chapter 7.

There are many historical examples of research centers and even schools developed to focus on a topical area and in order to address the social issues that arise in that terrain. One prominent case is schools of education. If education is an important social challenge, and if bringing all fields relevant to education together under one roof is the answer, then schools of education would seem to fit the prescription. In other words, the organization of schools of education resembles the interdisciplinary future envisioned by some reformers. Yet educational shortfalls and disparities remain stubbornly with us after a century of vigorous educational research based in schools of education (Labaree 2004). (Educational research is discussed in more detail in chapter 6.) A note of caution is thus in order: cutting a ribbon for a school of global health or a school of global warming will not automatically generate solutions to these vexing social problems.

Throttling Economic Growth

The image of colleges and universities as ivory towers governed by their own rules at a considerable distance from the "real world" coexists with the reality

that higher education is a major industry. The considerable public investment in universities naturally leads to questions about whether taxpayers'
dollars are being well spent. More broadly, the economic role of universities,
both locally and nationally, is being emphasized to a greater extent than ever.
Universities seek to replicate the part that Stanford University played as an
incubator for Silicon Valley start-ups and that of the Massachusetts Institute of Technology in nurturing computer and biotechnology firms in the
Boston area.

As Roger Geiger and Creso Sa (2009) put it, universities are increasingly
encouraged, indeed expected, to "tap the riches of science." The rationale for
this approach is simple and compelling. The economic success of advanced
countries depends on working smarter rather than working harder. In other
words, jobs that involve few skills, such as unskilled manufacturing, will gradually migrate to low-wage countries. To maintain and improve their standard
of living, affluent countries will have to lead in the knowledge sectors of the
economy.

There are many ways that universities can contribute to economic development, including the development of a skilled technical labor force, and
the advancement of basic research that over time would diffuse into various
products and processes. Historically, these indirect contributions have been
seen as among the university's primary missions. Increasingly, however, universities have been encouraged to play a direct role in the process of innovation. If economic success in a knowledge economy depends on maintaining
a competitive edge, and if this competitive edge requires a steady stream of
innovation, and if universities are to play a central role in this system, then it
stands to reason that universities should be encouraged to play a direct role in
the innovation process. In some fields, new patents have begun to take their
place alongside grants and publications as a metric for measuring faculty productivity (Berman 2012).

This theme becomes a strand of the interdisciplinarity narrative because
innovation increasingly becomes linked to product development, and research teams in the corporate setting are often multifunctional and multidisciplinary in nature (Rosenberg 1994, 152; Vissers and Dankbaar 2002; Olson
et al. 2001).[5] In other words, if the task at hand is to bring a new skin cream to
market, even one that is based on the latest in dermatological research, then
a diverse team is needed, including basic scientists, clinicians, specialists with
a background in managing clinical trials, financial analysts, and marketing
specialists, among others. The set of skills thus goes well beyond those likely
to be found in the faculty of a biochemistry department in a school of arts
and sciences or a dermatology department based in a medical school. Even

without the sales component, translating basic research into a product with market potential involves several broad skill sets.

Many of the most prominent new interdisciplinary centers on university campuses cited by Geiger and Sa are in the life sciences—Bio-X at Stanford, computational biology at Berkeley, genomics at Duke, life sciences technology at Cornell (Geiger and Sa 2009, chapter 5). Each of these offers the promise of a stream of new patents and potentially lucrative biomedical products.

These centers typically involve huge investments of resources in one main area, such as genomics at Arizona State, translational sciences at the University of Pennsylvania, and nanotechnology at the University at Albany–SUNY. Only a few universities, including Duke, Stanford, and the University of Pennsylvania, can make investments on this scale in more than one area. The risks are (a) the big bets may not pay off; (b) these examples will be taken as a model and applied to contexts where they do not apply; (c) there may be a lack of fit between these ventures and the educational missions of the university, and (d) the costly failure of commercial ventures will hurt universities over the long run.

Fragmenting Undergraduate Education

Despite its many successes, higher education in the United States has been criticized for a variety of reasons, with the complaints about disciplines just one among many. Colleges and universities are routinely castigated for their high cost, for limited student access, and for low completion rates (Martin 2011; Tierney and Hagedorn 2011; College Board 2011). The interdisciplinary critique often takes the form of an aggravating offense: not only is college too expensive, but it does not provide the fully rounded education it promises.

Here again there many interrelated lines of reasoning. A central argument is that the liberal arts disciplines are disconnected from one another, making an integrated undergraduate educational experience difficult to achieve. The problem is attributed to the incentive structure, which elevates departmental needs over the general good. A recent report on general education at the University of California paints a more nuanced picture:

> Over time, universities have delegated responsibility for courses and curriculum to academic departments, producing a situation of extreme decentralization. As a result, curricular development is seldom in the portfolio of deans' responsibilities. Departments may be motivated to offer general "service" courses to non-majors out of a desire to swell their enrollments, but departments are rarely motivated to develop general, interdisciplinary offerings.[6]

In chapter 9, evidence is presented on the prevalence of team teaching, cross-disciplinary courses, and cross-listed classes that points to a more complex reality.

A related concern is that distribution requirements that mandate a certain number of courses from different areas of the curriculum do not produce true intellectual integration (for example, see Czerniak et al. 1999). In interdisciplinary parlance, distribution requirements may generate a certain disciplinary range, and perhaps even a degree of multidisciplinarity, but not a truly integrated intellectual experience and certainly not a peak of trans-disciplinary synthesis. This perspective emphasizes the need for more connection among diverse academic subjects.

Some argue that there is too much emphasis on research in universities and not enough on teaching. In this vein, the reliance on graduate teaching assistants is often seen as deleterious to undergraduates, and inextricably linked to the organizational structure of the research university. For example, Taylor (2010) suggests that research universities depend on instruction by inexpensive teaching assistants. In this way, the emphasis on research and the neglect of teaching responsibilities by faculty go hand in hand.

Another line of argument focuses on the need for more integration between academic and real-world experiences.[7] This complaint begins with how material is taught rather than what is taught, but often ends with a revised agenda for a college education. There is evidence that students find it difficult to retain most of the content contained in lectures (Fink 2003), and that hands-on instruction has a more enduring impact. Some stress the need for more practical experiences to enable to students to connect their studies to their postcollege lives. Others stress the need for more volunteer experiences, more emphasis on education as a preparation for citizenship, and even for building more bridges between intellectual goals and spiritual understanding (Parker and Zajonc 2010). A related point is the need to inculcate in students the ability and desire to become lifelong learners (for example, Candy 1991; Vaill 1996).

A major point of divergence within the integrative education perspective is the issue of commonality versus differentiation. Many writers today focus on the individual student who is thought to require education that is individualized and directly engages his or her unique interests and abilities. This differs from the emphasis of an earlier generation of writers on a common intellectual core that provides each generation with a shared basis in contemporary culture (Bell 1966).[8] While of course it is possible to pursue both objectives to some degree, there is only so much time to devote to these concerns while students also find time to learn specialized subject matters and skills.

Moving past the criticisms of the current arrangements yields an even more diverse range of interdisciplinary prescriptions. These diverse philosophical perspectives can be embodied in a range of practical reforms. For some, integrated education takes the form of a truly synthetic capstone course combined with an interdisciplinary research project. Some seek to reorganize departments so that they focus on "problem-oriented programs" (Taylor 2010, 157), while others simply seek an expansion of service learning programs and other experienced-based initiatives (Eyler, Giles, and Astin 1999; National Service-Learning Clearinghouse 2012).

Applied and preprofessional education is usually not the main concern, as is the case with must discussions of interdisciplinarity. A theme developed in chapter 9 is that applied programs tend to be more integrated but at the cost of being narrower in scope than the liberal arts. This paradoxical pattern points to the ambiguities and complexities in the meaning of the term "integrative education."

Conclusion

Calls for more interdisciplinary connections on campus have a long history. A brief review of one set of such arguments from the late 1960s reveals many continuities with contemporary concerns.

While the current disciplinary arrangement of colleges and universities has been criticized from many vantage points, a central complaint is the inward focus of disciplines. Their resemblance to silos is at the core of a series of ostensible flaws. The chauvinistic, tribal, or inward orientation of disciplines is at the root of diverse complaints ranging from stifling innovation to fragmenting undergraduate education.

The American system of higher education encompasses thousands of schools, hundreds of thousands of faculty members, and millions of students. In any system this large, examples of shortcomings will not be hard to come by. The question is whether these problems are inherent in the nature of disciplines themselves. If disciplines are fundamentally flawed, then it is imperative that we search for an alternative. However, before we rush to tear down disciplinary silos, a closer examination of the reasons behind the current arrangements is in order. Perhaps the critics have not provided a complete and balanced appraisal. As we will see, many of the charges leveled against disciplines are not supported by the evidence. But first we will turn to a consideration of some theoretical arguments on behalf of a division of academic labor rooted in disciplinary arrangements.

3

Dynamic Disciplines

Thus far the discussion of interdisciplinarity has been proceeded in the absence of a formal definition of academic disciplines. In this chapter, a new definition of academic disciplines is developed. A discipline is defined as a broadly accepted field of study that is institutionalized as a degree-granting department in a large number of colleges and universities. This institutional theory of disciplines builds on the work of Stephen Turner but differs in some important respects. Whereas Turner emphasizes the way disciplines are closed and operate as employment cartels, the approach developed here highlights a number of features of disciplines that contribute to their dynamism and vitality.

In this institutional approach, the question of how many schools offer a degree in a particular field becomes a matter of central importance. Consequently, the empirical portion of this chapter focuses on counting the availability of degree offerings in various academic fields on college and university campuses.

The number of liberal arts disciplines is actually quite small. Broad fields such as psychology and history have attained the status of academic disciplines in the US system of higher education, whereas narrower fields of research, such as gerontology and demography, have not yet attained disciplinary status as defined here. The issue of stand-alone departments, versus sharing a department with another field of study, is also considered. The data suggest that joint or hybrid departments are remarkably common even for well-established fields such as physics. The presence of multiple fields coexisting under one departmental roof is especially common for foreign language instruction.

Evidence on the size of departments indicates that academic disciplines in their current form are remarkably recent developments in the United States,[1] dating back no earlier than the Second World War. Before that time, academic departments were so thinly staffed that they were more like lonely outposts rather than the buzzing centers of intellectual life that they have become. As disciplines grow they become increasingly differentiated internally; they also contribute to the emergence of related new fields. This pattern is illustrated with examples from the field of sociology.

The upshot of this discussion is to reverse the notion of disciplinary silos as applied to liberal arts fields at the most basic definitional level. Disciplines are broad, not narrow. Their breadth generates internal differentiation and competition, which contributes to their vitality. They frequently blur into each other, given the lack of clear jurisdictional boundaries; this is one among many factors that promote the borrowing of ideas and techniques across disciplinary lines.

Institutionalized Disciplines

The search for a satisfactory definition of academic disciplines typically begins with a search for their common intellectual properties (Krishnan 2009). This path is strewn with obstacles, since disciplines vary tremendously in the attributes of their theories, logics, and techniques, and the nature of their domains (Knorr-Cetina 1999). The fuzziness of disciplinary boundaries is often taken as a sign of the arbitrariness of the entire enterprise (for example, see Calhoun and Rhoten 2010, 103). Yet disciplines are recognizable entities, and they can be properly defined once their social and organizational features are given their due.[2]

A discipline is a form of social organization that generates new ideas and research findings, certifies this knowledge, and in turn teaches this subject matter to interested students. An institutional discipline is a recognized area of study that typically is identified with an academic department and an undergraduate major. An individual with a doctoral degree in a discipline is responsible for mastery of a certain body of knowledge, has contributed to that knowledge base in some way, and may be selected to teach the next generation of students in this field. There are no doubt brilliant insights obtained by individual observers of the natural or social world who have no formal training. For example, amateur bird-watchers surely know a great deal about the behavior of the species they observe, and their insights may match or even surpass those who have PhDs in biology or ecology. But institutionalized disciplines are different: they are organized groups that certify knowledge in the university context.

Defining a discipline is not unlike defining a profession.[3] It is a status that many fields seek and is one that is not always accepted by our institutions or the public at large. A long-standing debate in sociology has centered on which attributes of professions are essential in distinguishing them from other occupations (Greenwood 1957; Wilensky 1964). A similar approach might point to the common features of academic disciplines: they typically are organized into scholarly associations; their members meet at national and international conferences on a regular basis; and their research is typically published in peer-reviewed journals (Krishnan 2009, 9).

In the definition of institutional disciplines, it is the organizational arrangement of the field on university and college campuses that is most crucial. Disciplines produce PhDs who in turn are hired to teach undergraduates and graduates in the same field. Disciplines are based in departments and confer degrees. This attribute distinguishes broad disciplines from many important but smaller fields of scholarship that have not been able to attain control of their own academic departments. When departmental openings in a field are filled exclusively by PhDs with degrees of the same name, the field in question can be considered to have attained a great degree of autonomy and authority.

For Turner, to be a discipline, a field must have an "internal labor market," that is, a set of arrangements that make it typical to hire specialists in the field.[4] Without this, nonspecialists can obtain employment, and there is consequently less control over the specialized knowledge of the field. "Disciplines, this suggests, are cartels that organize markets for the production and employment of students by excluding those job-seekers who are not products of the cartel" (Turner 2000, 51). Turner's emphasis on disciplines as employment cartels, which emphasizes the exclusionary nature of disciplines, may lead a reader to assume that Turner has a negative view of disciplines. And indeed Turner does express concern over the risks of "fossilization" of disciplines.[5]

But Turner notes positive features of disciplines as well. For example, "The fact that a lot of people are trained in fundamentally the same way makes it possible for them to effectively make judgments about the quality of the work done by other people and for regimes of training to themselves be evaluated for their rigor" (Turner 2000, 52). The absence of an internal labor market, Turner suggests, makes interdisciplinary programs vulnerable to many external factors, which, he suggests, is "the answer to the question of why interdisciplinary efforts so often fail" (Turner 2000, 56).[6]

Turner's approach represents a good starting point because it emphasizes the social organization of disciplines. Yet this perspective can be improved upon by extending the analysis to more fully consider the conditions that contribute to the founding and persistence of disciplines. The two key elements Turner's approach misses are (1) the prerequisites for establishing an internal labor market in the first place, and (2) the continuing legitimacy needed to maintain it. To establish an internal labor market for a field, its advocates need to convince colleges and universities throughout the system to establish their program. Given the pressures of institutional isomorphism (institutions mimic and copy features from their peers, as explained by DiMaggio and Powell [1983]), fields are greatly advantaged if they are large enough for most, if not all schools, to adopt them. Thus, the pressures that derive from the need to be accepted on campuses throughout the country lead to the broad reach of disciplines; that is, they need to claim a large substantive or theoretical domain in order to warrant general adoption.

Institutionalized disciplines are thus distinguished from smaller fields by their larger size and scope. A small and specialized field is not likely to be established uniformly by colleges and universities across the country, and consequently it is not likely to have the scale needed to generate an internal labor market. According to this definition, physics is a well-institutionalized discipline while astronomy is less well ensconced. There were over 850 colleges and universities that offered degrees in physics in the United States in 2009, and tenured appointments are typically reserved for those with PhD degrees in physics.[7] In contrast, only eighty-seven colleges and universities in the United States offer degrees in astronomy, along with thirty-two additional schools offering degrees in the composite field of astrophysics. It is possible for a college or a university to forgo having an astronomy department, but it is more difficult to skip having a physics department. (See table 3.1.)[8]

Raising questions about the status of astronomy as a discipline may be jarring to some readers, given the signal place of the heavens as an eternal object of human fascination and the key role that astronomy played in the emergence of modern science. This example is chosen precisely to highlight the fact that the intellectual or epistemic status of a field of inquiry is not sufficient to make it an institutionalized discipline, which requires its widespread incorporation as a department on most college and university campuses.

No discipline is found in its own department in all colleges and universities. This distinguishes disciplines from the professions, since all states have doctors and lawyers, architects and engineers. A number of fields approximate universal adoption but most do not completely achieve this standard.

Turning to a more recent entrant, translational science is emerging as a field focused on the transfer of basic biomedical research into medications

TABLE 3.1. Number of schools featuring degree programs in liberal arts fields, 2009

	# schools offering	
	---	---
	Bachelors degrees	PhD degrees
Humanities		
English	1,378	134
History	1,267	150
Philosophy*	879	100
Classics	288	41
Art history	413	54
Linguistics	121	53
Classics	288	41
Natural sciences		
Astronomy	119	62
Biology	1,345	226
Chemistry	1,146	162
Computer science	601	26
Mathematics	1,233	83
Physics	812	191
Psychology	1,389	252
Social sciences		
Anthropology	462	92
Economics	827	153
Political science/government	1,073	124
Sociology	1,039	112

* Includes thirty-two philosophy and religion programs.
Source: *College Blue Book*, 36th edition.

and other cures for diseases and ailments. Translational medicine can boast of newly established journals (for example, *American Journal of Translational Research*), scholarly societies (for example, International Society of Translational Medicine), and research centers and institutes springing up on universities around the United States. For example, the University of Pennsylvania is opening the Institute for Translational Medicine and Therapeutics with over eight hundred investigators based in a new, state-of-the-art $370 million medical research complex.[9] However, despite the reference to "the discipline of clinical and translational science" by the Society for Clinical and Translational Science (2011), translational science is not currently an institutionalized academic discipline as I use the term here in that there are currently no PhD programs, no academic departments, and no undergraduates are as yet gaining degrees in this field.

By the same standard, sociology is an institutionalized discipline: most colleges and universities have a sociology department; sociologists with sociology PhDs are hired to teach sociology to graduate students (in universities) and to undergraduates (in both universities and colleges). In contrast to sociology, demography is a specialized area of research that is not an institutional discipline. Demography is a respected field of scholarship: it has scholarly associations (for example, the Population Association of America), peer-reviewed journals (*Demography, Population and Development Review*), and national and international meetings. But there are no undergraduate degrees offered in demography, no stand-alone demography departments, and only a handful of doctoral programs offering a degree in demography. Thus, graduate students specializing in demography must find an academic position in a related department, typically in sociology but sometimes in anthropology, economics, public health, or area studies. Demographic specialists may also seek employment in governmental agencies such as the US Bureau of the Census or nongovernmental organizations concerned with issues of population and health, such as the World Health Organization.

Undergraduate majors are thus a key component of this disciplinary system, since hiring decisions are based in part on enrollments. Without sufficient undergraduate majors, even the most venerable fields of study, such as astronomy, will have difficulty maintaining faculty positions and even a separate academic department. Similarly, while physics is among the most recognized and respected of academic disciplines, its small number of majors has resulted in the loss of independent departmental status at many colleges and even some universities. Fewer schools offer degrees in physics than they did thirty years ago, and physicists increasingly share a department with astronomers, as we will see in more detail below. Many students taking physics courses do so in order to fulfill general science requirements. In this way, physics takes on a service-department role with respect to undergraduate education even though the field is highly regarded in intellectual terms.[10]

The second amendment to Turner's approach is to note the importance of obtaining and preserving disciplinary legitimacy. Even though they represent somewhat closed employment enclaves, disciplines must continually maintain the support of a number of important constituencies: prospective studies, deans and administrators, and colleagues in other fields.[11] Without sufficient undergraduate majors, the number of faculty openings will come under pressure. Without a steady stream of graduate students, the field will be unable to reproduce itself. Without a degree of respect accorded by colleagues, candidates for promotion and tenure in a field will face an increasingly skeptical audience. Without various indicators of external legitimacy—grants, awards, and conferences—deans will grow wary of making additional investments. Thus, while Turner emphasizes the ways that disciplines resemble cartels, the fact is that they remain dependent on the recognition accorded by various publics. These external demands can offset the tendencies toward intellectual insularity and purity that can turn fields inward.

This definition of institutionalized disciplines distinguishes a limited set of liberal arts disciplines from much a larger set of smaller fields that are not part of the standard repertoire of academic degrees and departments. Compared with many smaller fields, liberal arts disciplines typically have a broad domain that is not precisely defined. For example, sociology is broader and more encompassing than a number of related areas of inquiry: demography, gerontology, public opinion research, or social network analysis.

The breadth of disciplines has two immediate organizational consequences, one internal, one external. Internally, the broad scope of disciplines results in the emergence of internal differentiation. For example, sociologists are currently organized into fifty different subgroups, and these in turn are each amalgams of many research nodes and specialties. Externally, disciplines' breadth and imprecise definition means that they frequently blur into each other.

The broad terrain covered by disciplines raises questions about their internal coherence. For example, in the field of sociology, there is little that connects experimental social psychology and comparative historical studies. Lattuca (2001, 244–45) suggests that members of a discipline sometimes disagree on its boundaries.

Thus, critics maintain, disciplines are loose assemblages of disparate specialties united only in their distinction from other fields. If disciplines are arbitrary arrangements that arose for accidental historical reasons, then breaking them down and reassembling them into interdisciplinary themes should be a relatively easy step.[12]

The fact is that the breadth of a field is one of the key prerequisites for its widespread incorporation by colleges and universities. It is only by making a convincing claim over a broad intellectual terrain that a field can make it onto the relatively short list of disciplines featured by most schools. While the intellectual distance between subfields often presents a challenge to faculty, it also represents a discipline's strength. The clash of disparate specialties and perspectives within a field generates intellectual sparks and efforts to bring intellectual order to the disparate units. Moreover, the competition of these subgroups for students and other resources helps to keep them moving forward. A field needs to demonstrate advances, or at least describe a narrative of advances, in order to draw in students.

In their discussion of the field of information systems, Avison and Elliot (2006) suggest that there is dynamic tension between clear intellectual lines of demarcation and intellectual vitality. Too rigid a definition of a field could stifle innovation, since certain questions or topics would be ruled out of bounds, yet if the scope of the field is too broad, it risks the loss of intellectual coherence. The sweet spot between these two extremes, they suggest, leaves room for creativity while allowing for sufficiently unified training to take place.

Andrew Abbott (2001) develops a theory of internal divisions within fields that emphasizes the elaboration of logical distinctions. Each field in the social sciences, he suggests, divides along a series of dimensions, each of which then divides again along the same lines. Thus, polarities such as pure versus applied, quantitative versus qualitative, and culture versus structure, serve as points of division, yet each divides again along the same lines, setting off a chain of distinctions that ultimately produces a fractal pattern.

The theory developed here is not inconsistent with Abbott's approach, although it does not depend on his fractal pattern, which some may misread as simply a merry-go-round of academics endlessly arguing with each other. The emphasis here is on what Metzger (1987) calls "domain expansion," that is, the development of new techniques, new methods, and especially new topics for exploration. The continual search for novelty is driven in part by competition between specialties and between fields for resources and legitimacy. This competition occurs across a variety of domains, including access to students, cultural influence, research grants, fellowships, and faculty positions.[13]

The institutional theory also emphasizes the size and scope of disciplines, which in essence serve as preconditions for Abbott's fractal processes. In particular, access to students is emphasized as a key resource that is often neglected in such discussions. In other words, academics must not only argue with one another over endless points of scholarly distinction but they must convince new generations of graduate and undergraduates students to join the party. Without their participation, and the broad legitimacy required to facilitate the regular recruitment of new generations of students, disciplines would not have the faculty positions and other resources needed to sustain themselves and the fractal process would come to an end.

Disciplines are self-organizing and do not have any formal legal status. In contrast, professions have legal standing. For example, laws in many states prohibit the practice of medicine without a license. There are no such sanctions for the practice of sociology or physics without a license. As Abbott (1988) has shown, even strict rules regarding professional boundaries are insufficient to prevent turf disputes. Where medicine ends and nursing and social work begin is often difficult to define, and in practice it becomes a matter of negotiation. The system of academic disciplines magnifies this pattern, since there is no system for policing the fuzzy boundaries between fields.

Thomas Gieryn (1983, 1999) drew attention to the issue of social boundaries in science. In Gieryn's usage, "boundary work" is principally about making claims about the authority of scientific knowledge, in other words, the distinction between science-and nonscience. This notion has been extended (Lamont and Molnar 2002) to efforts to maintain symbolic boundaries between a wide range of groups, including disciplines. The imprecise boundaries of academic disciplines facilitates competition among fields, and they allow for innovation without requiring the relabeling of disciplines. Thus, when economists began to explore the economics of the family (for example, Becker 1991), scholars from other disciplines, including sociology and anthropology, could not turn to any court for a cease and desist order. No injunctive relief was available for this type of academic trespassing. Rather, scholars of the family from other fields could incorporate insights from economists while arguing for the value of their own perspectives to various audiences, including prospective students, deans, and funding agencies.

The system of disciplines is thus characterized by extensive differentiation within fields and the lack of sharp boundaries between fields. There is no central authority that polices the boundary between sociology and political science, for example, the way border guards police national boundaries. Both fields examine social movements, public opinion data, civil wars and revolutions, the influence of corporate elites on political decision making, and a host of related issues. To take another example, the precise point where chemistry ends and biology begins has shifted over time as research questions have evolved and new techniques for studying biochemical processes have been developed. Thus, disciplines are not silos but rather can be thought of as sharing a dormitory space where they raid each other's closets and borrow each other's clothes. This system is dynamic; competition occurs on many levels within fields as well as across fields. The very structure of the disciplinary system tends to push in the direction of competition and over time will generally arrest any tendency toward intellectual fossilization.

Liberal arts disciplines are distinguished from applied and preprofessional fields by their greater emphasis on exploring the nature of its intellectual domain for its own sake. While disciplines are useful and devote tremendous efforts to solving social problems, they also attempt to systematize knowledge without having to focus on immediate vocational or practical concerns. Thus, disciplines are useful but are not exclusively oriented to immediate utility.

Disciplines differ from applied fields of study in the relative emphasis on the intrinsic value of knowledge. Academic disciplines emphasize their understanding of an intellectual domain and deemphasize the set of skills that will make degree holders immediately employable, whereas the emphasis in applied and preprofessional programs is the reverse. Yet this distinction should not be overstated. Academic disciplines, such as economics, for example, impart practical skills to undergraduates: it would thus be inaccurate and misleading to characterize liberal arts disciplines as devoid of utility outside of academia. Other fields impart a range of skills, including writing, research, and critical reasoning skills. Nonetheless, there is a difference in emphasis between an economics degree obtained from a school of arts and sciences and a degree in finance obtained in a business school. The emphasis in finance is on training the next generation of financial analysts, whereas the emphasis in economics is on teaching its subject matter. Disciplines pursue knowledge for its own sake to a greater degree than do other fields. This difference is a matter of degree and is not absolute on either side of a bright line.

A final element of the disciplinary system that warrants mention is that cooperation prevails as a norm on campuses. Disciplines surely compete with one another, but they do so as units within the same college or university. Thus, rival software companies compete more vigorously than do sociologists and psychologists. In the former case, defeat may mean going out of business. In the academic case, victories and defeats involve issues of status, resources, positions, and the like, but only in exceptional cases does the losing field go out of existence, and even then, it is usually hard to pinpoint a rival field that is responsible for its demise.

Committees with members from diverse disciplines meet routinely to decide matters large and small: to approve new courses, to award graduate fellowships, to advise the university administration on budgetary issues, and to make recommendations regarding promotion and tenure cases. Colleagues from different fields get to know and respect one another and gain an appreciation for the richness and diversity of campus intellectual life. Of course, disagreements often arise and conflicts ensue. Michèle Lamont (2009), for example, stresses the challenges that occur in the context of interdisciplinary grant review committees, but even she concludes that by and large decisions are made in ways that are broadly accepted by committee members. In short, the fact that cross-field committees function every day on campuses nationwide is often overlooked.

To return to the tribal metaphor so popular with critics of the disciplines, disciplines as tribes are remarkably peaceful and cooperative. Academic battles rarely go beyond wars of words. In the international arena, cooperation between formal adversaries is a noteworthy event. For example, the international space station was hailed as a remarkable feat of international cooperation between former cold-war rivals. By comparison, academic disciplines collaborate on a host of less visible projects on a routine basis. Thus, the notion of disciplines as rivals akin to tribes or nation states, while colorful, surely overstates the distance and degree of conflict between fields.

Departments and Research Centers

Academic departments are responsible for instruction across the terrain of each discipline. Given the breadth of most disciplines, this goal is difficult to meet in practice even for research departments based in the largest state universities, and it is completely out of reach of departments in small liberal arts institutions.

The need for broad coverage implies that departments are not first and foremost designed to maximize research productivity, since they must balance research objectives with the need for a sufficient range of skills to cover the field's teaching needs. In general, departments seek to strike some balance between a concentration of research skills and the breadth required to cover an adequate range of courses. The tension between these divergent objectives is one source of intradepartmental conflict for which universities are well known. Despite this and other sources of conflict, this hybrid system works because undergraduates help to provide funding stability and graduate students provide a source of research assistants. The combination of attending to teaching needs in conjunction with a substantial commitment to research enables university-based departments to take the long-term view needed for addressing the most fundamental and challenging lines of research and scholarship.

While academic departments are not necessarily designed to maximize research output, there are other units on campus that put this mission front and center. Research centers provide an important context for cooperation between fields, since most claim to be interdisciplinary. These centers can be developed to address a particular constellation of research issues or to address certain issues of the day, and they also represent a convenient arrangement for organizing external research funds. As we will see in chapter 5, research centers are ubiquitous in large research universities, and are often more common than discipline-based departments. In addition, research centers and other campus-based programs represent opportunities for cooperation between disciplines. Research centers are cross-cutting arrangements that are unique to academia. The system of professions has no analogue. Thus, there is no institution that connects the engineering and medical professions the way that academic bioengineering programs connect biology and engineering scholarship. Disciplines thus may be territorial and focused on political strategies that enhance their own standing, but via research centers and other programs across campus, they connect and cooperate with other domains of scholarship.

One might argue that the department has become an organizational convenience and is no longer an intellectual necessity because of the growing strength of international professional communities and the cosmopolitan nature of academics in most colleges and universities. But without a department, there is no hiring, no stable employment, and relatively little faculty input into decision making.

Scientific and Intellectual Movements

To become a defined field of inquiry, intellectual advances require more than a solitary scholar with a brilliant insight. Disciplines emerge because of the successful organizing efforts of a group of champions. Scott Frickel and Neil Gross (2005) introduced the term "scientific/ intellectual movement (SIM)" to describe the intellectual and social processes involved in the development of new intellectual fields and subfields. Frickel and Gross suggest that the development of a new field, such as the establishment of the discipline of psychology, or a subfield, such as the "status attainment model" in sociology, is analogous to the development of a new social or political movement, such as the civil rights or women's movements. In both cases, success depends on compelling ideas, sufficient financial and social resources, and effective organizational structures. Opportunities in the intellectual and social landscape are also indispensable.

Frickel and Gross suggest that new ideas are more likely to find a receptive audience when they resonate with established ideas. For example, when the founders of American studies sought to develop a more unified conception of American culture, they latched onto anthropological conceptions of culture that were already available. SIMs also benefit from social as well as economic resources. For example, Frickel and Gross note that new fields are more likely to emerge when high status actors "harbor complaints against what they understand to be the central intellectual tendencies of the day" (2005, 209). Advocates for a new field solicit the financial support needed to host conferences, edit newsletters and journals, and establish regional and national organizations. Key resources in the academic realm are research grants, fellowships, and especially tenured faculty positions.

An insurgent intellectual movement can help to bring about the creation of a new academic field. We will see this in action in chapter 8 with the emergence of American studies as an interdisciplinary area of research. SIMs can also help to overthrow an old approach and replace it with a new one. This too can be seen in the field of American studies, when a new generation entering the field in the late 1960s and 1970s overthrew the "myth and symbol" approach and brought in one that embraced women's studies, African American studies, regional analysis, and a critical stance toward American's position in the international arena. Finally, SIMs can also contribute to the differentiation of specialties within a field. This point will be illustrated later in this chapter with examples from sociology.

The discussion thus far has defined some of the essential features of university-based academic disciplines and the social forces that help bring them about. Now we can turn to the implications of this theory for our understanding of the disciplinary landscape in academia.

Institutionalized Disciplines: Organizational Measures

Liberal arts disciplines are thus distinguished from smaller fields or subfields by their breadth and ubiquity, and they are distinguished from applied and preprofessional fields by their greater emphasis on knowledge for its own sake. This approach makes disciplines as much a matter of their prevalence as their intellectual character. In other words, a field is more established as a discipline if it is represented in a wide array of colleges and universities.

Only a small number of fields have achieved the status of fully institutionalized disciplines in the college and university context in the United States. There are eight fields that are close to ubiquitous: the great majority of institutions that grant bachelors degrees offer these fields of study represented. These disciplines are biology, chemistry, English, history, mathematics, political science, psychology, and sociology—each one of these fields is ensconced in over one thousand institutions (see table 3.1).[14]

Three additional fields are nearly as common: economics, physics, and philosophy. While courses in these fields are widely available, degrees in these fields are occasionally not available. Economics sometimes falls under the purview of business schools, and thus some institutions offer degrees in business rather than economics. Physics and philosophy both suffer from low enrollments, and thus offerings in these fields are sometimes offered as supplemental to other science degrees (in the case of physics) or humanities degrees (in the case of philosophy) rather than as stand-alone degree programs. In any event, while not quite universal, these three fields are well established as liberal arts disciplines that largely define what it means to be a liberal arts school.

Another tier of fields follows rather substantially behind: computer science, anthropology, art history, and classics. Each of these is represented in hundreds of institutions, but not all institutions feel the need to offer a degree in each of these fields. These are all disciplines in Turner's sense of having a well-established internal labor market, but their presence is not currently viewed as an indispensable part of the liberal arts constellation.

A number of other fields are frequently found in research universities but are often absent in liberal arts colleges. Fields such as astronomy and linguistics are respected fields of inquiry that typically are present mostly in research universities. Consequently, without a market of positions available in liberal arts colleges, the number of PhDs produced in these fields is much smaller, and they do not constitute a defining element of the set of liberal arts fields.

The placement of biochemistry is an interesting one, since at first glance it would seem to be a hybrid field and thus by definition interdisciplinary. If counting degree-granting institutions were our sole criterion, then biochemistry would rank as a well-established discipline. In 2010, 463 colleges and universities granted a bachelor's degree in biochemistry, while 244 programs, including a number based in medical schools, offered doctoral degrees in this field. However, biochemistry often does not have its own department and thus is in a weaker position to control hiring decisions than are fields that typically control their own departments. (Data on the scarcity of stand-alone biochemistry departments are presented below.) In this schema, it is less a matter of biochemistry's intellectual vitality than its organizational position that raises questions about its disciplinary status. In some ways, biochemistry is its own fully established discipline, while in other ways it remains a specialty within the fields of chemistry and biology.

Ecology is another field with a great deal of scientific stature but limited representation as an undergraduate degree program. Only 114 schools currently offer degrees in ecology, and most are under the aegis of a biology department. A total of 534 bachelor's degrees were awarded in the field of ecology in 2008, compared with 54,384 in general biology. It may be that growing interest in the environment and climate change will increase interest in this field, but it seems most likely that ecology will follow biochemistry as an important area of inquiry with only partial autonomous disciplinary status.

The reason that having separate majors and departmental status is important is that these are the lynchpins of the disciplinary employment system. Autonomous disciplines have their own departments, their own majors, and their own doctoral degree programs. While journals, conferences, awards, and honors are all attractive accoutrements, an independent discipline cannot exist without an enclosed employment loop rooted in majors and departments.[15]

The last set of cases to be considered are languages, which help to illustrate several points. Let us agree that every language is equally worthy of study, although as a practical matter languages that are spoken by large numbers of people, and especially by economically powerful countries, are likely to garner more interest and resources. The fact that some languages are well ensconced in American universities says more about the university system and its priorities than it does about the languages themselves. While universities aspire to cover all knowledge, they often fall short of this goal in practice. Perhaps nowhere is this gap more evident than in languages. An estimated six to seven thousand languages are currently spoken, many of which are expected to become extinct over the next fifty years (Harrison 2007). Despite their large scale and considerable resources, even the largest American university can aspire to cover only a small fraction of them.

Ironically, for all the lofty rhetoric about addressing the challenges of globalization, only a few languages regularly have degree offerings in American universities. While considerable numbers of students take a course or two, since many schools maintain a foreign language requirement, the number of students majoring and receiving degrees in foreign languages is quite small. Brint and his colleagues (2012) report that Romance language programs bore a disproportionate share of programmatic cutbacks, even before the 2008 economic crisis.

Table 3.2 presents a variety of different indicators of foreign language instruction. Spanish is the most commonly available language in which students may obtain a bachelor's degree, with some 888 programs granting 9,278 degrees in 2009. Spanish may be considered a discipline in the sense that 65 doctoral programs granted 193 PhDs in Spanish language and literature. This field is large enough to support scholarly journals and to fill tenure-track vacancies for professors of Spanish. The only caveat is that Spanish is often located not in a Spanish department but in a department of Romance language and literature.

At present, degrees in Spanish and French can be obtained at most colleges and universities, with German trailing as a distant third. As a practical matter, Spanish and French are close to being defining members of the set of liberal arts fields, and thus the closure of a French department represents a serious challenge to this status. While we can speak of the discipline of Spanish language and literature, it is difficult to do so for many other languages

TABLE 3.2. Number of schools featuring degree programs in languages and literature, 2009

Language	Number of BA degree programs	Number of PhD degrees awarded (2011)	Number of BA degrees awarded (2011)
Romance languages			
Spanish	888	179	8,918
French	696	81	2,492
Italian	141	28	313
Romance languages, general	152	34	132
Latin	114	1	75
Asian languages			
Japanese	98	3	774
Chinese	72	8	449
Korean	5	3	28
Vietnamese	0	—	not listed
Hindi	1	—	not listed
Thai	0	—	not listed
Other languages			
German	440	43	1,019
Russian*	88	3	340
Arabic	13	1	141
Swahili	0	—	not listed

* Some may obtain relevant training in Russian via one of the twenty-four existing Slavic studies doctoral programs.
Source for degree programs: *College Blue Book*, 36th edition.
Source for degrees obtained: Digest of Education Statistics.
Source for course enrollment: Modern Language Association database.

in the United States. This is not a matter of disparaging these languages and the rich cultural traditions they embody, but simply because programs and students are so rare that there is not a sufficient numerical base for producing new scholars or for restricting new faculty positions to those with doctoral degrees in the field. For example, while seventy-two schools offer a bachelor's degree in Chinese, at present there are no doctoral programs conferring degrees in Chinese language and literature, and only eleven offering doctoral degrees in Chinese studies. Fewer than one hundred institutions offer degrees in Russian, Japanese, or Arabic. The situation is even worse for other important languages such as Arabic and Hindi. African languages such as Swahili and Yoruba are almost completely absent as degree options.

Thus, Chinese and Arabic have not yet reached the status of disciplines in the American university system because instruction is not normally restricted to PhDs in these fields. PhDs are being produced in small numbers, and the small number of schools with departments and degrees in these fields means that the market for PhDs remains small.

Disciplines, Degrees, and Departments

We have seen that only a relatively small set of fields has been sufficiently established that most colleges and universities offer degrees in them. It might be reasonable to assume that all schools that offer a degree in a field also have a college department. It is now time to examine this assumption. As we will see, the organizational configuration of many schools leaves important fields such as biochemistry as subunits of other departments, while the small scale of programs in other fields results in two or more disciplines sharing a department. The equation of discipline, degree, and department thus breaks down for some fields, especially in smaller and less elite colleges.

The presence of a stand-alone department is important because it gives members of the faculty a greater role in defining their academic needs. There is no need to persuade colleagues in a related field about one's priorities, or that a junior candidate is worthy of appointment. There is no risk of having the department chair being from another field, a chair who may not be able to fully appreciate or articulate the needs of one's field. Moreover, a department chair who hails from a neighboring discipline is likely to lack the personal disciplinary ties that facilitate many activities, from obtaining up-to-date information to soliciting tenure letters to assessing the quality and accuracy of letters of recommendation for job candidates. Disciplinary autonomy is clearly greater in a stand-alone department than it is when sharing a roof with another field of study. Securing a department of one's own is a basic indicator of the political strength of a discipline.[16]

I examined the 383 schools sampled by Brint and his research team by visiting each school's website to ascertain whether a degree was offered and whether there was a department that matched the degree program. Five fields were examined: anthropology, biochemistry, French, physics, and sociology. Of the 383 schools in this sample, 268, or 70 percent, offer a bachelor's degree in physics. But in a substantial number of them, physics is not a stand-alone department. It most commonly shares a departmental home with astronomy, but in other cases it cohabits a department with engineering or is part of a physical sciences unit. Only 45 percent of institutions in the sample had a stand-alone physics department. Schools without physics departments tend to be smaller and less elite.[17] Just under half of the sample of schools offered anthropology degrees (47.3 percent), while only one-third (35.0 percent) had stand-alone anthropology departments. Anthropology is most often paired with sociology. Sociology was housed in its own department in half of this sample of schools. It was housed jointly with another field in another 30 percent of schools, and was absent in the remaining 20 percent.

Biochemistry is an interesting case, as it has long been considered by some to represent a hybrid form, an "interdiscipline" (Hubenthal 1994). But while the intellectual contributions of biochemistry are indisputable, the field's organizational success is more limited, since stand-alone biochemistry departments are quite rare. Of the 147 schools in this sample offering degrees in biochemistry, only a small minority (21 percent) featured a stand-alone biochemistry department. The more common arrangements are (a) joint chemistry/biochemistry departments (28.5 percent); (b) biochemistry degrees offered by chemistry departments (21.2 percent); and (c) joint degrees offered by biology and chemistry departments (11.7 percent). The remaining degrees are issued under a variety of other auspices: departments involving molecular biology, departments with three of more fields, and programs under the heading of "general sciences."

French language instruction is in a similar position with respect to garnering independent department status. In this sample of 383 schools, 189 schools offered French degrees, but only 30 had stand-alone French departments. In the balance of cases, French was housed with Italian, Romance languages, modern languages, or foreign languages.[18]

These data have several important implications for disciplines. First, the equation of disciplines, departments, and degrees is not nearly as tight as many assume. It is not uncommon for degrees to be offered by subdepartmental units. Second, several prominent fields, including physics, are not as universally established as many discussions of disciplinary status assume. In other words, while physics is one of the most respected fields, its small enrollment hobbles it in the undergraduate context, and small colleges are often unable or unwilling to commit the resources needed to maintain a stand-alone physics department. Departments such as physics and anthropology are not infrequently asked to share space with neighboring fields, most often astronomy in the case of physics and sociology in the case of anthropology. Third, a minimum level of undergraduate enrollment is indispensable for disciplines as we have defined them. Analysts have long pointed to physics' intellectual breakthroughs and its long-standing federal support, but its weakness in terms of undergraduate enrollment puts it behind fields such as biology and psychology in terms of its presence on university and, especially, college campuses.

The importance of enrollments results in the need to slightly amend Frickel and Gross's approach to scientific and intellectual movements. While they focus on the elements of mobilizing faculty, grants, conferences, and the like, there is also a need for attracting a sizable number of undergraduates. This means that defining an area of study and making it attractive to considerable numbers of prospective students is an indispensable step in a field's successful transition to disciplinary status.

Contemporary Academic Disciplines as Recent Arrivals

Disciplines are often seen as ancient institutions. In discussions about interdisciplinarity, this sometimes appears as a rhetorical strategy to make disciplines seem antiquated and out of date (Klein 1990; Taylor 2010).[19] Yet disciplines as they appear in contemporary research universities are remarkably recent inventions.[20] Before the Second World War, the *idea* of discipline-based departments was well ensconced. As a practical matter, however, at most colleges and universities, departments were usually remarkably small in size. The most common arrangement was a single professor charged with providing expertise and guidance in all aspects of his field.

Taking my own field of sociology as an example, in 1936, over half (55 percent) of colleges featured sociology as a field of study.[21] Sociology was more common in universities than in colleges (two-thirds of universities offered sociology as a field of study, compared with just over half of colleges). In a number of schools, sociology was housed in a department with another discipline, most often economics.

In those schools with stand-alone sociology departments, the modal faculty size in 1936 was one. Just under half (49 percent) of schools employed a single sociologist; over 70 percent employed just one or two. In other words, the most common arrangement was to have a single sociologist representing sociology as a discipline. Even if we restrict our attention to universities, the typical sociology program was tiny. The presence of one or two professors was common there as well; the median faculty size was 2.0 (mean 2.7). The largest sociology department in 1936 had ten professors; only nine universities employed more than five professors of sociology.

Sociology was somewhat less established as a field in 1936 than were other fields of study, but departments in most other disciplines were just as small. Data were culled on biology, mathematics, and economics as comparison fields. In 1936, in mathematics and economics, the most frequent arrangement was one professor per department, while in biology two professors per department was slightly more common. Even if we set aside small colleges and focus strictly on research universities, the small scale of most academic departments is apparent. The median size of university-based biology departments in 1936 was just under two, while economics and mathematics departments averaged three professors each.

These small departments were very different social entities than the academic departments with which we are currently familiar. One or two professors would have had to cover a wide range of topics in their classes. The opportunity for discussion and debate with disciplinary colleagues was more limited. Fewer opportunities to specialize in particular lines of scholarship would have been available.

Research and scholarship predates the current arrangement of academic life. For example, Collins (1999) finds remarkable continuities in philosophical debates spanning a wide variety of epochs and continents. Yet contemporary academia stands out in terms of its size and scope and the creation of a disciplinary system that fosters innovation. Thus the present arrangement has been successful in part because of the scale of academic departments and not just their formal structure.

Disciplinary Growth and Internal Differentiation: The Case of Sociology

The growth of the academic enterprise in the United States since the Second World War is well documented. This is the terrain covered by Derek de Solla Price's transition from little science to big science. Cole (2009) summarizes many of these trends: the explosive growth in the number of students, research articles, peer-reviewed journals, and federal research support. American universities have been successful on a wide range of quality measures, including international rankings, the share of Nobel Prizes awarded to faculty at US research universities, and the number of foreign students seeking training in US graduate programs.

The emphasis here is more on specialization than growth, although the two are of course related. A faculty member in a large department can specialize to a much greater than her lonely predecessor would have been able to during the 1930s. Specialization is no doubt related to growth, but the relationship is far from one to one.[22]

Research specialties are far smaller than disciplines. While it is easy to count disciplines, it is far from clear how to count research specialties. The term "invisible colleges" has been used to refer to networks of researchers who work on the same issues and who follow each other's research but who are typically not located at the same research university (Price 1963; Crane 1972; Gmur 2003). We know that there are many such specialties in all liberal arts disciplines as well as in applied fields. It may be easier to paint a picture of internal differentiation within a single field, so I will turn again to sociology to illustrate some trends that apply more broadly.

In 1945, the *American Journal of Sociology* (*AJS*) celebrated its fiftieth anniversary with a set of eight essays that covered some of the main specialties of sociology. The specializations singled out for attention were social psychology, social pathology, population studies, race, theory, methods, and human ecology. In a review of the articles published in *AJS* during its first fifty years, Ethel Shanas used these same categories plus "social institutions and organization" and "social reform." These fields remain prominent to one degree or another in the discipline today, although "social pathology" now goes under the heading of "deviance and social control" and "social institutions" has evolved into the fields of organizational studies and economic sociology. Sociologist in many areas address issues of "social reform" although they are more likely to use terms such as "policy implications" or "public sociology" to describe this aspect of their research.[23]

The one lonely sociologist leading his own department in the late 1930s would thus have a bevy of topics for which he was responsible. By today's standards, we would view this scholar as a remarkable generalist. Yet even at the time, complaints were levied against excessive disciplinary specialization (for example, see McDowell 1948).

By 1950, sociology had grown considerably. Membership in the American Sociological Association had shot up from 1,000 in 1936 to 3,500 (American Sociological Association (Rosich 2005, appendix 12). While the modal department size remained just one, there were now forty-two colleges or universities with more than five sociologists, and fifteen with ten or more sociology faculty members.[24]

In the six decades since 1950, the sole sociology professor has been joined by substantial numbers of colleagues. In turn, specialization within sociology has continued to crystallize new areas of research. Members of the American Sociological Association (ASA) can become members of specialized groups of researchers called "sections" and one can create a new section with the support of two hundred ASA members. (In a number of academic organizations, these units are called "special interest groups" or SIGs.) There are currently fifty-three such sections. For example, under "M" we have Marxist sociology, mathematical sociology, medical sociology, the sociology of mental health, and sociological methodology. The most recent additions include disability and society; evolution, biology and society; and sociology of the body (American Sociological Association 2011). The ASA could boast of over fourteen thousand members in 2007. ASA membership tripled between 1940 and 1950, doubled again by 1960, and has doubled again since then (Rosich 2005, appendix 12).[25] An association with some fourteen thousand members is likely to have considerable internal differentiation.[26]

Sociology may be an especially diffuse field of inquiry, but it is by no means alone in the proliferation of specialties. The American Political Science

Association currently has forty-three sections, while the American Chemical Society is divided into thirty-three technical divisions. The American Mathematics Society currently lists seventy-one specializations within mathematics, while the *Journal of Economic Literature*, published by the American Economic Association, distinguishes twenty specialty areas within economics, many of which in turn have their own subdivisions.[27] This pattern is not restricted to liberal arts disciplines but is equally evident in interdisciplinary fields such as American studies (discussed in chapter 8) as well. American studies may well be even more differentiated per capita than sociology.

While some sociologists maintain their identity as generalists, most tend to specialize in a small set of these fields. Specialty areas in turn compete for positions in the top research departments, for space in the leading journals, and for grant support from the National Science Foundation and other funding sources. The internal differentiation of the discipline and the attendant competition that this generates contributes to its forward momentum.

The emergence of these specialties can be viewed as instances of the intellectual movements theorized by Frickel and Gross. In creating sections, activists have sought to assert the importance of these as areas of inquiry and made claims on the resources of the American Sociological Association, specifically, the opportunity to obtain a designated number of sessions at the annual meeting. In most cases, however, the goal has been to achieve recognition and a place at the table rather than to displace or overthrow established specialties.

Ulrich's Periodicals lists 605 active, peer-reviewed scholarly journals in sociology as March 2011, half of which were founded since 1990. While academic sociologists might question the inclusion of many of the journals on Ulrich's list, there are nonetheless more than before. My own list includes 120 sociology journals (Jacobs 2011). While a number of the leading journals are still generalist journals and review journals, the specialization of the field is increasingly evident in the journals, which focus on areas such as the sociology of education, health and social behavior, social psychology, gender, race, work and occupations, and so on. The theme of specialization is developed further in the next chapter.

Specialization in sociology remains a matter of research specialization rather than degree specialization. In other words, sociology is not divided into specialized undergraduate degree offerings, but becomes differentiated only for graduate students and researchers. In this way, it differs from applied fields of inquiry, which often exhibit extensive differentiation of specialty offerings for undergraduates.[28]

Internal specialization increases competition between specialties for resources and recognition. This helps to foster innovation. Furthermore, for those who maintain that diversity promotes creativity, the high degree of internal differentiation suggests that there is considerable room for diverse exchanges within a discipline.

Academic Specialization: The Contribution of Liberal Arts Disciplines to the Rise of Applied Fields of Study

The growth of disciplines results in internal specialization, but it also contributes to the emergence of new fields of study, many of which are applied in nature. Metzger's fine history of academic fields in the United States (1987) distinguishes between two types of growth. There is a tendency for fields to subdivide—first as they break away from natural and moral philosophy into their own specialties, and later as they divide into finer and finer subdivisions.[29] At the same time, there is a parallel process that brings applied fields into the academy, either through "affiliation" or "dignification." In other words, established professional fields such as law and medicine come to be affiliated with the university, while over time less well recognized subjects also become accepted as part of the university curriculum.

What Metzger's analysis misses is the ways in which arts and science disciplines have helped to lay the intellectual foundation for the creation of applied fields as well as the multiplication of internal subdivisions within each field. Metzger's two processes are thus more intertwined than he allows. Indeed, it is the very success of the traditional academic disciplines that has helped to develop the intellectual basis of the applied undergraduate fields with which they now compete for enrollments. Here again I present examples from the field of sociology, which has been prolific, but not unique, in spinning off specialties. Specifically, sociology has contributed to the development of communications, marketing, management, and criminal justice, all burgeoning applied fields, each with undergraduate enrollments that surpass those of sociology.

Social scientists over the course of the twentieth century developed the techniques to conduct surveys of public opinion based on statistically representative samples. This led to the founding in 1947 of the American Association of Public Opinion Research and its international counterpart, the World Association for Public Opinion Research, and to the creation of the journal *Public Opinion Quarterly*. Public opinion research, however, did not become its own discipline in the sense that there are no undergraduates who major in public opinion, no separate academic departments of public opinion, and no doctoral degrees in this field. Instead, public opinion research contributed to the formation of two applied fields, communications and marketing, even while continuing to play a role in sociology, political science, and psychology.

Sociologists with long memories celebrate the role that leading figures such as Paul Lazarsfeld and Herbert Hyman played in the development of public opinion research.[30] Sociology played an important role, but by no means was it the only influence on the formation of communications research, which today draws on many fields, including literary analysis, social psychology, and visual studies (Pfau 2008)

By the end of the 1960s, communication emerged not only as a field of study but also as a degree field for undergraduates. The communications major incorporated journalism but also addressed communication issues in other settings as well, including business and nonprofit organizations. The number of bachelor's degree recipients in the field of communications rose from just over ten thousand in 1971 to nearly seventy-seven thousand in 2008, which represents a rise from 1 percent to nearly 5 percent of undergraduate enrollments.[31]

Over time, however, communications has developed into its own field with its own concerns. (See Pooley and Katz [2008] for a brief history of the divergence of American sociology and communications research.) More important, communications began to produce its own PhDs. New fields often seek to create PhD programs since these are a sign that scholarship in the field is recognized as worthy of granting a degree. The production of newly minted doctorates in communications has moved this field into a position to be able to hire its own as faculty. In the early years of communications programs, faculty inevitably held degrees from various fields since there were few people with PhDs in communications.[32]

In short, communications began as an interdisciplinary field both intellectually and in terms of the training of its faculty, yet over time, faculty members were increasingly drawn from communications departments. In this way, applied fields such as communications gradually come to resemble disciplines. Communications as a field remains quite intellectually diverse, but this is principally because of the range of styles and approaches produced by communications PhD programs.

In order to consider the question of employment closure, that is, selecting faculty exclusively from those with a degree in the field, data on faculty hiring patterns by discipline from the National Survey of Post-Secondary Faculty (National Center for Education Statistics 2011) were consulted. By 2004, the year in which this survey was conducted, nearly 70 percent of faculty in communications programs had obtained their PhD in the field of commu-

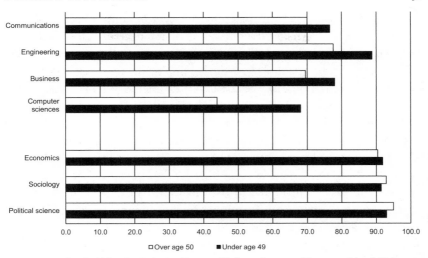

FIGURE 3.1. Faculty hiring closure by age: Percent with degree in same subject as teaching field. Source: 2004 National Postsecondary Faculty Survey Data (NSOPF).

nications. Thus, while sociology and other fields may continue to generate powerful ideas and interesting insights regarding communications processes, over time these will be incorporated into the field of communications only to the extent that faculty trained in communications accept these ideas and pass them along to their students.

Figure 3.1 presents data on the field of communications along with several other fields discussed here. The data suggest that applied fields—business, communications, engineering, and so on—increasingly tend to largely hire faculty from within their own fields. This level of self-recruitment (or doctoral-degree endogamy) in hiring is not as high as that found in the liberal arts disciplines, but nonetheless it has come to represent the majority of faculty appointments in each field. The closure, or self-recruitment, is more evident among the younger faculty. Thus, over time, interdisciplinary fields that endure and succeed in opening their own departments tend to become closed employment fields.[33]

Debates continue within the field of communications about its diverse intellectual roots. Herbst (2008) makes the case for communications as a post-disciplinary field of inquiry. Rogers (1999) bemoans the continuing division of the field between interpersonal communications and mass communications. Leydesdorff and Probst (2009) conducted a time series analysis of citation patterns and suggest that communications research is moving toward the establishment of a specialty of its own.[34]

Another consideration in mapping the field of communications is the many specialties in which undergraduates obtain degrees. As we will see in more detail in chapter 9, applied fields tend to splinter into a large number of degree programs oriented to particular employment opportunities. In the case of communications, degrees are currently offered in no less than thirty-two different fields, including journalism, media studies, radio and television, public relations, digital media, and animation technology. Thus, while communications research is somewhat interdisciplinary, this tendency coexists with internal differentiation in the form of the proliferation of degree offerings.

Sociology also contributed to the intellectual history of marketing research, management theory, criminology, and criminal justice (see Jacobs [2013a] for a discussion of these fields). These fields, once established, compete with sociology for student enrollments. Roughly thirty thousand undergraduates receive degrees each year in sociology. Marketing and criminal justice are each roughly as popular as sociology, while communications and management attract several times as many majors. These applied fields, to which sociology has contributed, now greatly surpass it in enrollments. Since the 1970s, the number of students obtaining degrees in business has nearly tripled, rising from 115,396 in 1971 to 335,254 in 2008. In 2008, over 135,000 students obtained degrees in business administration and management, a total that slightly surpassed all of the enrollments in the social science fields located in the liberal arts (anthropology, economics, political science, and sociology).

Sociology has contributed to the intellectual underpinnings of a number of other fields as well, including women's studies, African American studies, ethnic studies more generally, global studies, and so on. Similarly, one could trace the role that the discipline of economics has played in the development of business school programs, especially finance, as well as the increasingly dominant role that economics has played in public policy programs. The point here is not to attempt to map the full extent of sociology's impact or to recount sociology's greatest hits but rather to put the traditional counterpoint between liberal arts and applied fields in a new light. Arts and science fields such as sociology have helped to create specializations that end up as distinct undergraduate majors and, ironically, end up competing with their parent fields sociology for enrollments. In this sense, the liberal arts disciplines are often victims of their own accomplishments, as they succeed in providing the intellectual basis for applied fields that become competitors for students and other resources.

Conclusion

This chapter has covered a great deal of ground; consequently, a brief summary is in order. Institutional disciplines are defined as fields that are extensively represented in colleges and universities in the United States. This definition helps to identify disciplines as broad fields with extensive internal differentiation and fuzzy borders between them. Disciplines are dynamic, since colleagues compete for recognition and rewards within their chosen field even as disciplines compete with each other for status and resources. Disciplines in the modern sense date only to the Second World War. Before that, the disciplinary architecture was in place, but academic departments were too small to fully realize their modern functions.

As disciplines grow, they tend to subdivide into many specialties areas that often spill past the previously understood borders of the field. The difficulty in developing clear demarcations between fields, which is often taken as evidence of the arbitrariness of disciplines, is better understood as evidence of the vitality of a system that is continually forced to innovate. The dynamism of the system also has contributed to the growth in the number of preprofessional fields of study. While this trend is sometimes taken as evidence of the stodginess of the liberal arts disciplines, in fact they typically have provided the intellectual foundations of these applied fields. Once the liberal arts disciplines are understood to be dynamic entities covering broad fields with poorly defined boundaries, these patterns begin to make more sense. This theory also helps to explain the emergence of calls for interdisciplinarity. Disciplines in this sense are victims of their own success. They are continually uncovering new terrains to be explored and proliferating new specialized areas of inquiry only to be criticized for generating intellectual fragmentation.

Now that we have a clearer sense of the nature of disciplines and how they operate, the need for an academic division of labor can be explored in greater depth. The growth of the research enterprise and especially the proliferation of research journals is the focus point of chapter 4. The accumulated specialization built into contemporary academia raises questions regarding whether an emphasis on interdisciplinarity can in fact integrate knowledge. Ironically, efforts to create a more interdisciplinary academic journal system may make scholarly communication even more difficult.

4

Specialization, Synthesis, and the Proliferation of Journals

Academics specialize. James Watson and Francis Crick focused their attention on molecular biology, Ruth Benedict and Margaret Mead on anthropology, Jane Goodall and Dian Fossey on primatology. This has always been true to some extent, but it has become increasingly so since the rise of the modern university after the American Civil War, and especially since the Second World War. While polymaths and geniuses occasionally make breakthroughs in more than one field, the increasing knowledge base in most disciplines requires years to master and typically yields new insights only after lengthy immersion in a field.

The empirical inquiries summarized below take place in the context of a scholarly communication system with more the twenty-eight thousand active peer-reviewed journals.[1,2] Since no one individual could possibly keep up to date on this daunting and growing volume of research, some division of labor among academics is doubtless needed. The arrangement of research into discrete topics, domains, and themes of one sort or another seems inescapable. If the present set of scholarly disciplines and academic departments seems arbitrary and restrictive to some, the presence of some form of organizational structures designed to manage the domains of knowledge seems unavoidable, whether these are called divisions, schools, centers, institutes, or departments. The challenges posed by the growth of knowledge have been noted by others (Abbott 2011; Cole 2009; Price 1963), but rarely surface in the context of interdisciplinarity.

The analysis developed here begins a set of three chapters on scholarly communication. Whereas in chapters 5 and 6 the reception of individual books and articles will take center stage, in this chapter the general challenges of communication in a highly specialized academic system are considered.

The central question considered here is whether the journal system is shifting in the direction of a greater emphasis on interdisciplinarity. If so, scholarly communication, along with the closely associated system of academic rewards, might contribute to the blurring of disciplinary distinctions. Despite the substantial growth of research on interdisciplinary collaboration and intellectual exchange, relatively little attention has focused on interdisciplinarity in the context of the academic journal system.[3]

The presentation develops in four steps. First, academic specialization is shown to be a special case of the division of labor. Second, ironically, the inexorable advance of academic specialization may make interdisciplinarity an attractive ideal to some faculty members. Just as the division of labor in the factory can produce alienated blue-collar workers, it may be that an ever finer intellectual division of labor is contributing to a degree of discontent among researchers and scholars.

The empirical section of the chapter draws on a set of over 700 peer-reviewed journals that were established in 2008. Six distinct types of interdisciplinarity are developed in order to classify these journals. The evidence points to a rise in the number of interdisciplinary journals, but the large majority of such outlets are quite specialized in nature. The prospect of hundreds or even thousands of interdisciplinary journals is likely to make scholarly communication more difficult by spreading out similar papers over a wider set of sources. Finally, specialization and differentiation are partly balanced by powerful forces that pull in the direction of synthesis.

The Division of Labor

Intellectual specialization may be viewed as a special case of the division of labor, a topic that has interested scholars since before Adam Smith (see Sun [2005], for a collection of essays, half of which predate Smith). It may seem obvious to the contemporary reader that there are benefits to specialization, yet the nature of such benefits, as well as the costs of specialization, have preoccupied a number of prominent authors.

In *The Wealth of Nations*, originally published in 1776, Smith begins by proclaiming the advantages of specialization and illustrates the idea with an account of pin making. In his day, pin making involved at least eighteen steps—drawing out the wire, straightening it, cutting it, pointing it, affixing the head, and so on. By specializing in one or two of these tasks, each member of the production team could increase his or her skill and proficiency and thereby contribute to greater output in a shorter amount of time. Smith estimated that a team of ten pin makers could jointly produce forty-eight thousand pins in a day. Thus, each member of the production team could be credited with roughly 4,800 pins per day, far more than any individual would be likely be able to produce on his or her own. Thus, Smith declares, "The greatest improvement in the productive powers of labour, and the greater part of the skill, dexterity, and judgment with which it is anywhere directed, or applied, seem to have been the effects of the division of labour" (2007, 3).

Smith's division of labor takes place in a relatively simple factory setting using reasonably simple complex techniques. In other words, Smith's analysis of pin production rests on how to best arrange well-known steps, rather than the invention of a new, streamlined production technology. Even Frederick Winslow Taylor, the champion of "scientific management," concentrated on maximizing efficiency in the arrangement of tasks rather than the invention of new production processes.

Charles Babbage (1835) emphasized a different aspect of the division of labor, namely, the need to reduce the number of highly paid specialists. For example, in the medical setting, a doctor is trained in the entire range of skills, from taking blood pressure to diagnosing the underlying causes of the patient's symptoms. In this case, Babbage notes that costs would be reduced if a nurse or other technical assistant measured the patient's vital signs and conducted blood tests, thus allowing the physician to save time, see more patients, and to reserve her attention for the tasks to which she is uniquely trained. Thus, for Babbage, the division of labor is not only a matter of separating different procedures into their most efficient elements but of reducing the wage bill. By concentrating the energies of the most skilled workers on the most complex functions, each task is allocated to those with the appropriate training. Economizing on training is thus an essential element of efficiency in his arrangement of production.

Babbage had no hesitation in extending the logic of his analysis to "mental" as well as physical labor. In both cases, he insists, the division of labor "enables us to purchase and apply to each process precisely that quantity of skill and knowledge which is required for it" (201). When the job at hand is original research, Babbage no doubt exaggerates when he suggests that the skills and knowledge required for new discoveries and inventions can be specified "precisely." But there is surely something to the idea that even the most learned scholar cannot be expected to know all aspects of all things.

In the contemporary academic context, mastering the appropriate body of knowledge represents a major hurdle. In other words, if the case can be made for a division of labor in the production of a pin, surely advantages can be expected from the intellectual division of labor. In short, there are good reasons to train some individuals to be rocket scientists while others concentrate on biomedical advances while still others pursue esoteric subjects in the social sciences and the humanities.

In the case of pin production, specialization has its advantages even if it may not take a great deal of time to learn each procedure. In the contemporary academic context, the duration of training is a key constraint. The time to completion of a doctoral degree has been edging downward as graduate program directors strive to streamline their programs and reduce the number of "nth year" graduate students. Nonetheless, after more than a decade of such reforms, the median time to a doctoral degree in the United States in 2008 remained 7.7 years. The duration of graduate training currently ranges 6.7 years in the physical sciences to 9.3 years in the humanities to 12.7 years in education. Lest anyone jump to the conclusion that scientists are "getting off easy," postdoctoral training of two or three years in duration is common in the sciences: nearly half of doctorates in the life sciences pursue a postdoctoral position, along with over half of newly minted PhDs in the physical sciences. Indeed, it is increasingly common for scientists to apprentice in multiple postdoctoral positions before obtaining their own laboratories as assistant professors. The median age of doctoral degree recipients was 32.4, ranging from a low of 30.3 in the physical sciences to a high of 41.5 in education (National Science Foundation 2008). While there are no doubt ways to reduce the time to degree, no matter what steps are taken to improve graduate education, the fact of the matter is that there is just not enough time to learn everything.[4] And, as we will see in more detail below, the steady expansion of research makes the challenge of training new experts ever more challenging.

The length of graduate training reflects many factors, including the availability of financial support and the nature of the job market in different disciplines. In other words, the ten years it takes to get a degree in history or English reflects not only how much one needs to learn in these fields but also what it takes to stand out in a crowded labor market. Humanities PhD programs have been producing more PhDs than there are new academic openings to absorb them (Nerad, Aanerud, and Cerny 2004).[5] Thus, the rational strategy for an individual doctoral degree candidate is to stay an extra year in school in order to publish another paper and to make one's dissertation stand out as a particularly impressive piece of scholarship. Consequently, substantial reductions in the time to degree in humanities PhD programs need to go hand in hand with an improvement in the academic job market in these fields.

The Division of Labor and Its Discontents

Harry Braverman (1975) criticized the logic of Charles Baggage, and especially its implementation by "scientific management" specialists such as Taylor. The division of labor lauded by Babbage and Taylor can be viewed from the workers' point of view as a systematic process of "deskilling" work. By separating tasks into their smallest and most repetitive elements, the efficiency manager not only reduced wages but created untold thousands of narrow factory jobs, forcing legions of workers into mind-numbing and disengaged work.

Thus, while the division of labor improves efficiency, it risks producing alienated workers and fraying the social fabric. Intensive manufacturing may produce profits and benefit consumers, but such arrangements can be hard on workers. And continuous improvements in productivity make the workers' plight ever more perplexing. The more efficient the system, the more concentrated the workers' energy is directed to the task at hand, the more that can be produced, the more the market can become flooded with the product, the lower the workers' wage. It is easy to see how a factory worker could feel like a cog in a huge production system that is out of his or her control.

Braverman's book ignited a bevy of research on the "deskilling" of the labor force. The upshot was a mixed picture, with deskilling and upgrading coexisting in a complex pattern (Attewell 1987; DiPrete 1987; Jonsson 1998; Myles 1988).

Those who celebrate the arrival of the knowledge economy typically consider intellectuals exempt from such concerns. In the most optimistic account, we are living through the rise of the "creative class" (Florida 2004). Those who participate in, and indeed, those who drive the knowledge economy are engaged individuals who love their jobs and spend their days joyfully bouncing ideas off of each other.

Yet one can hear echoes of the industrial proletariat in the knowledge economy if one only listens. The titles of works by Stanley Aronowitz (*The Knowledge Factory* 2000) and Sheila Slaughter (*Academic Capitalism* 2004) play on the analogy between the lecture hall and the factory shop floor. Concerns about the speedup of intellectual labor and the endless day are not hard to find (Jacobs 2004; Misra, Templer, and Lundquist 2012). The growth of an "academic underclass" resonates with the older concept of the "reserve army of the unemployed" (American Association of University Professors 2003). Concern about the corporatization of universities are also in the air, with the specter of the ivory tower evolving into a glorified industrial research laboratory (Bok 2003; Slaughter 2004; Aronowitz 2000). While the economic insecurity of the industrial working class may not be as directly evident, given the rules of academic tenure in the American context, the rise of an untenured academic underclass contributes to unease, and reinforces the pressures on new PhDs: to earn one's way into the secure echelon of academia, one needs to work harder and longer and to publish more.

In this context, interdisciplinarity may have the same appeal to academics as efforts to resist the division of labor on the factory floor. In the case of the skilled factory worker, the search for a broader range of tasks is a way to make the experience of work engaging and satisfying. In the academic case, the professor seeks a broader intellectual terrain to call her own. In both cases, powerful forces seem to be hurtling toward an uncertain future. In both cases, autonomy and control are at stake: the workers' control of the labor process, the faculty's control over its academic domain. Specialization tends to increasingly limit academics' scope, just as the technical division of labor narrows the skill set of the industrial worker and limits the range of his daily tasks. While faculty at research universities earn more than do factory workers, both groups feel economically insecure for very good reasons.

Deskilling per se is not really dominant in either case. Just as today's factory worker needs more training than ever in order to deal with computerized production processes and other technological advances, academic researchers need to digest more and more esoteric literature, and to master new and more complex statistical and experimental techniques. Yet in both cases the specter of loss of autonomy and control, of having a narrower job description, is palpable. Thus, the appeal of interdisciplinarity in part may reflect this desire to stem or reverse the division of labor, to assert a broader domain of competence, to engage a broader set of questions with a bigger tool kit of techniques.

While faculty report high levels of satisfaction with their jobs, among their chief complaints is a lament about the difficulty of keeping current with research in their own field, let alone broad and deep reading outside their area of specialization (Jacobs and Winslow 2004). Consequently, concerns about disciplinary silos may resonate with individual scholars even if in fact ideas are constantly flowing between disciplines and departments.

In recent years, faculty members have come to accept the value of interdisciplinary knowledge. The results of a 2008 survey of over one thousand college and university faculty found that 70 percent agreed with the statement that "interdisciplinary knowledge is better than knowledge obtained by a single discipline" (Gross and Simmons 2008.) This view is shared by scholars in most fields, with only mechanical engineers and economists as exceptions.

The skepticism of economists for research from other disciplines found in Gross and Simon's study is consistent with the low rate of citation of other social science research by economists (Pieters and Baumgartner 2002).

Thus, interdisciplinarity may be appealing to faculty because it represents a way to resist the pressures of specialization. Unfortunately, as discussed in more detail below, interdisciplinarity does not really offer a way out of this particular conundrum, as it will not solve the problem of increasing specialization and is likely to increase centralized administrative control rather than to empower academics.

The Growth of Peer-Reviewed Journals

Taken as a whole, the volume of new research is overwhelming. No single person can possibly keep up with all of the new information pouring into research journals, not to mention books and other outlets.[6] A basic indicator of the extent of research is the number of peer-reviewed academic journals. The following analysis draws on data on academic journals compiled by Ulrich, which currently tracks over twenty-eight thousand peer-reviewed academic journals.[7] If journals publish a total of five hundred pages per year on average, then the determined omnivore would currently have to devour upwards of one hundred and forty thousand dense pages per year. Even if one could master the diverse technical information, the physical demands of this volume of reading would leave precious little time for anything else. New journals are regularly added to the list; one-third of all research journals have been founded since 2000. At the current rate of growth of approximately 3 percent per year, it will take less than twenty-five years to double the number of journals.

While the number of the journals by itself is daunting, the number of connections required to link each of these outlets is simply beyond reach. The number of possible two-way connections among the 789 journals established in 2008 alone is 310,866; three-way connectivity would require 81.5 million ties. Just under 400 million combinations are possible among 28,000 journals. Given a knowledge system of this scale, researchers and scholars must be forgiven if they are not fully up to date on the latest developments in fields outside of their expertise.

As Derek de Solla Price (1963) noted, it is foolhardy to project continued growth indefinitely as a straight line. At some point an inflection point will be reached. While the distant future cannot be predicted with any precision, a few conclusions and informed estimates about short-term trends in this area may be warranted. First, the growth in the number of journals in recent years continues unabated, although at a somewhat slower rate than was evident in earlier years. The average growth rate in the number of journals in the 1950–80 period was approximately 4.5 percent year; since 1990, the growth rate has averaged 3.0 percent per year.[8]

Second, a growing share of new journals are being published outside the United States in rapidly expanding educational systems. Since 1980, roughly 30 percent of new journals have been published in the United States. The substantial growth in systems of higher education throughout the world (Schofer and Meyer 2005) suggests that there may be continuing impetus for the creation of new journals. As educational systems compete for international recognition, publication rates have become an increasingly central indicator of recognition or prominence.[9] The drive to have journals in each subject area in each country of the world will continue to foster the proliferation of academic journals. Third, a new mode of publication—open access—has become a powerful force contributing to the expansion in the number of journals. Open access takes advantage of electronic communications in order to give free access to anyone around the world who has access to a computer and the Internet. In 2008, 40 percent of new journals were released in this format. In a number of instances, it seems that the open-access modality was a principal rationale for the formation of the journal. Thus, it is quite likely that the number of academic journals is likely to continue to grow for some time.

New Journals: The Prevalence of Interdisciplinarity

This review of journals began with the assumption that the very number of journals is antithetical to grand interdisciplinary syntheses. The scale of specialized knowledge makes the challenge of comprehensive synthesis hard to tackle as a practical matter. Nonetheless, the creation of new journals represents a research opportunity. What light will an examination of new journals shed on questions of specialization and interdisciplinarity? How many of these new journals emphasize interdisciplinary perspectives? Is interdisciplinarity being driven by the intellectual currents, as reflected in journals, the particular pressures of campus life, or some combination of the two?

The set of 789 new academic, peer-reviewed journals founded in 2008 was examined. The analysis was restricted to the 740 journals that were published in English or had abstracts in English and that had accessible websites.[10]

A principal goal of this analysis is to ascertain how many of these new journals are interdisciplinary in their orientation. The answer is quite a few in the social sciences, but surprisingly few in such major growth areas as biology.

TABLE 4.1. Peer-reviewed academic journals launched in 2008, by subject and percent interdisciplinary

	Number of new journals	% of journals by subject	% interdisciplinary (total)
Humanities comprehensive	4	0.6	100.0
Social sciences: Comprehensive works	17	2.4	88.6
Sciences comprehensive	8	1.2	62.5
Other humanities	31	4.5	60.0
Public health and safety	26	3.7	57.1
Communications	12	1.7	54.5
Sociology	12	1.7	50.0
Environmental studies	16	2.3	50.0
Other arts	19	2.7	44.4
Other engineering	15	2.2	42.9
Psychology	20	2.9	40.0
Other social sciences	32	4.6	35.0
Applied social science and social welfare	27	3.9	34.0
Political science	13	1.9	33.3
Chemistry	17	2.4	25.0
Business and economics	59	8.5	24.5
Computers	18	2.6	22.2
Engineering	30	4.3	20.0
Education	22	3.2	18.2
Other applied sciences	25	3.6	16.7
Law	12	1.7	16.7
Biology	64	9.2	12.5
Medical sciences	161	23.2	9.3
Mathematics	26	3.7	8.3
Physics	26	3.7	8.3
Pharmacy & pharmacology	13	1.9	0.0
Earth sciences	11	1.6	0.0
Other science	4	0.6	0.0
Total	740		25.9

Source: Authors' analysis, Ulrich database.

In some relatively new fields such as environmental sciences, interdisciplinary journals are the norm, while medical journals are often interdisciplinary in a rather narrow form as discussed in more detail below.

Table 4.1 lists the number of new journals by field (as classified by Ulrich) along with the percentage of journals that take an interdisciplinary approach. The principal criteria for classifying a journal as interdisciplinary is whether this term (or the term "multidisciplinary") is used in the mission statement on the journal's web page. In a modest number of cases, journals were classified as interdisciplinary even when this term was not explicit in the journal description when it was clear that the mission referenced multiple disciplines and fields of research as within the purview of the journal.[11]

In terms of the number of new journals, medicine and biology represents the largest groups, followed by business and economics. Some relatively new fields appear on the list, such as environmental studies and communications, as do some long-established fields such as mathematics and physics.

Overall, roughly one-quarter (25.9 percent) of new journals are interdisciplinary in one form or another. The definition of interdisciplinarity employed here is broader than what can be gleaned from the Ulrich classification system that includes no subject heading devoted to interdisciplinarity per se.[12]

The share of interdisciplinary journals varies markedly by field. In a number of substantive fields, the new journals were mostly interdisciplinary. These include communications, sociology, environmental science, and psychology. In contrast, new entrants in other fields, such as business and economics, biology, medicine, and physics, were much less likely to be interdisciplinary.

While the biomedical area is one of the main hubs for interdisciplinarity on university campuses, most of the new journals in the field of biology and medicine are specialized and focused on research in specific subspecialty areas. For example, the journal *Marine Genomics* covers "all structural, functional and evolutionary aspects of genes, chromatin, chromosomes and genomes of marine (and freshwater) organisms." This type of journal is not meant to be read by a general audience and does not specifically reach out to interdisciplinary contributors.[13]

Likewise, the *Journal of Innate Immunity* "covers all aspects of innate immunity, including evolution of the immune system, host-pathogen molecular interactions in invertebrates and vertebrates, molecular biology of cells involved in innate immunity . . . mucosal immunity . . . and development of immunotherapies."

Interdisciplinary journals in the biological sciences in this set of new journals were rare. One exception to this rule is the journal *Biosemiotics*, which describes itself as "dedicated to building a bridge between biology, philosophy, linguistics and the communication sciences. . . . Today, its main challenge is the attempt to naturalize not only biological information but also biological meaning, in the belief that signs and codes are fundamental components of the living world."

Medical journals represent an interesting case with respect to interdisciplinarity. On the one hand, they tend to be quite specific in their orientation toward practitioners in particular substantive areas. For example, *The Open Enzyme Inhibition Journal* is "an Open Access online journal which publishes research articles, reviews, and letters in all areas of enzyme inhibition studies. Topics covered in the journal include the mechanisms of inhibitory processes of enzymes, recognition of active sites, and the discovery of agonists and antagonists leading to medicinal agents." In medical journals, the emphasis is placed on streamlined and specific sources of information geared to immediate application in research and treatment by specialists and clinicians. These journals are not meant to be read by a general audience, but instead are focused to allow those within the field to have easy access to specialized information.

On the other hand, a number of medical journals do seek to integrate knowledge from a variety of types of approaches, including laboratory studies, clinical trials, and practitioners' observations. Thus, it is also possible to see some medical journals as interdisciplinary in the sense of combining basic, applied, clinical, and even behavioral aspects of a given illness. As the journal *Oxidative Medicine and Cellular Longevity* puts it, these medical journals attempt to "translate pioneering 'bench to bedside' research into clinical strategies." In other words, the goal is to connect laboratory research produced by specialized scientists with the work of clinicians and pathologists. In this way, some medical journals are more interdisciplinary than are journals focused more on basic science issues in biology.

Six Types of Interdisciplinarity

A perusal of the mission statements of these journals makes it clear that editors and publishers mean quite a range of things when they call a journal "interdisciplinary." Six distinct types of interdisciplinary journals emerged from the data.[14]

One group can be best thought of as "disciplinary plus." In other words, the journal is focused on a particular discipline but is willing to accept papers from related fields to the extent that they shed light on the core issues. For example, the journal *Collaborative Anthropologies* states that "it features essays that are descriptive as well as analytical, from all subfields of anthropology and closely related disciplines, and that present a diversity of perspectives on collaborative research." In this case, the focus of the journal is anthropology, and related disciplines are welcome to the extent that they address questions central to the mission of this journal, specifically collaborative approaches to anthropology.

A second type can best be thought of as "specialized interdisciplinarity." This term might seem jarring to those who assume that interdisciplinarity is inherently broad.[15] Nonetheless, it is clear that in many cases, papers from a range of disciplines are solicited to answer a rather focused set of questions. For example, the *Journal of the North Atlantic* (*JONA*) is "a multi-disciplinary, peer-reviewed and edited archaeology and environmental history journal focusing on the peoples of the North Atlantic, their expansion into the region over time, and their interactions with their changing environment." In this case, the journal is clearly interested in bringing together scholarship from a wide range of fields, but the focus is a particular part of the world at a particular phase of human history.

Similarly, the journal *Heritage & Society*, formerly *Heritage Management*, focuses on questions having to with the preservation of cultural heritage. It is "a global, peer-reviewed journal that provides a forum for scholarly, professional, and community reflection on the cultural, political, and economic impacts of heritage on contemporary society. We seek to examine the current social roles of collective memory, historic preservation, cultural resource management, public interpretation, cultural preservation and revitalization, sites of conscience, diasporic heritage, education, legal/legislative developments, cultural heritage ethics, and central heritage concepts such as authenticity, significance, and value." This journal seeks to bring together disparate scholarship as well as practitioners who work in the area of cultural heritage.

A third and broader type of interdisciplinary journal endeavors to cover the entire terrain of social and cultural phenomenon. This type of journal may be described as "social-cultural comprehensive." For example, the *Journal of Cultural Economy* is concerned with "the role played by various forms of material cultural practice in the organisation of the economy and the social, and of the relations between them. As such it will provide a unique interdisciplinary forum for work on these questions from across the social sciences and humanities."

Another example, *Theory in Action*, "is an interdisciplinary, peer-reviewed journal, whose scope ranges from the local to the global. Its aim is to provide a forum for the exchange of ideas and the discussion of current research (qualitative and quantitative) on the interconnections between theory and action aimed at promoting social justice broadly defined." This represents a more expansive notion of interdisciplinarity, and is perhaps closer to what some reformers have in mind. Whether such a journal is able to obtain cutting-edge contributions from economics, statistics, political science, and other fields remains to be seen.

An even broader approach to interdisciplinarity sets out as its terrain not only the social sciences but also the sciences and humanities as well. Thus, *The International Journal of Research and Review* "is an international, refereed, and abstracted journal that publishes empirical reports in the various fields of arts, sciences, education, psychology, nursing, computer science, and business." The scope of this and similar journals is comprehensive. The goal is truly to cover everything. Perhaps this (fourth) type of interdisciplinarity could be called "academic universal."

This type of journal seeks to facilitate the development of interdisciplinary connections. In other words, by juxtaposing contributions from diverse sources, the hope is that scholarly connections will be made that will jumpstart advances that would not otherwise be possible. This approach might seem to be an efficient approach to publication—one-stop shopping, with everything located under one roof. And perhaps the leading science journals such as *Science* and *Nature* do help to serve this role. But as the number of interdisciplinary journals increases, surely journals that span the entire gamut of academic inquiry reduce the efficiency of the scholarly search for new research. A key article might be located anywhere across a broad spectrum of such academic-universal journals.

The fifth type of interdisciplinary journal focuses on a particular public issue or social problem.[16] This "problem solving" approach is designed to bring together research that addresses diverse aspects of a given social issue. For example, the journal *Ethnicity and Inequalities in Health and Social Care* (2011) seeks to

> promote race equality in health and social care. It is a vital source of information with its themes clearly located in practice and includes coverage of:
>
> - identifying and preventing inequalities
> - access to services
> - support, care and quality of service provision and outcome.

This type of journal does not necessarily expect any given paper to be interdisciplinary in approach. Instead, the assumption is that there is an interdisciplinary audience that shares an interest in the same issue, problem, or topic, and is willing to learn from diverse disciplinary and substantive approaches to the shared area of concern.

Other journals seek to address not just a single set of issues but social problems more generally. For example, the *International Journal of Society Systems Science* describes its goals as follows:

> Society faces many significant challenges nowadays: pollution, poverty, pain, terrorism, crime, greenhouse effect, war, disease, starvation, road accidents, inflation/deflation, unemployment, pornography, great suffering, ignorance, pesticide poisoning, and falsehood, to just name a few. . . . IJSSS eliminates the following "six barriers":
>
> - the barrier between social and natural sciences
> - the barrier between theory and applications
> - the barrier between hard decision models and soft ones

- the barrier between different disciplines in the business world
- the barrier between government and industry
- the barrier between the ivory tower and real society

The goal is quite broad but very different from that envisioned by *Theory in Action* and other interdisciplinary journals that are not focused on social problems.

A sixth and final type of interdisciplinary journal focuses on a particular theory or approach. In sociology, the journal *Rationality and Society* seeks to connect broad areas of social behavior under the rubric of rational action. In this way, it seeks connections with similar approaches in economics, political science, management studies, and other social science fields. In order to distinguish this approach from the others considered here, the term "theoretical" interdisciplinarity will be employed.

In some ways this type of journal may come the closest to pursuing the notion of transdisciplinarity sought after by advocates of reform. The idea is to unify diverse areas of study under a single, synthesizing perspective. As a practical matter, however, these approaches are often theoretically broad but substantively thin. They achieve breadth at the expense of considering the multifaceted nature of each topic under consideration. In this way, they are the opposite of the problem-solving approach to interdisciplinarity. The emphasis is on expanding the scope of the theory rather than fully examining any particular topic.

One journal in the data set exemplifies this approach: *Derrida Today*. The mission of this journal is to explore "what Derrida's thought offers to contemporary debates about politics, society and global affairs. Controversies about power, violence, identity, globalisation, the resurgence of religion, economics and the role of critique all agitate public policy, media dialogue and academic debate. *Derrida Today* explores how Derridean thought and deconstruction make significant contributions to this debate, and reconsider the terms on which it takes place."

This approach is certainly interdisciplinary in scope, as its domain ranges from politics to culture to economics. Yet it represents interdisciplinarity in a very different sense from the journal that focuses on health care inequalities. The latter seeks to explore every aspect of a particular issue with the goal of alleviating a specific social injustice, while *Derrida Today* emphasizes social critique more generally without necessarily seeking to lay out the detailed steps needed to fix any particular social problem.

As classified by this schema, journals that take the "specialized interdisciplinarity" approach are by far the most common, comprising just under 50 (48.1) percent of the sample. Together with "disciplinary plus" (13.5 percent),

TABLE 4.2. Journals launched in 2008 by type of interdisciplinarity

Journal type	Example	Number	Percentage of interdisciplinary journals
Specialized interdisciplinarity	*Heritage & Society*	64	48.5
Socio-cultural comprehensive	*Journal of Cultural Economy*	23	17.4
Disciplinary plus	*Collaborative Anthropologies*	18	13.6
Issue-focused/ problem solving interdisciplinarity	*Ethnicity and Inequalities in Health and Social Care*	15	11.4
Academic universal	*International Journal of Research and Reviews*	10	7.6
Theoretical interdisciplinarity	*Derrida Today*	2	1.5
Total		132	100.0

Source: Authors' analysis, Ulrich database.

these two groups represent more than three in five of the new interdisciplinary journals. The least common were those taking the theory driven approach (1.5 percent), followed by the very broad "academic universal" group at 5.5 percent. Rounding out the list, the social-cultural comprehensive group was more common (at 17.3 percent) than new journals focused on social issues (11.3 percent).

This typology suggests that most interdisciplinary journals are specialized in one way or another. Whether the journal adopts a "disciplinary plus" approach, a "specialized interdisciplinary," a "problem solving" or a "theoretical interdisciplinarity" strategy, each of these groups of interdisciplinary journals are intended to address a particular audience of researchers.

The "socio-cultural comprehensive" and "academic universal" approaches to interdisciplinary journals are more in line with the goals of interdisciplinary analysts in terms of endeavoring to promote communication and exchange across a wide set of disciplines, but it remains to be seen how successful these journals will be. Why would a team of biologists or engineers submit their research report to a journal that mostly publishes social science and humanities essays? Journal visibility and ranking are self-reproducing: researchers naturally tend to send their best papers to the highest ranked journals because these journals offer the best prospects for visibility for their research. In this respect, all of the new journals have an uphill battle to climb. An interdisciplinary journal with a comprehensive or universal strategy would be likely to face even greater challenges in obtaining high quality submissions and becoming recognized as an important outlet for scholarly communication.

Internationalization and Specialization

Does the internationalization of publishing tend to promote the publication of broader journals? The reasoning behind this question is as follows: the first sociology journal published in Ghana is likely to be broader in scope than is the fiftieth sociology journal published in the United States. One of the key goals of launching the first journal in a discipline in a given country is to help put the intellectual output of scholars from that nation on the map. A generalist orientation is more likely to suit this objective. Moreover, the volume of scholarship is likely to be too low to support a wide spectrum of specialist research outlets. Thus, the internationalization of academic publishing might contribute to the growth in the number of generalist or even interdisciplinary journals.

It is the case that new journals established in small countries likely to be broad based. For example, the journal *Epiphany* is a refereed semiannual journal and a publication of Faculty of Arts and Social Sciences of International University of Sarajevo. This interdisciplinary journal focuses on aspects of Bosnia and Herzegovina and also provides an outlet for scholars from this part of the Balkans. The journal, founded in 2008, publishes original articles in the arts and the social sciences.

A similar pattern may be observed for new sociology journals in Belarus, Slovenia, and other countries. But the fact is that there are many more new journals published in larger and more affluent countries, including the UK, Australia, and Canada. Consequently, the growth in the number of journals published outside the United States does not lead to the proliferation of journals from small upstart countries.

Interdisciplinary journals born in 2008 were classified by their country of publication. Journals published in the United States were slightly more likely to be interdisciplinary than those initiated in other countries (odds ratio of 1.28). Just focusing on the three leading countries of origin (United States, UK, Netherlands), the same patterns holds (odds ratio of 1.34). Consequently, the speculation that interdisciplinary journals are growing because they represent broad new contributions from countries without many specialized outlets does not hold.

Interdisciplinarity and Open Access

The next question for consideration is the possibility of a connection between the rise of open-access publishing and interdisciplinarity. Both of these trends are powerful forces that are reshaping scholarly communication, and it is natural to hypothesize that these two trends may reinforce one another. It is easy to cite examples of journals where the emphasis on interdisciplinarity and open access seem intertwined. For example, the *Scholarly Research Exchange* "is a peer-reviewed, open access journal that publishes original research articles in all areas of science, technology, and medicine."

Yet as a general proposition, the connection between open access and interdisciplinarity is open to dispute. In fact, interdisciplinary journals are actually less than half as likely to be open access than are other journals founded in 2008 (odds ratio of .45). This result makes sense when one considers the distribution of journals across subject areas. Journals in the natural sciences are more likely to be open access, and these are less likely to be interdisciplinary, especially in high-growth areas such as the biological sciences and medicine. Consequently, it is best to understand the trends of open access and interdisciplinarity as distinct currents rather than as aspects of the same intellectual movement.

Interdisciplinary Journals and the Splintering of Knowledge

Interdisciplinary journals can help to disseminate research across the boundaries of diverse research communities. A small number of leading journals, such as *Science* and *Nature*, play such a role. Even less visible interdisciplinary journals can also play a positive role, for example, by helping to foster standards of scholarship that overcome the customs of particular fields of study. However, there comes a point at which the proliferation of interdisciplinary journals must become dysfunctional. By scattering the results of studies across diverse outlets, a sharp increase in the number of interdisciplinary journals will make it even harder for scholars to track down and evaluate current research.

The evidence suggests that most interdisciplinary journals are targeted in one way or another, with only a small minority attempting a broad reach across the social sciences, humanities, and natural sciences. But let us consider what the consequences might be of the creation of more journals with truly diverse missions.

If the thirty thousand mark for peer-reviewed journals is rapidly approaching, then 5 percent (a conservative estimate based on Ulrich's classifications) of this total would represent some 1,500 interdisciplinary journals. Surely having the gems of new breakthroughs scattered across 1,500 outlets would not serve to consolidate knowledge but would instead help to insure that it would be splintered. In this case, it is clear that 1,500 specialized journals would help scholars keep up to date more efficiently than 1,500 journals that each ostensibly covered everything.

As we have seen, among new entries, the share of interdisciplinary journals is now roughly 25 percent. Over the next ten to fifteen years, we can expect the establishment of perhaps another ten thousand journals. If interdisciplinary journals maintain their current share, this will result in 2,500 new journals, to be added to our current 1,500. If these were all interdisciplinary in the broadest sense, then research findings would be scattered over some four thousand interdisciplinary journals. The regular publication of thousands of interdisciplinary journals would make the task of following the journals themselves exceedingly difficult if not impossible. At some point the journals themselves become irrelevant—they are just a storage device to be tracked by search engines. As the use of search engines increases and the tendency to read journals from cover to cover declines, the interdisciplinary journals's goal of sparking new insights by juxtaposing articles form diverse fields in a single issue is undermined.

Synthesis

The flood of information seems to be overwhelming and inexorable. Keeping up with the latest developments across each and every field would seem to be hopeless. In particular, the torrent of information would seem to force researchers and scholars to be increasingly specialized. But there are powerful countervailing forces that pull research in the direction of breadth and synthesis. These include high visibility generalist outlets, review articles, the rewards for theoretical advances and synthetic contributions, and the synthetic demands of teaching.

In chapter 5, a brief list of outlets that facilitate interdisciplinary communication will be discussed in conjunction with the evidence on interdisciplinary communication. These included generalist journals such as *Science* and *Nature*, quasi-academic outlets such as the *New York Review of Books*, and a number of other campus-based publications designed to trumpet the accomplishments of researchers and scholars from diverse fields on campus.

While these vehicles may help to promote a degree of awareness of disparate research activities, there are more systematic ways to keep up with selected literatures. In particular, review articles have become increasingly instrumental in helping researchers keep up to date. When written effectively, essay reviews synthesize and distill the most significant findings from recent research in a field. Specialists review dozens if not hundreds of research papers and summarize the main findings for the reader. In this and other ways, scholars seek to keep up to date with the latest scholarship in an efficient manner.

Journals that specialize in publishing review articles have become among the most highly cited journals in many fields. The publisher Annual Reviews fields a set of journals that focus on reviews of recent research for forty scholarly disciplines. They report that their publication is the most highly cited journal in twenty of the forty-four disciplinary comparisons listed and within the top five in another seventeen cases.[17] This remarkable pattern of visibility actually understates the case because the Annual Reviews is not the only publisher of review journals. For example, in economics, the *Journal of Economic Literature*, is the most cited journal in its field, yet this journal is not published by the Annual Reviews. It is also the case that some outlets publish occasional review essays while not devoting the entire journal to this purpose.

A second powerful countervailing trend is the value of theory, especially synthetic theory. Scholars who are able to connect disparate findings into a coherent synthesis are highly rewarded. Indeed, there is a clear interdependence between synthesis and specialization, between theories and facts. Specialized research needs to be embedded in overarching frameworks, which in turn need detailed empirical investigation to be valid and meaningful.

Some of these theories will be interdisciplinary in the sense that they offer intellectual insights that are not confined to a single discipline. For example, behavioral economics offers insights that pertain to topics in sociology, political science, anthropology, and a number of applied social science fields.

But synthetic theories need not be interdisciplinary. Broad syntheses can be successful within disciplines, while a considerable amount of interdisciplinary scholarship can be very specialized and narrow in scope. The attempt by some to equate the term interdisciplinary with "broad" or "synthetic" or "integrative" is misplaced.

Another powerful force tipping scholars toward broader and more integrative approaches to their field is the need to teach students. The modern research university combines research and teaching. In this sense, it is a hybrid form that is not solely focused on research as are some independent institutes. Mommsen (1987) dates this hybrid model to the founding of the University of Berlin in 1808, although, as we saw in the chapter 3, modern disciplines become fully realized only after the Second World War.

The breadth needed for teaching leads some faculty members to write textbooks. It leads many highly focused scholars to read more widely in search of examples that can be successfully used in class. Many faculty report that class discussion leads to novel and fruitful research questions.

The breadth of teaching stems from the fact that a university's teaching needs do not fully match the specialization of scholarship. Area studies may offer a useful example. A scholar whose research focuses on eighteenth-century Bulgarian plays may be one of only five or six Slavic faculty who are obligated to cover a dozen or more Slavic languages and a dozen or more Slavic countries. This scholar will thus spend most of her time teaching far afield from her specialty in Bulgarian theater. Breadth is often forced on faculty who strive to master the burgeoning body of knowledge in several substantive areas.

Large departments enable faculty to teach a narrower set of classes, with scholars more able to teach a set of courses more closely aligned with their research specialties. In an English department with one hundred professors on the faculty, as is the case at Ohio State University, several faculty members might specialize in eighteenth-century British authors, others might focus on early English poets, while still others focus on nineteenth-century American authors. But even in such a mega-department, the demands of teaching, especially teaching undergraduates, tend to pull faculty in the direction of greater breadth.

Several conclusions regarding synthesis are thus in order. The pressure toward specialization and even fragmentation is countered by the tendency toward synthesis, which often occurs at the disciplinary or even subdisciplinary level. While sustained advances require both detailed investigations and general theory, it is probably the case that there is a pattern of oscillation between these two poles. In some periods, more general theorizing tends to predominate, while in other periods the accumulation of specialized findings tends to outstrip the ability of theories to rein in the relevant data.

The effort to equate disciplines with fragmentation thus misses the mark in several respects. It is not the broad disciplines but rather the proliferation of subdisciplinary specialties that poses the main risk of fragmentation. And efforts to synthesize most commonly occur within fields rather than in an interdisciplinary context.

Conclusion

Mastering the cutting-edge research techniques in all fields is simply beyond the reach of any individual; indeed, simply keeping up with thousands of journals, conference papers, books and blogs is plainly not feasible. Consequently, scholarly life necessarily becomes divided into different fields of scholarship, with specialists mastering diverse bodies of knowledge and focusing on different lines of inquiry.

The continued growth of new journals provides important insights into the trajectory of scholarship. Most new journals are specialized, allowing experts to track developments in particular areas of inquiry. A substantial minority of newly established journals are interdisciplinary, but even these are mostly specialized in one way or another. The review of journals presented here raises questions about whether the term "interdisciplinary" should be understood as synonymous with "broad." Interdisciplinary journals often seek to be "integrative" in one manner or another, but the meaning of this term is open to diverse meanings as well. In some contexts, "integrative" represents an attempt to address an important social problem, while in other contexts, "integrative" may represent an attempt to bring diverse phenomenon under the aegis of a single theoretical perspective.

The proliferation of truly interdisciplinary journals would seem to represent more of a challenge than an opportunity for scholars, since it would sharply increase the number of journals that need to be scanned to keep up with specialized developments. At some point, search engines rather than journal titles would become central to scholars' efforts to keep up with the literature. Perhaps that point has already been reached.

This chapter has not explored questions regarding open-access article repositories. The posting of papers online has become an important alternative way to access research (Prosser 2004; Registry of Open Access Repositories [ROAR] 2012). Major research universities are creating repositories of research produced by their faculty, and subject matter repositories represent an alternative organizational model. The Social Science Research Network has recently boasted of passing a milestone: the papers in its collection, numbering over 385,000 and growing, have been downloaded over 50 million times (Social Science Research Network 2012). Thus, access to research reports and scholarly articles is no longer confined to the pages of scholarly journals. However, journals are likely to continue to play an important role because they help to certify knowledge, differentiating approaches and findings that are more likely to be trustworthy from other writing that may be more suspect (Mabe 2009). A full assessment of the future of interdisciplinary scholarly communication will have to take into account the relationship between scholarly journals and the online access to research via open-access repositories, authors' websites, and forms of online communication.

This chapter emphasizes the central role of specialization in the development of new research journals. Yet the march toward specialization does not necessarily doom academia to intellectual fragmentation. Ideas continually percolate between fields, and powerful forces push in the direction of fusion as well as specialization. The rewards for intellectual synthesis are high, and detailed studies make the most sense when conducted within the rubric of an overarching framework. However, a full assessment of the relationship between forces that promote specialization and those that lead to integration or synthesis is beyond the scope of this chapter.

Over the course of the last two chapters, the context for interdisciplinary communication has been established. In chapter 3, a theory of disciplines was advanced that showed these to be enduring units with extensive dynamic forces operating both internally and externally. We have just seen how the enormous volume of research results in specialized channels of communication even when these are self-consciously interdisciplinary. It is now time to turn to evidence on the extent of communication between diverse fields of study. This will be the focus of chapters 5 and 6.

5

Disciplines, Silos, and Webs

Thus far the case for interdisciplinarity has been reviewed and contrasted with a newly developed theory of institutional disciplines that emphasizes their breadth and dynamic quality. We have also considered the tremendous volume of research and its relationship to academic specialization.

In this chapter the empirical assessment of the permeability of disciplinary boundaries begins. The analysis proceeds as follows. The discussion starts with a consideration of how citation data relate to key concepts employed by advocates of interdisciplinarity. Empirical findings on the flow of ideas between fields are presented, followed by some brief comments on how universities seek to facilitate the exchange of ideas across fields. The prominence of interdisciplinary centers in research universities is then discussed. The chapter concludes with a consideration of the claim that disciplinary insularity results in the neglect of important public policy challenges facing the country and the world.

Hierarchy of Interdisciplinarities and the Flow of Ideas

Before presenting findings on the extent of interdisciplinary exchange, it may be useful to explain where this evidence fits in the constellation of interdisciplinary ideas and terminology. Interdisciplinarians use a range of terminology; indeed, discussions in this area sometimes seemed plagued by an overabundance of terms. For example, with reference to the status of women's studies, Alice Ginsberg's list of terms includes "multidisciplinary, interdisci-

Portions of this chapter draw on and further develop themes addressed by the author and Scott Frickel in their 2009 essay in the *Annual Review of Sociology* (Jacobs and Frickel 2009).

plinary, nondisciplinary, antidisciplinary, neo-disciplinary, transdisciplinary, cross-disciplinary, critical interdisciplinary, intersectional, intertextual, and pluridisciplinary" (2008, 13). Missing from Ginsberg's list are the terms "post-disciplinary," "supra-disciplinary" (Balsiger 2004), "de-disciplinary" (Klein 2010b, 23), "postnormal science" (Funtowicz and Ravetz 1993; Bramwell and Lane 2005), and "Mode2 knowledge production" (Gibbons et al. 1994), among others.

This plethora of terminology is often celebrated by reformers. For example, Joe Moran writes

> I want to suggest that the value of the term "interdisciplinary" lies in its flexibility and indeterminacy, and that there are potentially as many forms of interdisciplinarity as there are disciplines. In a sense, to suggest otherwise would be to "discipline" it, to confine it within a series of theoretical and methodological orthodoxies. (2010, 14)

Out of this extensive lexicon, three terms are most commonly used: multidisciplinary, interdisciplinary, and transdisciplinary.[1] These concepts can be arranged to represent a hierarchy of interdisciplinarity, ranging from the more minimal to the more complete.[2]

Multidisciplinary is the slightest form of cross-disciplinary linkage; indeed, it is not really interdisciplinary at all. For example, Julie Thompson Klein describes it in mostly critical ways (Klein 2010b). She writes that multidisciplinary education is often little more than a "mélange" of courses from different fields. Multidisciplinary research may use one field (say history) to set the context for other work but is not genuinely integrative. Klein is also critical of catalogs or encyclopedia: simply compiling essays from a variety of fields into a single compendium is not truly interdisciplinary.

The term "interdisciplinary" can be confusing because it can refer in general to cross-field exchanges (this is the way it is generally used throughout this book) or more specifically as an intermediate level of interdisciplinary connectivity. In the latter sense, interdisciplinary is more interactive, collaborative, and sometimes "proactive" than are multidisciplinary undertakings.

Klein distinguishes methodological from theoretical approaches, with the latter ranked as a more fully interdisciplinary than the former. Bridge building versus restructuring are prominent metaphors in this area, with the latter again further along on the interactive continuum than the former. The terms "hybridization" and "cross-fertilization" often appear in these discussions as well.

The notion of "transdisciplinarity"—sometimes "postdisciplinarity"—is intended to convey a higher, or the highest, level of truly transformative scholarship. Compared to other types of intellectual exchanges, transdisciplinarity attains a degree of synthesis and integration that sets it apart. Whether this advance represents a new intellectual synthesis or a solution to a practical problem, the end result is fundamentally different from the original components. The achievement requires disparate elements but each is transformed when combined with insights from other areas.[3] In both cases, ideas, techniques, and perspectives from different fields are brought together in a transformative way.

The house of interdisciplinarity as commonly discussed thus has three floors, but much of the real action is going on in the basement. The flow of ideas between disciplines occurs all of the time but is often missed by critics. For example, a sociologist might employ a new set of techniques developed by statisticians, first used by economists and widely employed by cancer researchers, but this fact would likely be missed, as it is not part of the set of collaborations depicted in the interdisciplinary hierarchy. The degree to which disciplines are porous at the level of ideas is a basic indicator of the openness and flexibility of disciplines.

Figure 5.1 helps to contrast this approach with the more typical analyses of interdisciplinarity. This graph illustrates how interdisciplinarians view the nature of communication across disciplines. Merely juxtaposing ideas from different fields—multidisciplinarity—does not get very far in terms of blending and recombining these ideas, and thus falls at the bottom of the

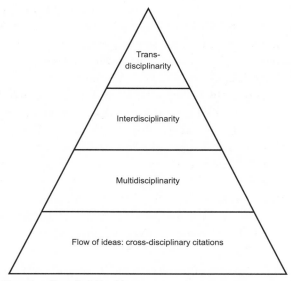

FIGURE 5.1. Hierarchy of interdisciplinarities.

interdisciplinary pyramid. Transdisciplinarity, in contrast, represents an effort to use ideas from different fields in a new and synthetic way, and thus sits atop the interdisciplinary hierarchy.

The point of this illustration is that, beneath the three echelons of interdisciplinary typically considered, lies a deeper, more basic level of exchange, namely, the flow of ideas across fields. Interdisciplinarians too often essentialize disciplines and ignore or downplay the intellectual dynamism that can be readily seen at this foundational level. Figure 5.1 can help to situate the findings presented below on citation analyses and the receptivity curves presented in chapter 6 while pointing to the dynamic character of arts and science disciplines.

When a sociologist studying divorce rates uses a statistic widely used by oncologists, she is engaging in interdisciplinary communication. She is deploying a technique that neither of these fields owns or created. She can pick up an article on cancer survival and notice the analytical technique familiar from her own research. This will occur without formal interdisciplinary collaboration, without a joint appointment, without the creation of an interdisciplinary training or certificate program. It occurs simply because survival analysis has become part of the tool kit of cancer researchers and the contemporary quantitative sociologists trained at major research universities in the United States and around the world.

The use of survival analysis occurs at the basement level of interdisciplinarity. This type of exchange occurs every day without fuss or fanfare, without the intervention or assistance of vice provosts for interdisciplinary research. It is one way, but by no means the only way, that disciplines advance, but it is largely ignored by those who advocate the interdisciplinary restructuring of the university.

Another way to make this point is to pursue the analogy between disciplines and tribes more fully. The suggestion is that disciplinary scholars somehow resemble primitive people, not only ignorant of knowledge of the world outside their department's corridor but actively seeking to block it out. Anthropologists, however, have for some time questioned the idea of "pure" primitive culture. Indigenous cultures in many if not all parts of the globe are hybridized in a myriad of ways, borrowing religious ideas here, technology there, thus making it difficult (if not completely meaningless) to say what a tribe's pure, essential or "traditional" culture might be (Sahlins 1999). Globalization has made complete cultural isolation increasingly difficult if not impossible. In this context, it seems odd to suggest that the last bastions of cultural isolation occur in the modern university, in other words, in the central precincts of the information society. Just as indigenous cultures around the world have absorbed external influences, so too has sociology (and every other field) incorporated ideas and techniques from across the university.[4]

Empirical Data: The Web of Science

The idea that disciplines have become isolated silos is often quickly agreed to, a simple and basic assumption that conversational partners assume will be accepted as a point of departure. In discussions with colleagues about inter-disciplinarity, I have found that some (but by no means all) believe that the notion of silos is an established fact.

Yet, at other times, a very different assumptions is invoked. Specifically, when university departments are threatened with closure, the interconnect-edness of the academic enterprise is often summoned as a reason to preserve the unit in question. In this context, the notion of academia as a seamless web comes to the fore. If the intellectual enterprise is an elaborate weave, then the closure of a given department represents a tear in that fabric that can unravel learning far beyond the point of incision. Thus, when the University at Albany announced that it would no longer offer a degree in French, the chorus of defenders emphasized not only the importance of French in a global economy but also the spillover effects of ripping one strand of inquiry from the larger tapestry of knowledge.

> First, no department is an island. Universities are places where scholars in one field have opportunities to debate, collaborate with, and learn from scholars in very different fields. The loss of any department is a loss to every depart-ment at that institution. . . . It looks like you are merely clearing away some of the underbrush. But you are damaging the ecology of the entire institution. (Menand 2010b)[5]

The central problem with the "silo" model is that it does not fit the facts. In this case, Louis Menand is correct in asserting that all fields are connected to one another, to varying degrees.

Citation analysis has emerged as a technique for tracing the connections between researchers as indicated by their own references. The principal data-base in this area, now called the Web of Knowledge, includes references on thousands of journals in the sciences, social sciences, and the humanities. This database is quite extensive but by no means completely comprehensive. These data are familiar to many scholars and journal editors as they form the basis for the Journal Citation Reports (Thomson Reuters 2011).

Thed Van Leeuwen and Robert Tijssen (2000) draw on these data in their analysis of connections across fields. They classified 2,314 journals into 119 subject categories, and report that most (69 percent) references are cross-disciplinary, that is, the *majority* of references in a given journal are drawn from journals in other disciplinary fields. This remarkably high rate of cross-field exchange in part reflects the detailed classification scheme they employ. In other words, had they grouped journals into twenty or thirty fields rather than 119, van Leeuwen and Tijssen would have reported a lower rate of cross-disciplinary citations. Nonetheless, their research fits with the "web of science" imagery much more closely than with the "isolated silos" premise.

Additional pertinent data on the degree of intellectual contact between fields has been tabulated by the National Science Foundation. Imagine a matrix of origin and destination fields of inquiry; the entries in each cell are citations in scholarly journals. Table 5.1 presents a summary of this matrix that focuses on the diagonal cells, that is, the fraction of citations occurring within a discipline. While this classification scheme suggests that most citations occur within fields, a substantial minority of references cross disciplinary boundaries. For example, over 30 percent of citations to research in chemistry appear in journals outside the field, as do nearly 40 percent of citations to biological research.

Table 5.2 presents similar data on the social sciences and related areas of research:[6] specifically, the percentage of citations occurring within a given field as well as the percent occurring within the social sciences. As was the case in table 5.1, it is clear that there is considerable intellectual exchange across fields. For example, over half of the studies that draw on sociological research are published outside this field, and over 40 percent appear outside the social sciences. Extensive external contacts via citations are evident for applied as well as basic fields of inquiry.

TABLE 5.1. Citation patterns across broad scientific fields

Scientific field	% citations within field	% interdisciplinary citations
Physics	81.7	18.3
Chemistry	69.0	31.0
Earth and space science	83.2	16.8
Mathematics	77.4	22.6
Biology	61.7	38.3
Biomedical research	75.4	24.6
Clinical medicine	71.4	28.6
Engineering & technology	61.9	38.1
Psychology	65.5	34.5
Social sciences	77.3	22.7
Other	67.1	32.9

Source: National Science Foundation, 2000. Science and Engineering Indicators, appendix table 6–54.

TABLE 5.2. Citation patterns within the social sciences and professional fields

	% within field	% within social sciences
Anthropology	52.8	61.5
Area studies	28.3	89.8
Criminology	41.7	55.8
Demography	40.7	73.6
Economics	80.9	87.2
General social science	23.4	60.7
Geography and regional science	51.3	82.9
International relations	65.8	98.8
Planning and urban studies	29.2	62.0
Political science and public administration	58.7	90.7
Science studies	47.8	57.1
Sociology	51.9	75.1
Miscellaneous social sciences	23.9	35.6

Health and professional fields	% within field	% within health and professional fields
Communication	59.7	73.5
Education	68.9	75.4
Gerontology & aging	18.5	34.8
Health policy & services	26.5	39.4
Information & library science	75.5	84.5
Law	78.2	84.0
Management & business	77.8	79.2
Nursing	33.0	48.7
Public health	22.8	33.4
Rehabilitation	53.2	63.2
Social studies of medicine	16.7	37.0
Social work	41.2	50.8
Speech, language pathology, audiology	53.0	60.8
Miscellaneous professional fields	54.2	64.9

Source: National Science Foundation, Science and Engineering Indicators, 2000, appendix table 6–54.

The findings presented in tables 5.1 and 5.2 should be considered rough and approximate, as they depend on the classification of scholarly journals. Reclassifying a particular journal will alter these findings. For example, the journal *Sociology of Education* could be placed either with education or with sociology; either choice will affect the rate of internal citations in each field. Nonetheless, some clear patterns emerge. Some fields, such as economics, tend to be more internally oriented, while other fields, such as area studies, rely heavily on scholarship from other disciplines. Some of these differences reflect the size of fields: demography is a relatively small field, and thus a high rate of citations outside this specialty is to be expected.

These data on cross-field citations raise an important question for advocates of interdisciplinarity, namely, whether the fields that are most open to external ideas are also the most intellectually dynamic. If this were true, area studies would be the envy of the social sciences, and economists would be busy trying to figure out how best to emulate the success of area studies scholars. In fact, the reverse is true: economics is the most influential field in the social sciences, and it is also the most inwardly focused. Area studies is a much weaker field in no small part because of an inadequate base of students and financial support, and its openness to research from other fields is not necessarily an indication of the vitality of the field.

Alan Porter and Ismael Rafols (2009) suggest that science as a whole is becoming more interdisciplinary. They report that in 2005, compared to 1975, research papers in six science and engineering fields studied (a) had many more coauthors (roughly 75 percent more); (b) cited 50 percent more papers; and (c) cited papers from more diverse subject classifications (also an increase of 50 percent).[7]

This study suggests the advent of computers, search engines, and electronic access to the scientific literature is altering the very nature of scientific publications. Researchers have far more literature at their fingertips than was the case a generation ago. As we have also seen, they also have more to keep up with. These results point to the quiet yet fundamental changes in the nature of research that have occurred in the context of ostensibly stodgy disciplines.

Analysts of the connections between journals have developed maps of science. They maintain that these maps reflect the actual behavior of scholars rather than distinctions made by philosophers or the official fields in which researchers may have received their degrees. Figure 5.2 is one such map, drawn in 2004, based on over 6.4 million citations in over six thousand journals (Eigenfactor Project 2011). In this particular analysis, molecular and cell biology form a powerful node with strong links to neuroscience, medicine, ecology, and chemistry, with many other fields branching off from this central complex. For our purposes, the main point is that there are connections between all fields.[8]

These results are based on the patterns of citations found in the bibliography sections of academic journal articles. Critics of citation studies rightly point out that the precise meaning of citations is elusive, with some references taking on a symbolic or ceremonial role (Nicolaisen 2007; van Raan 2005; Cole and Cole 1987). Authors cite research for a variety of reasons, and the expectations regarding appropriate citations vary across disciplines (Hargens 2000).[9] There are good reasons not to rely too heavily on citation statistics to evaluate individual scholars or to make tenure decisions. But for our

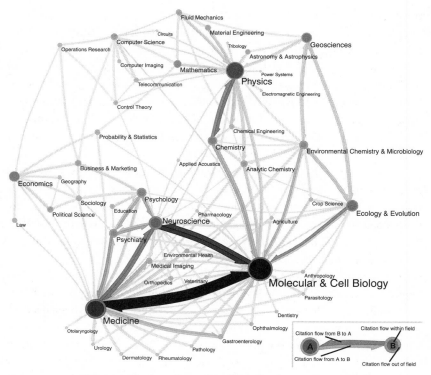

FIGURE 5.2. A citation map of science. Source: http://www.eigenfactor.org/map/maps.htm.

purposes, citation patterns are not so easily dismissed. Critics of disciplines who claim that they are inwardly focused would have difficulty explaining why scholars cite so much research from outside their own field. The present discussion does not depend on the ranking of one article over another based on its citation count or even the accuracy of any given reference. The conclusion offered here is that the volume of cross-disciplinary references is simply too large to be ignored.

Another line of criticism is that citations are too often the result of social pressure to cite the most celebrated scholars in the field. This line of reasoning would suggest that citation statistics may well understate the prevalence of cross-disciplinary references. If the pressure is to cite local heroes, then the reasons that scholars so often cite foreign dignitaries need to be elaborated.

There are many technical issues involved in drawing the maps of research specialties. For example, Gmur (2003) shows that in depicting the layout of a field, the precise configuration will depend on a series of decisions about how to assess cocitation data. Maps can describe connections between individual papers or ties between journals. In addition to citations, one can map specific scientific terms or coauthorships. Maps based on overlap in the usage of particular terminology (coword analysis) display the conceptual connections between papers while avoiding the concerns over "ritualistic" citations (Callon, Courtial, and Laville 1991; Moody and Light 2006; Moody, Light, and Leahy 2012). Every type of map of intellectual connections depicts a web of knowledge, even if the exact position of particular fields may vary.

The Diffusion of Ideas across Disciplines

Another way to study the connections between fields is to examine the diffusion of particular concepts or terms. Rather than sum all citations by journal or discipline as the studies noted above have done, examples of the prevalence of specific ideas or terms in various fields can serve as a useful barometer of interdisciplinary communication. The data strongly support Crane's (2010) contention that some concepts diffuse across the humanities and sometimes the social sciences as well. As was noted in chapter 2, Klein (1996) and Moran (2010) present case studies in the humanities that include substantial evidence of blurry boundaries and extensive communication across fields.

Consider the diffusion of a single term: the prevalence of the term "postmodern" in academic journal articles cataloged electronically by the Web of Knowledge (see table 5.3). This term appears in thousands of journal articles spread across disciplines in the humanities (for example, literature, religion, philosophy), and the social sciences (sociology, geography, psychology), as well as various applied fields such as education, business, and law. This tabulation by no means captures the full range of diffusion of this term since the Web of Knowledge data are restricted to journal articles and omit books and other forms of writing.

The analysis presented includes the term "postmodern" as the result of a "topic" search. The procedure was repeated using a narrower search that focused on article titles (results not shown). The latter approach yields a slightly different ranking of fields but leads to the same substantive conclusion. Even in the specialized context of academic journal articles, the term "postmodernism" diffused broadly. Indeed, the concept appears in research journals from over one hundred areas of research.

Since the term "postmodern" may mean different things to different scholars, this analysis was repeated with a narrower term that is less vulnerable to this concern, namely, Bruno Latour's "actor-network theory." This term has been the topic of 1,373 journal articles. As is evident in table 5.3, this concept has diffused across a number of disciplines, from business and economics to computer science. In addition to the fields listed in table 5.3, this

TABLE 5.3. Diffusion of terms and concepts in the humanities and social sciences

A. *Presence of term "postmodern" in the title of an academic journal article, by field of journal*

7,637 total articles	Percent
1. Literature	23.1
2. Religion	8.2
3. Sociology	8.8
4. Psychology	7.9
5. Arts/humanities (other)	6.5
6. Philosophy	6.0
7. Social science (other)	5.8
8. Government/law	4.6
9. Education research	4.5
10. Business/economics	4.1

B. *Actor-network theory (Bruno Latour) as a title or subject area of an academic journal article, by field of journal*

1,373 total articles	Percent
1. Business, economics	22.5
2. Sociology	19.6
3. Geography	13.0
4. Environmental science/ecology	9.3
5. Public administration	7.4
6. Social sciences (other)	6.5
7. Computer science	5.8
8. Information/library science	5.7
9. Government/law	4.8
10. Educational research	3.9

Source: Author's analysis of Web of Knowledge data compiled September 2012.

concept appears in many other areas of research as well, including anthropology, psychology, public health, and international relations.

This analysis was broadened to include citations to Latour's two most influential books—*Laboratory Life*, with Steve Woolgar (1986 [1979]) and *Science in Action* (1987) (results not shown). Again, each book is different with a slightly different set of disciplines, but the same thrust remains: Latour's work is discussed by researchers in many fields. Whether these concepts diffused too quickly (becoming a fad) or too slowly (due to unwarranted resistance) is not something these data directly address. Assessing this would require a baseline indicator of how much reception there should have been. Nonetheless, these data do appear to counter the simple assumption that ideas developed in one discipline are rarely adopted in another.

The data on references to Latour can also be viewed as a case of the incorporation of interdisciplinary ideas into disciplinary contexts. Latour's work is stridently and explicitly nondisciplinary or postdisciplinary. This case thus raises questions about whether the acceptance of ideas by scholars and researchers depends on whether these ideas originate in a discipline compared with an interdisciplinary origin.

This analysis was repeated using the works of such prominent humanists as Jacques Derrida and Michel Foucault, along with prominent social scientists including Charles Tilly and Robert Putnam (results not shown). While each of these authors has been influential in a somewhat different set of disciplines, each has nonetheless been the subject of articles in many fields in the social sciences and humanities.

Research methods, especially statistical techniques, are frequently adopted by a broad set of fields. (See Abbott [2001, 143], for a list of scholars responsible for the importation of several statistical methods into sociology.) For example, as noted above, survival analysis is a statistical technique that has been used in tens of thousands of published journal articles since the 1990s. These papers appeared in public health journals; many types of medical journals, including oncology, cardiology, and surgery; statistics journals; and studies in such diverse fields as computer science, demography, economics, and ecology. In examining the wide diffusion of this powerful statistical technique, it is hard to see evidence of academic silos that impede the diffusion of this methodological innovation. Is this diffusion too slow? Perhaps, but it is hard to specify what the "right" rate of diffusion would be.

And survival analysis is by no means alone. Survey research methods, experimental designs, and regression analysis along with its many variants and enhancements, have become commonplace in journals ranging from public policy analyses to psychology. Prospective authors complain that publication in the leading journals is difficult without the use of the latest methods even when simpler analyses would lead to the same conclusion.

There are of course cases in which disciplines differ on matters of substance. Not all ideas are equally embraced in all quarters. Michèle Lamont and Myra Strober both underscore the cultural divisions among disciplines, especially in the social sciences and humanities (see also Becher and Trowler 2001). Yet it is not clear exactly how interdisciplinarity will succeed in overcoming these dividing lines.

One noted case involves the opposing explanations of improvements in health and declines in mortality advanced by McKeown and Preston. A prominent British epidemiologist, Thomas McKeown (1976), argued that economic development was more important than medical advances or even public health measures in contributing to the advancement in human longevity. Samuel H. Preston, an internationally renowned demographer, at nearly the same time (1975), argued that economic development was less important than commonly thought and that public health measures were more important. It is commonly believed that epidemiologists have tended to accept McKeown's side of the argument, ironically devaluing their own field, while demographers have often rallied to Preston's position. In a 2007 symposium on his original 1975 paper (International Journal of Epidemiology 2007), Preston notes one possible reason for the continued difference of opinion, namely, that both studies were based on indirect evidence. Both scholars advanced their arguments largely by the process of eliminating alternative explanations rather than providing data directly supporting their conclusions. An analysis of citation patterns suggests that both the Preston and McKeown papers were cited in journal articles in epidemiology, public health, and demography, among others, and thus differences of opinion were not the result of lack of visibility of these studies.

The examples provided thus far draw from the social sciences and humanities, reflecting topics I am familiar with as well as those that have been suggested in the course of conversation with colleagues. Nathan Rosenberg, an economist at Stanford University, provides parallel examples of diffusion across fields in the natural sciences, including examples from physics, chemistry, biology, and engineering (1994, 154–56). Rosenberg emphasizes the diffusion of scientific instrumentation (1994, 253–55) as particularly salient in leading to important innovations. For example, nuclear magnetic resonance developed by physicists for studying the magnetic movements of atomic nuclei was adopted by chemists, biologists, medical clinicians, and neuroscientists, for whom imaging technologies, including magnetic resonance imaging, have become important tools.[10]

Is there a "citation penalty" for interdisciplinary research? In other words, do scholars pay a price in terms of the recognition of their work by pursuing interdisciplinary topics? Studies on this topic yield conflicting results. For example, Levitt and Thelwall (2008) find a disadvantage for interdisciplinary studies in the natural sciences but not in the social sciences. In contrast, Rinia et al. (2002) report no cost to interdisciplinary publications. The difference between these two arguments depends in large part on the status of interdisciplinary journals. If one adjusts for the relatively low status of interdisciplinary journals, as Rinia and colleagues did, then there is little or no additional penalty for interdisciplinary publications compared with similarly ranked disciplinary journals. However, advocates of interdisciplinarity would point out that there are relatively few interdisciplinary journals that have obtained high status, thus inhibiting scholars from pursuing interdisciplinary research.[11]

Universities as Information Hubs

Academics not only have a variety of motives to learn more about intellectual developments across the academy, they also have at their disposal many means to do so. One way to keep up is by reading. A number of general-interest outlets enable American academics to keep tabs on developments in a wide range of areas. *Science*, the journal of the American Association for the Advancement of Science, has a print circulation of 130,000 and an estimated readership of 1 million. The *New York Times* circulation is 1 million daily on Tuesdays when the Science Times is published and over 1.4 million when the Sunday Book Review section is published. The *New York Review of Books* has a circulation of approximately 135,000. The *Chronicle of Higher Education* has 68,000 subscribers, an estimated readership of 250,000, and a total of 1.7 million unique viewers of its web page.[12]

Scholarly exchange also occurs through audio and visual channels. National Public Radio's program Science Friday boasts of 1.3 million listeners. For certain topics, TED Talks has proven to be an effective means of disseminating ideas.[13]

Many faculty members receive two or three alumni magazines: one from their undergraduate institution, a second from their graduate school, and a third from the school in which they are currently employed. Alumni magazines provide campus news and faculty profiles along with accessible reports of recent developments in far-flung research fields. For example, Harvard alums can find in the *Harvard Magazine* stories on new scholarship about the Civil War in the United States, a new institute for biologically inspired engineering, the social consequences of polygamy, and how one learned to dance in Jane Austen's time. In addition to alumni publications, Penn offers faculty a daily e-mail blast with brief summaries of ongoing faculty research and scholarship.

It is unlikely that those who learn about far-flung scientific advances in the pages of the *Chronicle* or those who listen to Science Friday for an hour will somehow become able to do cutting-edge research. But they are likely to become aware of developments in other fields. They are likely to know, if they have any interest, that nanotechnology and neuroscience are areas undergoing rapid advances, and they may well learn enough to determine whether they want to inquire further.

Newly available technology is making it easier to keep up with the unending supply of peer-reviewed journals. Many schools offer journal alerts, that is, the table of contents of new issues. At Penn, in 2012, 444 faculty received updates on a range of journals.[14] I currently receive alerts from ten journals; a colleague claims to keep tabs on fifty journals. Journal publishers including Sage Publications are increasingly offering similar services.

In the past, one could go to the library and browse in the reading room where new periodicals arrived. Research assistants could be sent to copy selected articles; some university libraries have provided this service to faculty. Thus, the availability of journal tables of contents in one's e-mail reader may not be as big a departure from the past as it may seem. Yet e-mails alerts may be a more regular event than a leisurely trip to the library reading room, and the decision to receive regular alerts indicates an interest in keeping up with the literature.

Given the volume of published research discussed in chapter 4, most faculty members have long since ceased trying to keep up with all publications that may be of interest . . . unless there is some help from one's friends. Passing along items of interest electronically is an important means by which faculty help one another keep informed. For many, blogs, Facebook, and Twitter make passing along information quicker and easier. Research groups often circulate newsletters with brief summaries of items of interest.

In recent years, new channels of communication have become readily accessible. Search engines are able to search specialized databases such as the Web of Knowledge and Google Scholar. As noted in chapter 4, open-access repositories make a rapidly growing share of research findings accessible to all who have access to the World Wide Web. In short, it has become easy to locate more research papers than there is time to read and digest.

Joint and secondary appointments also facilitate communication. Just as faculty like to accumulate honors and awards, they also like to collect affiliations. Connections to various campus programs and other departments are surprisingly common. To illustrate this pattern, the websites of the universities with the top ten sociology departments were consulted. The university affiliations of full professors were counted. Overall, 84 percent of senior sociology faculty in these schools listed affiliations to various programs and other departments; two or three secondary affiliations were not uncommon. For comparison, the same information was compiled for economics departments in the same institutions. Economics faculty were not as likely as sociologists to list multiple affiliations; nonetheless, a majority (52 percent) did so. Again, the evidence suggests that faculty members actively seek connections outside their own specialties.

Research Centers

As noted in chapter 3, research centers represent an important feature of contemporary research universities that has largely been neglected in the discussion of interdisciplinarity (see Ikenberry and Friedman 1972; Friedman and Friedman 1982; Klein 1996, chap 6; and Rhoten 2003 for exceptions). Centers are often organized around applied topics, such as the problems of an aging

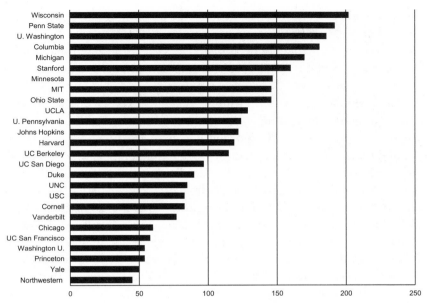

FIGURE 5.3. Research centers at top 25 US universities, 2012. Source: Gale Ready Reference Shelf.

society or the challenges of bioethics, but there are also many centers that focus on topics of enduring academic interest, such as the Minda de Gunzburg Center for European Studies at Harvard.

Research centers are an increasingly common feature of US higher education. Data from the census of organizations compiled by the Gale research group (Gale Cengage Learning 2012) reveals that there well over ten thousand research centers located at colleges and universities in the United States in 2012.[15] Research centers are most common at the leading research universities. The data indicate that there were on average over one hundred research centers (119) per school in the twenty-five leading research universities in the United States (see figure 5.3).

A remarkable total of nearly three thousand research centers are found at these twenty-five universities, representing nearly one-quarter of the total found in all US colleges and universities. The number of research centers generally follows the volume of research grants, although institutions with medical schools typically have considerably more centers and institutes than other schools.

Consequently, at the largest research institutions, there can be as many, if not more, research centers as there are disciplinary departments. Examination of a sample of these centers from university websites suggests that the vast majority are interdisciplinary, at least in name and in self-presentation.

Given their sheer number and tendency to identify institutionally with inter-disciplinary goals, research centers may function—imperfectly to be sure—as intrauniversity "boundary organizations" (see Guston 2000) that help to bridge disciplinary divides and serve as an organizational counterweight to academic departments.

Strong disciplines combined with the flexibility to create diverse research centers as needed may be an attractive organizational solution to the challenges of organizing rapidly growing bodies of research and knowledge. Among a variety of functions, centers provide "micromobilization contexts" for recruitment into emerging interdisciplinary fields (Frickel and Gross 2005). Thus, while advocates of interdisciplinarity have lambasted the ostensibly hidebound nature of academic disciplines, it is clear that university-based academic departments coexist with an increasing number and dizzying array of research centers that at minimum represent an organizational context for bringing together scholars from diverse backgrounds with shared interests.

Do such centers facilitate communication across disciplinary boundaries? Ikenberry and Friedman report that the vast majority of the applied and natural science centers they studied emphasized interdisciplinarity, but they found that only about half of the social science centers professed this as a goal (1972, 44–49).

In a more recent report, Diana Rhoten (2003) offers a guardedly pessimistic analysis. On the positive side of the ledger, faculty in the six interdisciplinary research centers she studied reported spending half of their work time on center-related interdisciplinary activity, and 83 percent said that their relationships with other center members had positively influenced their own research agendas. She also reports that those centers with larger numbers of affiliated faculty generate more information sharing but fewer substantive interdisciplinary connections.

Despite these encouraging findings, Rhoten's overall appraisal is pessimistic. She complains that the centers tended to be organized around "catch-all themes" rather than unifying problem definitions, and consequently fall short of achieving the transformative level of interdisciplinary synthesis. While this valuable study identifies some important organizational problems, the question of whether research centers represent efficacious solutions to generating interdisciplinary research is far from settled. A more modest standard of interdisciplinary awareness and cooperation puts her data in a more positive light.[16] Furthermore, if voluntary participation in research centers does not produce true interdisciplinarity, it is worthwhile considering what types of organizational settings might be more conducive to interdisciplinary research and scholarship.

The Proliferation of Research Centers

How interdisciplinary are interdisciplinary fields? In other words, one possibility is that the rapid growth of a new interdisciplinary field results in internal differentiation. Successful interdisciplinary research areas thus may generate a new set of journals, subspecialties, and internal conflicts over resources, in short, the same fragmentation that reformers hoped could be overcome.

Bibliometric research on nanotechnology has explored this issue but is thus far not definitive in resolving it. An early study suggests a high degree of interdisciplinary citations in nanotechnology research (Meyer and Persson 1998). However, a more recent study of coauthorship patterns (Schummer 2004) suggests that nanotechnology is a not a single field but rather offshoots of physics, chemistry, electrical engineering, mechanical engineering, and materials science. Schummer's strong conclusion is that nanotechnology's "apparent interdisciplinarity consists of largely mono-disciplinary fields which are rather unrelated to each other and which hardly share more than the prefix 'nano'" (Schummer 2004, 425).

Interdisciplinarity is likely to produce its own type of fragmentation. In other words, the promise of bringing large numbers of academics together around a relatively limited number of research themes is illusory. The multifaceted nature of the vexing problems of the day allows for diverse definitions of these issues, which enables academic entrepreneurs to build research empires around their own particular approaches. Social problems are often supported by a wide range of funding sources, leading researchers to pitch their studies to the interest of a range of donors and granting agencies.

One example of the proliferation of research centers under the umbrella of a single social issue may help to illustrate this point. Since 9/11, Pennsylvania State University has endeavored to promote research related to homeland security. This worthy goal does not fall within the purview of any single academic discipline and thus is typical of the examples used by interdisciplinary reformers to argue for the development of new organizational models. Yet the Penn State example suggests that interdisciplinarity does not mean the unification or integration of knowledge. This university has developed no less than twenty-one research centers focused on various aspects of homeland security (see table 5.4). These many centers were not a secret but indeed were prominently displayed on the university's website (Pennsylvania State University 2011). These include the International Center for the Study of Terrorism; the Center for Information Assurance, which addresses issues of cybersecurity in the context of threats to computer systems; the Protective Technology Center, which focuses research and development activities with

TABLE 5.4. Homeland security research centers, institutes and laboratories at Pennsylvania State
University

- Anechoic Chamber and Laboratory Facility
  Provides the environment to encourage research between Penn State, industry, and government
  agencies to solve the many types of communication systems (radio) interoperability issues currently
  plaguing emergency first responders in America.
- Applied Research Laboratory
  As a DoD-designated, Navy UARC (University Affiliated Research Center), the Applied Research Lab
  serves as a university center of excellence in defense science and technologies, with a focus in naval
  missions and related areas.
- BioNanoMaterials Laboratory
  Developing a sensing platform that uses organophosphorus hydrolases (OPH) to detoxify a broad
  range of organophosphate pesticides and the chemical warfare agents.
- Center for Chemical Ecology
  Researchers explore the role chemistry plays in predator-prey, parasite-host, herbivore-plant, virus-
  vector, and intraspecific interactions.
- Center for Infectious Disease Dynamics
  CIDD is a "virtual" center bringing together theoreticians and empirical scientists in a wide variety of
  disciplines to collaborate and innovate in the area of infectious disease research.
- Center for Information Assurance
  Conducts broad-based research on various aspects of information and cybersecurity.
- Center for Info and Communications Technology Research (CICTR)
  Generating solutions to current and future technical challenges in the transmission, storage,
  transformation, switching, networking, and security of digital information.
- Center for Network Centric Cognition and Information Fusion
  A new center is being established at Penn State. We will apply multidiscipline and interdiscipline
  research to address large-scale applications such as homeland security, national defense, medical
  diagnosis, and environmental monitoring.
- DETER Laboratory
  Effort to create, maintain, and support a collaborative and vendor-neutral experimental environment
  for cybersecurity research.
- Gas Dynamics Laboratory
  Conducts research on gas dynamics, flow visualization, optical flow diagnostics, and a variety of
  thermal-science topics important to national security.
- International Center for the Study of Terrorism
  In the Worldwide Universities Network, theories and research from a wide range disciplines are applied
  to studying terrorism and to developing effective means of responding to the threat of terrorism.
- Indoor Environment Center
  Scope includes building security from intentional and unintentional large-scale releases of toxic and
  infectious agents.
- Institute for Non-Lethal Defense Technologies
  Supports development of nonlethal options for both military and civilian law enforcement.
- Intelligent Agents Laboratory
  Development of intelligent agent technologies—specifically, team-based agents and market-based
  agents—is the focus of this lab.
- Navigation & Research Development Center
  Conducts research for new technology navigation sensors and systems for application in air, marine,
  and land vehicles.
- Networking and Security Research Center
  The NSRC provides a research and education community at Penn State for professors, students, and
  collaborators from industry interested in networking and security.

- North-East Visualization & Analytics Center
  One of five Regional Visualization and Analytics Centers (RVACs) that are bringing academic expertise to the nation's efforts to discover information that may warn officials of a terrorist attack.
- Protective Technology Center
  Focuses research and development activities with the goal of protecting people and infrastructure from terrorist attacks.
- Spatial Information and Intelligence Laboratory
  Creating systems that will enable even nonexpert users to access highly complicated geographical information resources and will facilitate decision making among teams.
- Systems and Internet Infrastructure Security Laboratory
  Focused on the discovery of the next generation of technologies that will secure computer systems.
- User Science and Engineering Laboratory
  The focus of this lab is the interdisciplinary work domain of emergency crisis management/crisis planning.

Source: Pennsylvania State University website, 2011. Homeland Security Initiative.
Home : Research : Centers, Institutes and Laboratories.http://homelandsecurity.psu.edu/discovery/centers/index.html.

the goal of protecting people and infrastructure from terrorist attacks; and other centers focused on crisis management, infectious diseases, nonlethal defense technologies, and a host of other issues. Each of these may represent a laudable endeavor, but the proliferation of these research centers, institutes, and laboratories underscores the fact that there are many aspects of any issue and that interdisciplinary initiatives can lead just as easily to the multiplication of academic units as to their consolidation. This is especially true if interdisciplinary units are added to the university landscape without removing the traditional disciplinary departments.

Abbott (2001, 135) makes the point that social issues are far more numerous than are disciplines, and an interdisciplinary university would thus have to be far more fragmented than the current discipline-centered arrangement. He further notes that that a problem-centered university would engender its own forms of duplication, as numerous problems connect with the same underlying bodies of knowledge. The Penn State example takes Abbott's point one step further. Even a single social concern, such as homeland security, is amenable to many organizing principles and can easily be embodied in a diverse and competing array of units on campus, each with its own intellectual lineage, its own committed supporters, and its own funding streams.

The contemporary university accommodates this diversity by combing a limited set of discipline-based departments with a much more varied set of research centers. This flexible arrangement allows for faculty and other researchers to come together in a center or institute to work together on particular problems while still developing and inculcating disciplinary skills through their service in departmental roles. While this arrangement may not fully live up to expectations in particular instances (Rhoten 2003), a problem-based approach would compound rather than resolve the problem of too many intellectual units.

Are Social Issues Neglected by Disciplinary Specialists?

A central concern of Campbell and others is that important social issues are not addressed because they are not located at the core of their disciplines. The inadequacy of disciplines in addressing social problems is taken up by the Network of Transdisciplinary Research, a project of the Swiss Academies of Arts and Sciences (2011).

> Transdisciplinary Research (TR) responds to the observation that "the world has problems, universities have departments" (Brewer 1999, 328). This means that TR is oriented towards problem fields in the life-world. . . . Examples of such problem fields are migration, violence, health, poverty, global environmental change and cultural transformation processes, among others. (http://www.transdisciplinarity.ch/e/Transdisciplinarity/)

The suggestion, then, is that disciplines divert their adherents from addressing the issues of the day. Yet the fact of the matter is that there is no shortage of research on important social problems. The data presented in figure 5.4 provide a very rough indication of the extent of scholarly attention to selected issues. The data were obtained from searches of the Web of Knowledge. The analysis was restricted to the period 1990–2010 in order to make the findings informative. Figure 5.4 provides both low-end and high-end estimates of the number of articles addressing a particular topic. The low-end figure is based on a title search; the high-end figure represents a subject search.

Have researchers shied away from health care reform and health care policy as a social issue because it does not fit neatly into the confines of one discipline? The data suggest otherwise. Over the last twenty years, over fifteen thousand academic papers have been written on this topic. The same level of scholarly interest has been devoted to questions of educational reform and educational policy.

The fact is that university-based researchers are deeply engaged in the issues of the day, whether the topic is AIDS, immigration, climate change, racism, sexism, domestic violence, homelessness, or terrorism. In each of these areas, thousands of papers have been written attempting to grapple in one way or another with these important social challenges.

The data presented in figure 5.4 are likely to understate the extent of scholarly attention to these issues, as they reflect the use of only one or two

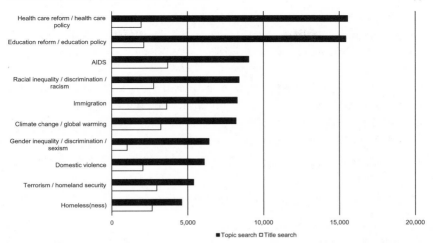

FIGURE 5.4. Academic research on selected social issues, 1990–2010. Source: Author's analysis of ISI-Web of Knowledge data.

terms for each topic. The results are further understated because the Web of Knowledge database does not include books, reports, congressional testimony, or essays written for newspaper op-ed pages or other important outlets. Searches on these topics were repeated using Google Scholar, which encompasses books and dissertations as well as a wider set of journals than does the Web of Knowledge. The results of a title search in Google Scholar generally at least double the number of entries presented in figure 5.4. For example, the term "global warming" appears in 12,100 titles in Google Scholar compared with 3,200 in Web of Knowledge. And even Google Scholar excludes items written for the general public, for example, essays written for the opinion columns in newspapers and general interest magazines.

In conducting this analysis, the emphasis was placed on specific terms that would reduce the prevalence of false positives. A search on a more general term such as "poverty" returns tens of thousands of entries, including studies of poverty within advanced countries as well as poverty in poor countries. The results presented thus represent conservative estimates of the extent of scholarly interest in public issues.

An advocate of more integrated studies might counter these data by noting that these issues still confront us, that poverty remains stubbornly with us. Reformers insist that more interdisciplinary approaches are needed to resolve these challenges. But this argument is not compelling because the solution to social issues is not simply a matter of the knowledge base. Much excellent research has been conducted on poverty in the United States, but the fact of the matter is that poverty rates are much lower in western European welfare states that are more committed to social and economic equality (Atkinson, Smeeding, and Rainwater 1995). It is not simply a matter of divided disciplines and insufficient knowledge but lack of political will that makes poverty a social challenge.

Moreover, while many important social issues are multidimensional, the conclusions that one should draw from this fact are not so obvious. In attacking multifaceted problems, one might best pursue specific lines of research armed with discipline-specific skills. The question of how to best approach social issues that are broad in scope is discussed in more detail in chapter 7.

Why the "Silo" Metaphor Is Appealing

Despite the considerable evidence to the contrary, some remain skeptical about the degree of openness of academic disciplines. Support for the idea of intellectual silos may well stem from the vast scope and rapid accumulation of research rather than the fortress-like nature of academic disciplines. As we saw in chapter 4, the torrents of new information force a certain degree of specialization. One key fact of academic life is that it is hard to keep up with all of the latest developments in one's specialty, let alone the entire range of one's discipline. Even the most devoted scholars will thus find themselves only with only a passing acquaintance with many pieces of research they feel they should know. In national surveys of US universities, the difficulty in keeping up with one's field of research is among the leading complaints professors have about their jobs.[17]

Taking my own field as an example, currently at least 120 peer-reviewed sociology journals are published (Jacobs 2011.) In addition, books remain as important as articles in the field. *Contemporary Sociology*, the main book review journal, reviews over three hundred books per year (and lists perhaps triple this number as books received but not reviewed). Few scholars are able to read all of these reviews, and no one could possibly read all of these books. And of course this list is far from comprehensive with respect to sociological scholarship based outside the United States.

Given how hard it is to keep up with one's own field, it is a fact of life that most academics read only selectively outside their areas of expertise. As a result, the fact is that there are many developments in other disciplines that they may have heard about but have not fully mastered. Thus, from the individual scholar's point of view, it is understandable if she feels less than fully up to date in fields outside of her main areas of inquiry. However, from the point of view of the field or the discipline, there are always new ideas being developed and others percolating in from other fields.

Conclusion

If the charge of "siloism" is to be leveled at academic disciplines, the evidence compiled here suggests that disciplines are not guilty. Of course it is hard to provide a clear standard against which communication should be measured. One can always complain that there should have been even more communication. There are a variety of indices, from citations to coauthorships to interjournal connections, each of which can be adjusted to reflect the size of each field, its growth rate and funding levels. Nonetheless, it is clear from the evidence summarized here that academic research reports routinely reference studies outside their domain. Specific terms and ideas can be mapped in dozens of disciplines. Particular techniques, especially statistics, are adopted from the medical lab to the social science research center. The knowledge base of field after field is an amalgam of homegrown developments and imported ideas.

There are many channels for communicating the latest developments. While it is not possible for any single individual to keep up with everything, general interest journals, university magazines, and various other sources provide the means to become acquainted with developments that may be of interest. The advent of the Internet and search engines has broadened the scope of scholarly interchange. The notion that disciplines are hermetically sealed silos can be laid to rest. If disciplines fall short by some other metric of communication, then this standard must be specified and tested empirically.

Universities are complex organizations with many constituencies and intersecting structures. A large set of interdisciplinary research centers, often addressing broad social issues, coexists with traditional academic departments. These units, far more numerous than the disciplines themselves, help to promote exchanges across fields.

The evidence also points against Donald Campbell's suggestion that the issues of the day lie neglected because of the inward focus of disciplines. Narrowly focused searches produced tens of thousands of studies on social issues ranging from education to health care to poverty. These problems remain in part because there is more to know, because funding for research on important issues is not always available, and because the political system does not always capitalize on the most promising directions of social reform.

In the next chapter we will pursue the question of scholarly communication further by examining the flow of ideas across fields in more detail especially the timing of reception in different disciplinary contexts.

Receptivity Curves:
Educational Research and the Flow of Ideas

As we have seen in chapter 5, the notion that disciplines represent isolated silos that completely block the flow of information and ideas is overstated, if not completely in error. Bibliographical data indicate substantial rates of citations outside most authors' principal field of study. Moreover, one can trace the diffusion of particular ideas from its origin discipline to a variety of topical destinations.

In this chapter, the issue of intellectual exchange is taken one step further by asking not whether ideas move but when they do so. In other words, the question is whether the reception of particular ideas is fast or slow. If certain fields are particularly slow in accepting new ideas, one may affix to them the label of "intellectually remote." While some may view this as a harsh term, it is not nearly as harsh as the notion of a silo, which implies that new ideas rarely if ever seep in. Before we specify how to operationalize the concept of an intellectually remote domain, let us first consider the field of educational research and how it fits into the broader discussion of interdisciplinarity.

Education Research and the Study of Interdisciplinarity

As we have seen, advocates of interdisciplinary collaboration suggest that scholarship should be organized around topics rather than disciplines (Saltiel 2011; Geiger and Sa 2009). For example, graduate fellowships at Stanford are intended to help train researchers to address interdisciplinary social problems (Sullivan 2011). This approach, it is suggested, will enable researchers to learn about indispensable ideas being developed by scholars in neighboring fields of study. Breaking down arbitrary disciplinary boundaries holds the key to solving our most pressing and important problems, from poverty to pandemics to global warming.

If a topical rather than a disciplinary focus were truly sufficient to solving our most vexing intellectual challenges, then schools of education would be at the forefront, a model for the rest of academia to emulate. They bring scholars together from disparate fields, including specialists in developmental psychology, language instruction, reading, student counseling, and administrative leadership, as well as a relatively small number of anthropologists, economists, historians, sociologists, and academics from other fields. No one discipline claims ownership of all aspects of education, and thus the interdisciplinary ideal is alive and well in schools of education.[1]

Critics of education scholarship are not hard to find, especially among historians of educational research. For example, David Labaree (2004) and Ellen Lagemann (2000) bemoan the fact that education typically finds itself at the bottom of the academic pecking order.[2] Thus, it would appear that organizing scholarship around topics rather than disciplines by itself is not sufficient to overcome the intellectual challenges associated with improving our educational system.

A related complaint has been raised concerning the lack of connection of education scholarship to the liberal arts. For example, Lagemann laments "the isolation of educational study from other branches of university scholarship" (2000, 232). For Lagemann, the low status of education in the academic hierarchy is both the cause and the effect of its distance from other fields. "Clearly deriving from multiple sources, the low status that has plagued educational scholarship from the beginning has had several discernible and unfortunate effects, the most important having been the distance it has encouraged between educationists and their peers in the arts and sciences and other professional fields" (2000, 233).

This comment is puzzling from the vantage point of debates about interdisciplinarity. The problem as Lagemann sees it is that education suffers from not enough disciplinarity, since the arts and sciences are the prime sources of intellectual dynamism. The irony, then, is that the more applied divisions of the academy are calling for tighter connections with the liberal arts at the same time that others are criticizing these same disciplines for their insularity and lethargy.

This chapter investigates the complaint that education suffers from too great a distance from the vibrant sources of intellectual innovation located elsewhere on campus. The goal is to ascertain whether there is truth to this particular charge. The analysis will take a historical approach to ascertain whether educationists are unaware of the latest academic developments, and whether they fail to incorporate the latest ideas and statistics in their research. In other words, do the intellectual currents coursing through the main ivy-covered quadrangles lack sufficient wind behind them to carry over to the education courtyards? There has been little empirical research on this issue. This analysis seeks to fill this gap, and, in so doing, to shed light on broader issues of cross-disciplinary communication.

Of course the opposite complaint has also been leveled: that educational research is too focused on raising the status of schools of education in the academy, and consequently this scholarship becomes too removed from the everyday concerns of improving schools. Indeed, the sentence by Lagemann quoted above includes both charges: "the isolation of educational study from other branches of university scholarship as well as its relative remove from practice" (2000, 233). The goal here is not to suggest the best research strategies for education scholars to pursue but simply to assess the degree of intellectual distance between scholarship in education and that in other areas of academic of inquiry.

Education represents perhaps an extreme test case regarding the diffusion of ideas across fields. Schools of education are applied preprofessional units that are often located at a physical distance from the arts and sciences. And, as noted above, critics have specifically complained of the intellectual insularity of the field. If the evidence shows rapid diffusion of scholarship both into and out of the field of education, it will represent powerful support for the proposition that the diffusion of ideas throughout academia is not as problematic as critics suggest.

Defining Intellectually Remote Fields via Receptivity Curves

Let us define an intellectually remote field as one where new ideas are slow to filter in and even slower to be discarded. This definition depends on the relative rates of receptivity to new ideas. Not only is it a place where new ideas are slow to be accepted, it is also a place where old ideas stay in currency long after they are discarded in adjacent fields.

To make this description more concrete, we can compare the impact of a major innovation in two fields, education and psychology. Specifically, the reception of a specific new idea (one may think of an important book or article by Piaget, Bandura, or Wechsler) will be considered as an indicator of the receptivity to new ideas, and of the adherence to old ones. If education were slow to pick up an important new idea or intellectual development, then there would be fewer citations to this work in the years immediately after its publication. If psychologists were quicker than educationists to absorb these new insights, then this might be taken as one indication that education is outside the main currents of intellectual advancement. Similarly, let's imagine that, after a lengthy delay, educationists finally pick up the new idea but then continue to adhere to it long after it had been abandoned by psychologists and other scholars. Again, this could be taken as evidence that the field of education is behind the curve of related academic fields.

The logic sketched out here is represented in graphic form in figure 6.1. The graph displays hypothetical data on the annual citation rates to a new idea in two fields, education and psychology. In this figure, education is depicted to be slow on the uptake of a new idea, relative to psychology. Thus, in the first few years after its publication, citation counts to the new article mount quickly in psychology but accumulate only slowly in education. As the citation life cycle of the article begins to peak in psychology, scholars in education finally catch on and begin to pay attention. Ironically, the idea in question has already begun its downward slope in psychology, as it has begun to be superseded by newer ideas and intellectual developments. However, even as psychologists are moving on to greener intellectual pastures, scholars in education are just coming to embrace the discarded notion. Thus, for a period of time, psychology is turning away from an idea even as it is still on the upswing in education. In the hypothetical example depicted in figure 6.1, the

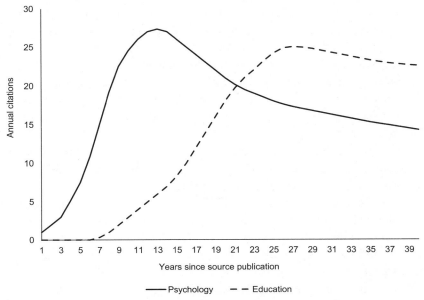

FIGURE 6.1. Interdisciplinary citations: A model of delayed diffusion.

idea in question is on a downward trajectory in psychology after (postpublication) year 13, when the idea peaked in popularity and influence. However, educationists continue to flock to this idea for more than another decade. In our hypothetical example, it takes until year 27 for the idea to reach its apex in education after which it continues to linger in education journals. This gap can be observed on the right-hand side of figure 6.1, where the downward slope of citations is gentler in education than in psychology.[3]

I will refer to the graphs representing citation trajectories as "receptivity curves" since they track the timing and level of discussion of an idea in a given field. The question posed is whether the receptivity curve in education lags behind its companion in psychology and those in other adjacent fields. This question will be scrutinized with regard to the early diffusion period on the left side of the graph as well as the persistent adherence stage on the right side.

Of course there is no gold-standard measure of how fast an idea should diffuse, nor is there a measure of how long that idea should remain in currency. All these curves can indicate is the relative pattern observed in different intellectual domains. If new ideas emerge in such liberal arts fields such as psychology, economics, anthropology, and sociology, then any lag in citations may be taken to represent delayed receptivity in the field of education. Specific examples will be considered so that readers can judge the appropriateness of this assumption in particular cases.[4] The movements of ideas in the reverse direction will be considered as well. In considering the export of ideas from education to other fields, we will add yet another technique to our kit, namely, the analysis of citation rates of entire journals. The research strategy employed here follows the lead of Rinia et al. (2001), who examined citation lags across subject classifications. They showed that intradisciplinary citations, that is, citations occurring in journals in the same field as the original publication, tended to appear slightly earlier than that published in other fields.[5]

Pamela Walters and Annette Lareau (2009) provide a list of the eleven most cited authors based on a survey of 129 education journals during the period 1981–2002. The openness of education as a field to research conducted in other disciplines should be evident from these entries. Most of these highly visible scholars are not faculty members in schools of education but rather were affiliated with departments of psychology. If education were closed to outside influences, this compilation would be dominated by educationists.[6] The useful list compiled by Walters and Lareau does not indicate whether the same research is cited in other fields, nor does it indicate which fields latched onto these ideas first. This study builds on their research by expanding the list of influential studies and by comparing the reception of research in different fields.

The analysis reported here draws on annual citation counts and disciplinary classifications from the ISI Web of Knowledge. This database is not entirely comprehensive: it does not include all academic journals, and it does not include citations that appear in books (see Jacobs 2009 for a discussion of these issues). Nonetheless, the Web of Knowledge covers millions of citations to research papers published in thousands of journals, and offers a consistent system for classifying journals by discipline. It is the basis for many studies published in the area of library science, information science, and bibliometrics, and thus represents a reasonable place to begin.[7]

Education and Psychology

To develop empirical examples that fit the logic mapped out in figure 6.1, annual citation data are needed, along with a specific original publication date. Thus, it makes sense to examine citations to a particular article or book.

The first example considered is the reception of a major scholar in the field of developmental psychology, Jean Piaget, who developed a stage theory of children's growth that encompassed their intellectual, social, and moral development. Figure 6.2a maps the trajectory of citations to Piaget's book *The Origins of Intelligence in Children* (1952a) in the fields of education and psychology. This particular work of Piaget has accumulated a large number of citations in the more than sixty years since its publication in English in 1952. It is remarkable that the influence, or visibility, of this work increased steadily for thirty years after its publication, and citations to this work endure through the present: a staggering 150 citations per year to this book are regularly recorded in academic journals indexed by the ISI Web of Knowledge.[8]

The reception patterns of Piaget's book in psychology and education resemble each other a great deal. There are fewer citations in education than in psychology, but that is just a matter of the relative size of the two fields. There was no delay in the receptivity to Piaget in education journals, as indexed by scholarly citations. If anything, the upward trajectory of citations to Piaget in education journals was a bit steeper over the first fifteen years postpublication than it was in psychology journals, where citations to Piaget increased through year 30. Education also saw a spike in citations in year 30, although the peak citation year in education is actually a few years earlier. Psychologists appear to be a bit more reluctant to move on from Piaget than their educational colleagues: over the last twenty years, the slope in citations appears to be slightly downward in education but close to flat, with annual fluctuations, in psychology.

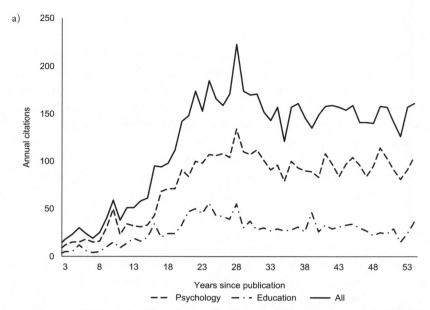

a)

FIGURE 6.2A. Citations to Jean Piaget, *Origins of Intelligence in Children*, 1952. Source: Author's analysis of ISI-Web of Knowledge data.

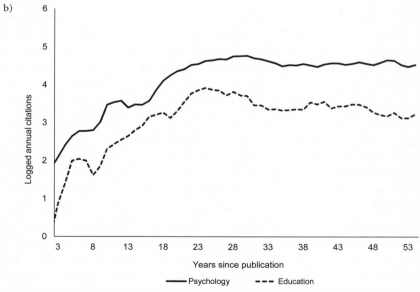

b)

FIGURE 6.2B. Jean Piaget, logged three-year running average. Source: Author's analysis of ISI-Web of Knowledge data.

The parallels between education and psychology appear even more clearly in figure 6.2b, which presents the natural log of citation counts. This adjustment makes it easier to compare curves with marked differences in scale. These citation data are also presented as a three-year running average in order to smooth out year-to-year fluctuations. Figure 6.2b shows a similar rate of receptivity to Piaget's work in psychology and education over the first twenty-five years after publication. After year 25, there was continued interest in psychology and a slight decline in interest in education. The observed pattern of receptivity for this particular work of Piaget does not fit the "intellectual remote" pattern outlined in figure 6.1.

The reception of two other prominent books by Piaget, *The Construction of Reality in the Child* (1954) and *Play, Dreams and Imitation in Childhood* (1952b), follow much the same pattern: more citations overall in psychology than in education; a similarly rapid rate of early adoption; a peak of interest in education a bit earlier than in psychology; and long-term enduring interest in psychology compared to a slight downward trend in citations in education (results not shown).

Figures 6.3a and 6.3b take up the same questions in a more recent period with a very different figure in psychology: Albert Bandura, whose study "Social Learning Theory of Aggression," was published in 1973. Bandura's "social learning theory of aggression" departed from the behaviorism of B. F. Skinner by stressing the way human behavior, especially among the young, could be understood as modeled on the activities of others. His study peaked in influence about fifteen years after its initial publication in both education and psychology. (Figure 6.3a and subsequent figures present only the logged and smoothed results.) This example is somewhat unusual in that there was a resurgence of interest in Bandura's book twenty-five years after its publication, and another surge in interest at year 35. Perhaps the publication of Bandura's 1995 book helped to rekindle interest in his earlier work.

The same pattern is evident in citations to Bandura's edited collection, *Self Efficacy in Changing Societies*, published in 1995, which emphasized the capacity of individuals as agents to organize and self-regulate their behavior. Bandura's book is rapidly on its way to receiving seven hundred or more citations per year, a truly remarkable degree of influence, with education journals generating approximately one hundred citations per year and psychology journals three hundred. As seen in figure 6.3b the climb in citations is roughly a straight line in both fields with no clear inflection point. The logged citation graph makes it clear that the main difference between education and psychology is scale: the trajectory is similar for these two fields, while the

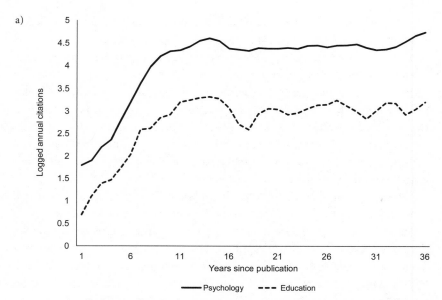

a)

FIGURE 6.3A. Citations to Albert Bandura, *Social Learning Theory of Aggression*, 1971. Source: Author's analysis of ISI-Web of Knowledge data.

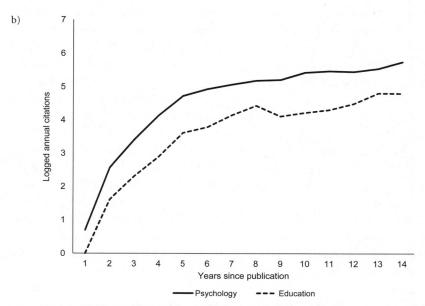

b)

FIGURE 6.3B. Citations to Albert Bandura, *Self Efficacy in Changing Societies*, 1995. Source: Author's analysis of ISI-Web of Knowledge data.

absolute volume of citations is higher in psychology. Here again, there is no evidence of delayed reception in education.

Reception of the research of another prominent psychologist, David Wechsler, whose 1991 work on the measurement of intelligence has been very influential is yet another example (results not shown).[9] The citations to this publication actually rise a bit more quickly in education than in psychology. By the third year after the publication of Wechsler's work, it was already widely cited in education; the peak citation year in education journals occurs ten years after publication. The rapid assimilation of Wechsler's intelligence scale may be due to the fact that it was an updated version of scales that he had developed years before. Psychologists were also quick to cite Wechsler's 1991 work, and the citation count continued to rise in psychology through 2007.[10]

Some might object that the strategy of selecting these top-cited figures unduly emphasizes those papers that have managed to span disciplinary silos.[11] An important question, then, is whether less cited papers have a similar pattern of interdisciplinary as these exceptionally influential works.

This question is addressed in table 6.1. Here the top-cited papers in each of five journals are compared with less influential research. In four of the five cases, there is as high a rate of interdisciplinary citation for the less visible papers as for the top-cited articles. These results suggest that the interdisciplinary trajectories for less cited papers may not be terribly different from the top-cited papers discussed here. *Educational Evaluation and Policy Analysis* has a higher share of citations outside of education for top-cited

TABLE 6.1. Diffusion of top-cited articles versus all articles

	100+ citation articles			All articles	
Journal	Education (percent of citations)	Other (percent of citations)	# articles	Education (percent of citations)	Other (percent of citations)
Harvard Education Review	57.8	42.2	9	48.8	51.2
Education Evaluation and Policy Analysis	59.8	40.2	5	64.4	35.6
Teachers College Record	66.5	33.5	8	68.2	31.8
American Education Research Journal	55.5	44.5	47	54.2	45.8
Review of Education Research	51.8	48.2	103	52.2	47.8

Sources: Author's analysis of Web of Knowledge data.

articles than for all articles (40.2 percent versus 35.6 percent), but the differences for all of the other journals are either in the opposite direction or not statistically significant.

There is a second, important reason for targeting these top-cited papers. Academic scholarship is a skewed activity: a relatively small number of figures have a terribly disproportionate degree of visibility or influence (Brouthers, Mudambi, and Reed 2012). Given this pattern, a focus on these most influential works is appropriate, since they have the most influence on the direction of research.

Education and Sociology

As we have seen, there are extensive intellectual connections between psychology and education. The evidence suggests the relatively free flow of ideas from psychology into education, which counters the disparaging suggestion that schools of education represent an intellectually remote outpost in the otherwise dynamic institution of higher education. The same question is considered with respect to sociology, whose leading figures have long been interested in educational issues, dating back at least to the writings of Talcott Parsons and Emile Durkheim.

There are good reasons to expect that, compared with psychology, sociological research may not flow as easily into educational journals because of the scarcity of sociologists on the faculty of schools of education. Data on doctoral degree fields of faculty drawn from the National Survey of Post-Secondary Faculty (US Department of Education 2011) show that only 0.6 percent of professors in schools of education have a degree in sociology. In contrast, more than 6 percent (6.65 percent) of education faculty have degrees in psychology, if one combines psychology degrees (1.69 percent) with educational psychology degrees (4.96 percent). This fact no doubt facilitates the permeability of ideas between psychology and education.[12]

The analysis for the field of sociology proceeds in the same manner as for psychology. Figures 6.4a and 6.4b present the receptivity curves for two influential contributions by James Coleman. His famous 1966 study, "Equal Educational Opportunity," widely referred to as the "Coleman Report," suggested that parental social background was more influential in shaping students' educational destinations than school factors such as spending per pupil. This study raised many concerns on the part of educators, and introduced regression analysis to a generation of education researchers.

As shown in figure 6.4a, Coleman's work became visible more quickly in education journals than in sociology journals, but in both fields the influence

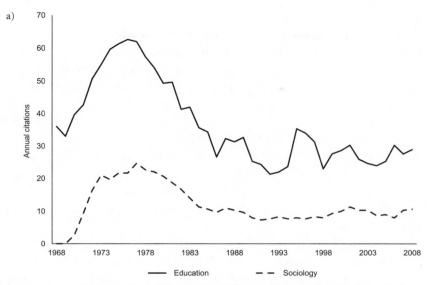

FIGURE 6.4A. Citations to James Coleman, *Equal Educational Opportunity*, 1966. Source: Author's analysis of ISI-Web of Knowledge data.

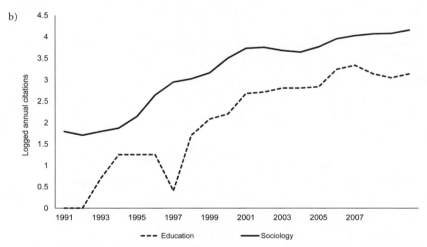

FIGURE 6.4B. Citations to James Coleman, "Social Capital," 1988. Source: Author's analysis of ISI-Web of Knowledge data.

of this research peaked during the 1970s. The similarities in these two receptivity curves is easy to see in figure 6.4a.

Figure 6.4b examines the reception of Coleman's 1988 paper in the *American Journal of Sociology* on "social capital," which outlined a general theory of social influence operating via social networks, and illustrated the impact of parents' social networks on children's educational achievement. Coleman's 1988 paper has been cited more extensively in sociology than in education, but again there is little evidence of a delayed reception of this research in either field. The logged curve shows a largely parallel reception in sociology and education, with a brief downward blip in education journals during the late 1990s.

Pierre Bourdieu is another interesting scholar to consider. There are good reasons to expect that Bourdieu might not be widely read by education scholars. He was French; his writings can be difficult to digest; and his largely theoretical work may apply more to France than to the United States. Nonetheless, Bourdieu's work has been rapidly absorbed by educationists. The reception of Bourdieu and Passeron's *Reproduction in Education, Culture and Society* (1977) is a good example to consider, since it focuses directly on issues of education disparities of great interest to both sociologists and education researchers. The receptivity curves for education and sociology closely overlap one another. In fact, this volume is cited somewhat more frequently in education than in sociology. Similar patterns are evident for other influential studies of Bourdieu, including his book *Distinction*, a highly cited book that addresses broad cultural themes but bears less directly on issues of educational policy.

Based on the reception of Coleman and Bourdieu's contributions, we may conclude that the barriers to communication between sociologists and educationists are easily surmounted. The most influential and visible work in sociology is read, cited, and apparently absorbed remarkably quickly by educational scholars.

Education, Economics, and Statistics

While the connections of education researchers to their counterparts in psychology and sociology seem quite strong, the ties to economics are much weaker. The relatively slow reception of economic ideas in education journals may reflect the very small number of scholars trained in economics with appointments in schools of education. Drawing again from the National Survey of Post-Secondary Faculty, only 0.25 percent of faculty in schools of education have degrees in economics. Nonetheless, while economic ideas do find their way into education journals, they do not arrive as quickly as is the case with psychology and sociology.

The term "human capital" was coined by economists during the 1950s to emphasize the economics aspects of educational decisions. In this regard, "investing" in human capital is analogous to investments in physical capital, namely, plants and equipment. While some critics complain that the human capital perspective is too narrow in emphasizing only the economic aspects of education, over time the human capital school has made a powerful case for additional investments in education and the expansion of educational opportunities.

The number of academic journal articles on the topic of human capital were traced across three fields: economics, sociology, and education (results not shown). Publications on this topic naturally appear first in economics journals, since economists coined the term and developed this framework. By 1975, roughly fifteen articles were appearing annually on this topic in economics journals. While a few papers were published annually on this topic in education during the 1970s and 1990s, it was not until 1995 that a sustained increase in articles on this topic appear in education journals. This rise in education journal articles coincides with a jump in articles appearing in sociology journals, and is roughly five years after a major spike in articles in economics journals.

These findings suggest that education has indeed lagged considerably behind economics in the area of human capital. Specifically, a sustained increase in education journal articles published on this topic does not begin until 1995, approximately thirty years after economics articles began to be published on this topic.

This conclusion is modified somewhat when the focus shifts from journal article topics to the citation of particular studies. In fact, articles in education journals were citing Gary Becker's book *Human Capital* (1964) in considerable numbers as early as 1973, and were a bit quicker to do so than were their counterparts in sociology. By the end of the 1970s, citations to Becker's work in sociology began to slightly outpace those in education. Thus, educationists were aware of the human capital perspective and were citing it quite frequently from the 1970s onward, even if they were not publishing papers in this area until some years later.

Taken together, these results suggest that economics is a field where educationists lag somewhat behind, although we should be clear that the lag is relatively modest in duration given the scarcity of economists in schools of education who were positioned to receive these ideas.

The emphasis on statistics and measurement in education has a long and somewhat contested history (Lagemann 2000). It is hard to obtain a comprehensive view of the adoption of statistics in contemporary education scholarship since a wide variety of statistical methods are employed. The conclusion offered here is that the incorporation of new statistics into education research is a routine development that has been aided by the wide availability of computer software "packages" that facilitate the use of the latest techniques. In some cases, statistical innovations diffused quickly in the field of education because they were developed by educational statisticians.

Jacob Cohen, whose 1977 book *Statistical Power Analysis for the Social Sciences* appears on Walters and Lareau's list of the most cited sources in education, has been widely employed by psychologists and researchers in many fields. Within five years of its publication, Cohen's work was cited twenty or more times in education journals, a remarkable level of visibility that continued with only the slightest downward slope over the ensuing thirty years (results not shown). In psychology journals, Cohen's book continued to grow in influence for nearly thirty years after publication, reaching a peak of 130 citations in 2004. The initial reception curve is rapid in both education and psychology, but it quickly flattens out for education while continuing a long ascent in psychology.

The analysis of a particular statistical text is informative but not decisive, since scholars in various fields may rely on different references to inform their statistical choices. The adoption of specific techniques may help to fill in the picture. The term "structural equations" has appeared as a topic over thirty thousand in academic journals articles across a wide swath of the social sciences, and nearly six hundred times in education journal articles. The results indicate that research using structural equations is more common in psychology than in education, and the trajectory of reception is roughly parallel to that in psychology and in other fields of research. Structural equation models appeared during the 1980s in a smattering of articles in diverse fields, but once this technique became popular in the early 1990s, its usage in education grew at a roughly parallel rate to that in other fields of research.

A second example, hierarchical linear models (HLM), was adopted by education researchers with an even shorter delay. It may be that the location of the inventor of this technique in a school of education facilitated its adoption by educationists. Stephen Raudenbush and Anthony Bryk, both of whom earned their degrees in educational statistics at Harvard, held faculty positions in schools of education. Sustained citations to HLM first appear in the Web of Knowledge in 1991 and begin their upward ascent in education in 1993 (Raudenbush and Bryk 1986; Bryk and Raudenbush 1992). Since then the use of this technique has grown in parallel between education and other fields.

Meta-analysis is another homegrown statistical approach diffused rapidly in the field of education. Larry Hedges, who played a prominent role in inventing meta-analysis, obtained his degree in educational statistics from Stanford and held a faculty position in the University of Chicago School of

Education for many years. Meta-analysis combines the results of a group of small studies into a single statistical analysis, giving researchers more statistical power by combining many relatively small individual studies into a single, larger statistical generalization (Hedges and Olkin 1992). Meta-analysis has been used in some fifty thousand academic articles over the last thirty years in fields from the medical sciences to psychology, nearly four hundred (391) of which have appeared in education journals.

Education researchers were relatively early adopters of this technique: articles using this technique began to appear in education journals during the 1980s. Over time, the use of meta-analysis outside the field of education has soared, while its use in education remained relatively constant at an average of twenty articles per year from the early 1990s through 2006. Thus, if educationists were somewhat slower than other researchers to employ structural equations in their research, they exhibited no delay in adopting meta-analysis.[13]

The last case considered here is one of significantly delayed adoption, but it represents an exception to the general pattern. Lee J. Cronbach, who taught at the Graduate School of Education at Stanford University, developed a method for assessing the internal reliability of scales developed from multiple indicators. His seminal paper, published in 1951, was quickly cited in a wide variety of fields, but it was employed by education scholars only a handful of times before 1970. This case represents one of those relatively rare instances in which research is absorbed more quickly outside the originator's field than it is inside.

This relatively long lag in the adoption of this approach in all probability reflects the period in which it occurred. Since the 1970s, statistical software packages have been developed and become widely available. Programs such as SAS, SPSS, and STATA are inexpensive and easy to use, thus lowering the "startup costs" of learning new statistics for new users.[14] The publication of user-focused manuals (for example, Bryk and Raudenbush 1992; Hedges and Olkin 1992), no doubt also facilitates the widespread diffusion of new statistical methods.

It may also be the case that large statistical data sets contribute to the diffusion of new statistics. In the field of education, a number of large-scale longitudinal studies, such as the National Educational Longitudinal Study, have provided the empirical basis for thousands of research papers. It is fair to say that an interdisciplinary research community tends to form around each of these data sets. When statistical advances are introduced by some users of a given data set, this rapidly sets the standard that others must match.

A skeptical reader might wonder how education faculty are able to keep up with so many new statistical developments. The point is not that every researcher is up to date on every innovation, but rather that these new techniques find their way into the field and become available as part of researchers' tool kits.

Overall, the past forty years has seen a range of statistical techniques flow into educational scholarship. In some cases, educationists have been a few years behind other fields in adopting these techniques, but in other cases they are fully up to date compared with their colleagues in psychology and other fields. Here again, it is hard to square the view of education as an isolated silo with these data on the broad-based adoption of a range of statistical research techniques by scholars publishing in education journals.

Exporting Educational Research

In considering the question of the intellectual isolation of schools of education, it is important to remember that ideas can flow two ways. Thus far we have examined the extent to which ideas flow into education. Let us now consider flows in the opposite direction in order to explore how well the research of education scholars travels outside its field of origin.

The clearest cases of export from education to other fields involve the development of educational statistics discussed above. New statistical methods developed by scholars in schools of education, including Cronbach's alpha, HLM, and meta-analysis, were quickly adopted by scholars in diverse fields, in some cases even more rapidly than in the field of education itself. The origination of statistical innovations in education rather than in a department of statistics has not presented a barrier to the adoption of these techniques by researchers in a broad spectrum of fields.

Outside of education statistics, however, the diffusion of educational research into other fields of scholarship has been less prominent. It is not a case of delayed reception so much as it is limited reception. Two cases in the area of higher education support the conclusion that there is relatively little delay in the reception of educational research by other fields. Vincent Tinto is a social psychologist who specializes in issues of higher education whose work on the adjustment to college has been influential among students of the college experience. Receptivity curves were drawn for his important review essay, written in 1975, and his book on who leaves college, published in 1987. Tinto's scholarship has been more visible in education than in other fields, but the receptivity curves for these two works indicate that, in terms of timing and trajectory, the reception of his work is similar outside of education.

Alexander Astin of UCLA has directed a large-scale data collection project on college freshmen since the late 1960s. The media often cite the results of this project when discussing trends in the experiences of college students. Astin's most influential line of research follows freshmen through their years in college. The reception of Astin's 1977 book, *Four Critical Years*, shows an initial peak in interest about ten years after publication, followed by a second peak about twenty years later. There are more references to this work in education journals than in journals in other fields. While the reception curves in education and other fields resemble each other, there is more continuity in interest in education than in other fields.

In order to further explore the flow of ideas from education to other fields, I drew on Rinia et al.'s approach by comparing the timing of the interdisciplinary citations with those occurring within the same discipline. This approach avoids reliance on prominent examples and seeks to assess the entire corpus of papers published in a set of journals.

Table 6.2 examines the citations to ten journals, seven in education and three in educational psychology. All articles published between 1990 and 2000 were examined. The analysis sought to ascertain whether citations occurring

TABLE 6.2. Lag time for citations to articles published in education journals between 1990 and 2000

A. Generalist journals

	Citation: lag: median years since publication		Citation gap, in years* (Other journals— education journals)
	Education journals	Other journals	
Review of Education Research	7.069	5.358	−1.711
American Educational Research Journal	6.236	6.996	0.760
Journal of Higher Education	7.349	7.952	0.603
Harvard Education Review	10.970	11.083	0.113

B. Education psychology journals

Child Development	10.664	9.549	−1.115
Journal of Learning Sciences	8.569	8.031	−0.538
Journal of Counseling Psychology	5.002	7.162	2.160
Sociology of Education	7.327	8.357	1.030

C. Specialized education journals

Health Education Research	6.354	8.272	1.918
Computers and Education	6.432	7.336	0.904
Total			0.412

* A net positive indicates that the citations were faster in education than in other journals.
Source: Author's analysis of Web of Knowledge data.

in education journals appear earlier or later than those in other fields. Summing over all ten journals, articles were cited in education journals more rapidly than they were cited in other locations. However, the gap was quite small—less than six months (0.4 years).

Four generalist journals in education were examined. In three of these journals, education scholars cited the research a bit more quickly than did researchers in other fields, but the gap was less than one year. In one journal, the *Review of Education Research*, the opposite was true: scholars outside education actually cited educational research more rapidly than did researchers in education.

As a point of comparison, four journals published outside of education, three in psychology and one in sociology, were examined. The "intellectually remote" label would imply that ideas from these sources would diffuse more slowly into education than in the field in which the research originated. This pattern holds in two cases, but in two other cases citations actually appear more quickly in education than in the field where the research originated. These exceptions are the *Journal of Counseling Psychology* and *Sociology of Education*: in each case, educationists appear to pick up on this research more quickly than did other researchers.

Two of the journals in the list were specialized education journals: *Health Education Research* and *Computers and Education*. In both cases, references appeared in educational outlets before they appeared in health or computer journals. This evidence does suggest a delay in communication between those teaching about education in fields like health and computers and those conducting research in these areas.

The data presented in table 6.2 confirm the general pattern of findings we obtained earlier from tracing the reception trajectories of individual papers. Broadly speaking, it only takes less than half a year longer on average for education scholarship to travel outside of the field compared to the time it takes the same research to be recognized within education journals. And the absorption rate by educationists of research produced by scholars in neighboring fields appears to be even faster.

Summary

Despite concerns raised about the intellectual isolation of schools of education, the evidence compiled here suggests that, no matter their source, ideas and techniques are rapidly assimilated by educational researchers. Ideas flow easily from psychology into education, and the same can be said for sociology and statistics.

The adoption of a particular statistical advance by educational researchers may be slightly faster if the innovation was developed by a colleague based in a school of education, but these differences are minor relative to the broader pattern of rapid diffusion across fields. Economics is probably the clearest case where there is a lag between the development of new ideas and their reception in education, but even here the lag is not as long as one might think and depends on whether it is measured in terms of citations to particular studies or journal article titles.

The evidence for movement from education to the broader academic community is mixed. Research by prominent educationists, as well as research published in education journals, does travel to other fields, although in most cases the majority of readers are other scholars of education. It is not principally a matter of timing but rather a limited degree of visibility. Educational statistics is a clear exception to this pattern, as statistical advances in education have been adopted rapidly by scholars in diverse field of research.

The thrust of this analysis suggests that disciplinary "silos" are not nearly as limiting as some critics assume. The field of education has not been unduly hampered by its intellectual and social distance from the rest of the academy. Whatever the merits of interdisciplinarity as an organizing principle, the claim that it is needed to overcome disciplinary myopia is not well supported by the receptivity trajectories presented here. Whether the focus is on individual books and seminal articles, specific technical terms, or broad concepts, scholars in the field of education are quick to assimilate ideas developed in related disciplines. The movement of ideas in the opposite direction may not be as extensive, but here again there is little evidence of a time lag. Citations to articles published in education journals occur at roughly the same time in other fields as they do in education. The accumulated data from a variety of distinct approaches, taken together, suggest that the field of education should be absolved from the charge of intellectually remoteness.

The case of education also raises questions about the desirability of a topic-based organization of knowledge, since educational researchers continue to import ideas from arts and science disciplines, while movement in the opposite direction is more limited. Interdisciplinarians might respond by noting that schools of education are not fully integrated, that scholarship within these units remains segmented by disciplinary divisions. While that is no doubt the case, the question is why we should expect future issue-based programs to be any different. If the division of labor within schools of education reflects the need for some degree of specialization, then we can expect a similar pattern to emerge in other topic-based or issue-based programs.

There is nothing that prevents applied fields from being successful and from contributing to the university and to society in tremendously important ways. One such example is agriculture departments located in land-grant institutions. The important research conducted in these settings provided the basis for the green revolution of the 1960s and 1970s, which enhanced agricultural productivity and by some accounts played a key role in averting widespread famine in developing countries including India. This example is discussed in more detail below in chapter 7. There are no doubt many other successful examples that could be noted from engineering, medicine, and management, among others. The point is that bringing research together around a major social issue, such as education, by no means guarantees a solution to the problem. And, conversely, specialized research can make major strides in addressing multifaceted social problems.

The principal theme developed throughout the analysis thus far is that there is much to be valued in the contemporary arrangement of academic disciplines. There is of course nothing in the current arrangement to prevent disappointing outcomes on the part of individual researchers or even particular fields of research, as it is unrealistic to expect a constant flow of breakthroughs in all fields. Moreover, critics should consider the possibility that the problems observed represent deficiencies in execution rather than fundamental flaws in the system.

There is enough stability in university-based employment to allow individual scholars to make considerable investments in esoteric lines of inquiry, yet the system is not simply an agglomeration of faculty sinecures. Taken as a whole, the system of disciplines has many dynamic elements built into it. Broad disciplinary domains foster competition not only between individual researchers but also between diverse groups within disciplines. Disciplines are often built on an amalgam of ideas and techniques that have been assimilated from diverse sources. If some interdisciplinary bridges are worth building, they should not be erected on the premise that disciplines are inherently flawed.

With regard to the central concern disciplinary insularity, the evidence presented in the last two chapters suggests that this criticism is overstated if not completely unsupported. Interdisciplinary connections are quite common in the American research university. Ideas flow back and forth with remarkable speed and techniques developed in one field are rapidly adopted in other domains. This pattern is even true of units in the academy such as schools of education that have been criticized for their intellectual distance from arts and science disciplines.

The focus of the book will now shift to a consideration of interdisciplinarity as an alternative mode of organizing the modern university.

PART TWO

Interdisciplinary Alternatives

7

Antidisciplinarity

Interdisciplinarity is everywhere—neuroscience, nanotechnology, bioengineering, behavioral economics, and the digital humanities, not to mention various racial, ethnic, and gender studies programs. All of these are exciting developments; all have been heralded for their current authoritative knowledge as well as their dramatic potential for future advances. The cumulative power of these examples can easily lead an observer to the conclusion that the era of the interdisciplinary university is upon us. "Mode2 knowledge," "post-normal science," and the "post-disciplinary university" are among the terms that have been deployed to characterize the new era (Gibbons et al. 1994; Funtowicz and Ravetz 1993). Some have called for a new interdisciplinary philosophy of science (Schmidt 2010), while others outline new methods for conducting research (Repko, Newell, and Szostak 2012).

Advocates of a postdisciplinary university maintain that disciplines are a relic of a bygone era. Some call for a wholesale reorganization of the structure and purpose of the university, even if the outlines of its replacement remain poorly defined. "Attempts to understand the world or any part of it need to be inter- and transdisciplinary in nature—even if this means that we lose the comfort of disciplinary guarantees of expertise" (Frodeman 2010, xxxv).

Frodeman is by no means alone in heralding the arrival of the postdisciplinary university. For Julie Buckler, our current postdisciplinarity reality is "an intellectual university in which we inhabit the ruins of outmoded disciplinary structures" while the transdisciplinarity future she envisions "is the highest level of integrated study" (2004, 2). In Paul Forman's succinct formulation, "modernity entailed disciplinarity, postmodernity entails antidisciplinarity."

Is interdisciplinarity merely a "popular buzzword" (Schmidt 2010, 39), or does it represent a fundamental break with the frameworks of knowledge that have prevailed since Newton and Darwin? Are we entering a new age in which disciplines are no longer needed? There are of course many middle positions short of these extremes, and there are no doubt positive ways to incorporate interdisciplinarity into the contemporary university without major organizational changes. Indeed, one can argue that the system of discipline-based departments coupled with interdisciplinary research centers already accomplishes this objective

Unfortunately, the interdisciplinarians themselves have not agreed on a set of principles, let alone the organizational template for the design of the postdisciplinary university. As we will see, some maintain that this cacophony of terminology, frameworks, goals, and aspirations is a necessary and even desirable state of affairs.[1] In a number of places, this lack of agreement is actually celebrated. In other words, whereas reformers call for a greater synthesis of knowledge from others, they apparently absolve themselves from this standard.

Thus, the powerful examples of successful interdisciplinary endeavors somehow need to be reconciled with the often weak and self-contradictory analyses and arguments developed by analysts and reformers. Since a clear outline of what a postdisciplinary university might look like has yet to emerge, a careful consideration of how it might be structured is the task of the remainder of the book.

Thus far, the spotlight has been on disciplines and communication between them. The critique of disciplines presented was followed by an institutional theory of disciplines that emphasized their breadth and dynamism. The theme of specialization was explored with an analysis of newly formed journals. The extensive flow of ideas across webs was documented in a variety of ways, and the remarkably rapid pace of communication across fields was illustrated with examples from the field of education and its neighbors.

We have seen that disciplines work well in part because they represent loosely affiliated sets of research groups working together in many ways but also competing with each other for resources and rewards. American universities succeed because they have created a system of disciplines which has produced remarkable and sustained creativity. It is not simply that individual fields of inquiry have spawned successful research communities, but that the broader system fosters a remarkable balance of competition and cooperation. University employment allows scholars to devote tremendous time and energy to esoteric issues knowing that there is a career system that will support such work. Faculty positions are allocated based on enrollments, funding streams, and intellectual promise, with discipline-based departments playing a large role in faculty hiring decisions. The presence of a multiplicity of research centers at major research universities gives the current arrangement added flexibility by advancing specialized research programs that span disciplinary boundaries. Undergraduate and graduate education undergirds this system, fostering intergenerational continuity even as each generation of students enters the academy with its own preoccupations and interests.

Now we are in a better position to consider interdisciplinary alternatives. The remainder of the book considers whether interdisciplinarity can be structured in a way that builds on these strengths. In other words, to make interdisciplinarity work, would quasi-disciplinary systems have to be created? There can be no doubt that individual scholars successfully borrow ideas from other fields. Despite their many challenges, some interdisciplinary collaborations are successful. The questions here concern on how one builds on successful cases of interdisciplinarity.

This chapter begins by distinguishing some of the goals identified for an interdisciplinary university that leads into an extended discussion of the varied meanings of the term "integration." The central issue here is whether interdisciplinary knowledge is indispensable for the solution of the world's great challenges.

The bulk of the chapter considers whether interdisciplinarity represents a permanent organizational form or is instead a transitional phase that quickly reverts into disciplinary patterns. The issue is whether interdisciplinarity is inherently self-limiting or self-defeating. The discussion stresses the importance of research communities in the advancement of scholarly research. The cumulative force of these arguments and evidence is that interdisciplinary programs succeed to the extent that they recreate the organizational systems and support enjoyed by traditional disciplines and departments have obtained.

In the next chapter, the case of American studies, a long-standing field that was among the first to embrace interdisciplinary as an ideal, will be scrutinized for evidence regarding the feasibility and desirability of interdisciplinarity as an alternative to disciplinary structures. In chapter 9, the relationship between interdisciplinarity and effective education for undergraduates is considered. Finally, in the concluding chapter, specific steps to promote interdisciplinarity, such as cross-disciplinary faculty appointments and cluster hiring, are examined. Concerns about the contribution of interdisciplinarity to centralized university decision making are raised as well.

Interdisciplinarity, Theoretical Synthesis, and Integrated Problem Solving

As was noted in chapter 5, interdisciplinarity can be ranked in terms of the degree to which knowledge from disparate fields is brought together in a synthetic or integrative manner. The terms "synthetic" and "integrative" are sometimes taken to be synonymous with interdisciplinarity. It has been suggested that "the majority of definitions of interdisciplinarity focus on integration" (Repko 2008, xiii), citing Lattuca (2001). William Newell regards "synthesis or integration" as "the distinguishing but elusive characteristic of interdisciplinary studies" (2001, 1).

Just as the concept of interdisciplinarity has many meanings, the term "integration" is also used in a variety of ways. The two main uses are "theoretical synthesis" and "integrated problem solving." The former connects ideas without a specific claim to practical utility, while the latter typically refers to the need for integrated solutions to complex social issues.

Both of these senses of the concept of integration are evident in the definition offered by the National Academy of Sciences report:

> Interdisciplinary research (IDR) is a mode of research by teams or individuals that integrates information, data, techniques, tools, perspectives concepts, and/or theories from two or disciplines or bodies of specialized knowledge to advance fundamental knowledge or to solve problems whose solutions are beyond the scope of a single discipline or area of research practice. (2004, 2)

Another instance can be found in a discussion of undergraduate education:

> We define interdisciplinary understanding as the capacity to integrate knowledge and modes of thinking in two or more disciplines or established areas of expertise to produce a cognitive advancement—such as explaining a phenomenon, solving a problem, or creating a product—in ways that would have been impossible or unlikely through single disciplinary means. (Boix Mansilla, and Duraising 2007, 219, as quoted in Golding 2009)

The following discussion considers theoretical synthesis and applied integration in turn. In both cases, defining interdisciplinarity in terms of these concepts appears unwarranted.

Interdisciplinarity is neither necessary nor sufficient for theoretical synthesis. First, this goal should be viewed in relative terms. Few domains of knowledge are completely integrated and few completely lack integration. Few theories are completely general, and so, short of unifying everything, we can only talk of contributions that are more or less synthetic.

Second, tremendously important intellectual synthesis can occur within a discipline; conversely, many interdisciplinary studies fail to achieve any real degree of integration. For example, if physicists were able to develop a unified theory connecting weak forces and strong forces in a "grand unified theory," this would represent a remarkable achievement (Weinberg 1994), but it would not necessarily be interdisciplinary in nature. It would very likely have implications for other disciplines, but it would not itself draw from biology, the humanities, or most other fields with the exception of mathematics. The Clay Awards, given in recognition of major breakthroughs in the field of mathematics, provides another example (Clay Mathematics Institute 2012). A number of these honors have been justified on the grounds that the recipient's contribution unified two or more domains of mathematics.

As we saw in chapter 3, disciplines are quite broad in scope with considerable internal differentiation. In this context, there is often substantial room for intellectual advances that connect disparate subfields. The research and theorizing that contributes to intellectual integration should be recognized as important whether it occurs within a field or at the intersection of different disciplines.

Intradisciplinary syntheses can be extensive in their reach, yet many interdisciplinary domains are quite limited in scope. The analysis of newly formed academic journals presented in chapter 4 revealed that interdisciplinarity is often quite specialized in nature. The notion that narrow interdisciplinary bridges should be privileged over broad disciplinary syntheses seems unwarranted. Thus, the tacit assumption that interdisciplinary is necessarily broad and synthetic is often not the case. And the fact that a given research study happens to be interdisciplinarity does not make it important or successful. To summarize, with respect to intellectual or theoretical synthesis, the equation of this concept with interdisciplinary fails on many accounts. Synthesis can and does occur within fields and often fails to materialize in research that spans fields. In short, efforts to equate "interdisciplinary" with "synthetic" are misdirected. They overstate the case for cross-field connections, and ignore the synthetic nature of developments that occur within fields.

Interdisciplinarity and the Solution to Complex Problems

A second sense of the term "integration" refers to problem solving. The argument here is that armchair academic theorizing represents disconnected abstractions unless and until it is brought together to solve practical problems. The connection to the world's most daunting issues is made even more explicitly by Repko, Newell, and Szostak, who maintain that "developing a comprehensive understanding of complex societal problems, and especially resolving them, requires interdisciplinary thinking and research. . . . integration is the best way to address complex problems" (2012, xv).

The practical rewards of interdisciplinarity feature prominently in discussions of scientists especially in the biomedical area (Dauphinée and Martin 2000). Frodeman also places special emphasis on utilitarian considerations. "Interdisciplinarity is simply a means. But to what end? Pragmatically put, toward the ends of greater insight and greater success at problem solving" (2010, xxxii).

The argument that interdisciplinarity yields integrated solutions is attractive and widely mentioned, yet it too quickly melts under closer examination. Here it may be useful to consider various stages that span asking a research question to generating a useful solution. Integration may occur at the level of the research finding, for example, the discovery of a new drug. Next is integration at the level of developing a product or program, in this case, bringing that drug to market. Integration at the level of policy making is another matter entirely. In this case, integration might refer to a system for enhancing adherence by patients to a drug regimen, or more broadly to financing prescription drugs, or even to a comprehensively integrated health care system.

Distinguishing between these stages helps to make clear that complex problems do not necessarily require interdisciplinary research teams. The fact that large problems are multifaceted does not mean that research pursuing a single, integrated solution is the way forward. There are typically partial solutions that can usually be integrated with a larger whole only after progress in various specialized areas is made.

Second, it is important to keep in mind that integrated solutions from one point of view are often clearly limited or incomplete from another point of view. Depending on how "the problem" is defined, a given strategy may represent a comprehensive solution, a partial solution, or the source of unintended consequences. For example, if the energy problem is defined as excessive reliance on foreign oil, then the promotion of offshore drilling in the United States might seem to be an appropriate solution. However, if the energy problem is defined as a clean energy problem, then more drilling may take us in an entirely wrong direction.

Third, a problem may require many disciplines, but an interdisciplinary research agenda may not be the most fruitful. Answers to problems emerge when the knowledge base is "ripe" or "ready." Thus, while a problem may have many facets, the connections between these elements may not be the best place to look for solutions. It may well be that diverse research groups with diverse skills and agendas may succeed in tackling certain aspects of the problem, which in turn shapes subsequent strategies for research and policy strategies.[2]

Fourth, as we have seen in chapter 5, problem-oriented interdisciplinarity tends to splinter into many different approaches and units. This is because of the very multifaceted nature of problems that it is designed to solve. The many homeland security research centers at Pennsylvania State University underscore the fact that there are many important and useful angles of research that contribute to the overall issue of homeland security. But these useful approaches do not result in the consolidation of research under a single umbrella but rather proliferate in response to diverse funding streams and definitions of the problem under consideration.

A more basic point is that the large, complex, and multidimensional university cannot be organized solely or even principally to address the social problems of the day. The university's mission must include the pursuit of basic research whose utility may not be evident for an extended period of time. In this way, universities in some respects resemble a seed bank. While refining the crops currently in use may prove useful, it is also wise to store additional seeds that may be needed sometime in the future. These additional seeds may have useful traits, and their cultivation may help us to understand plant processes in a more basic way. Thus, neither the humanities nor basic mathematics may offer immediate solutions to the world's problems, yet both may prove instrumental in the future in ways that are not fully anticipated today. The arts and sciences must reserve at least a portion of its energy and creativity to basic issues and long-term goals.

Disciplinary distinctions sometimes represent competing frameworks. This fact is at the root of Sherif and Sherif's (1969) insistence that what is true in one field must be true in other fields. They viewed discipline-specific frameworks as a weakness, a sign of intellectual fragmentation. Strober (2011) makes a similar point when she documents how difficult interdisciplinary conversations can be. While outsiders may have little patience for such academic squabbling, the fact is that we don't know which set of ideas will win in the end, or even whether some unexpected synthesis will emerge. Again, the seed bank analogy may be useful. The partial shelter offered by discipline-based labor markets allows for diverse ideas to develop in the academic context like seeds to be stored for future use. Thus, the failure of diverse researchers in a university to be on the same page should be recognized as a strength rather than a weakness, because this system produces a larger set of ideas and possibilities that may help us to address unexpected contingencies.

Specialized Contributions to Multifaceted Problems

The solutions to multifaceted problems depend on specialized research, even while at particular junctures integrated policy solutions may be helpful and even essential. The case of global warming may help us to illustrate some of the distinctions just outlined. Global warming is certainly a multifaceted problem, but it does not necessarily follow that any given research project in this area requires an interdisciplinary team. This example will help to underscore the difference between integration as applied to research versus policy making.

Climate change represents an existential challenge to the future of humanity. The changes to the physical environment are likely to include increasing levels of greenhouse gases in the atmosphere, climbing temperatures, rising sea levels, oscillating weather patterns, droughts, and related phenomena. Climate change will likely impact complex ecosystems, human food supplies, and the habitability of coastal and low-lying areas, not to mention the possibility of rising social tensions and conflicts over water and other resources that may become scarce and expensive. Researchers have explored the viability of alternative energy technologies, carbon sequestration, and the reduction of methane emissions from cattle ranches and dairy farms. While of course it is a good idea for researchers and scholars to be informed of developments in related fields, the fact is that global warming and other issues often draw on specialized research conducted by specialists trained in particular disciplines.

While Roy Bhaskar and his colleagues (2010) make a convincing case that climate change is multifaceted, they do not succeed in showing that advances in particular aspects of this domain require interdisciplinary knowledge on the part of researchers. For example, an oceanographer who refines models of sea currents (Rahmstorf 2002) does not necessarily need to be at the cutting edge of new battery technologies (Soloveichik 2011). Similarly, those who study access to water in sub-Saharan region (de Wit and Stankiewicz 2006) do not need to be at the forefront of research on polar bear populations (Stirling, McDonald, and Richardson 2011). The analysis of ice-core samples to better understand climate history is its own area of specialization (Petit et al. 1999). Researchers who specialize in this area may not need to know the fine points of economic and political debates over the strengths and weaknesses of "cap and trade" approaches to the control of carbon emissions (for example, Stavins 2003; Lohmann 2006).

These assertions are borne out by empirical research on climate change studies. Bjurstrom and Polk (2011) examined citations to climate change research in ninety-six journals, and find that while some fields draw on a wide variety of disciplines, most climate-change fields draw on research from closely related areas of research (which they refer to as "narrow interdisciplinarity"). An awareness of developments in other facets of climate change would not hurt anyone; yet this is quite different from suggesting that climate change needs to be an "integrated" area of research housed in its own center, department, or school.

Immediate action on climate change is urgently needed because the momentum of global warming is exceedingly difficult to reverse. Once greenhouse gasses are emitted, they can remain in the atmosphere for centuries. Current forecasts suggest that the planet may continue to warm for hundreds of years into the future. The coordination of efforts, across countries and across areas, is thus of the utmost importance. Yet it is useful to distinguish the knowledge policy makers need to coordinate current efforts, and the knowledge and skills researchers need to have in order to make the next set of breakthroughs. Public policies related to climate change will need to take many factors into account, yet the knowledge and insights needed for successful policy making are likely to be quite different from those needed to make scientific advances in the many specialized questions raised by climate change. For example, it is useful from a policy perspective to understand the relative contributions to greenhouse gasses of raising farm animals, driving cars to work, and generating electricity for home use, but this knowledge is different in kind from having the skills needed to advance research on any of these issues.

This case highlights two distinctions: between the scope of a problem and the scope of relevant research; and between specialization in the research lab and integration in the context of product development or policy making. These points are consistent with the proliferation of research centers that address the issue of homeland security at Pennsylvania State University documented in chapter 5.

The discussion of global warming remains speculative in part because the research and policies that will contribute to solving this problem still lie in the future. A second example, drawing on a historical case, may provide further support for these distinctions. Specifically, the case of the "green revolution" may be informative regarding how basic and applied fields of research can be brought together to solve the world's challenges.

As it was perceived in the 1960s, the problem of feeding the world's growing population was multifaceted. Contributing factors included a rapidly growing population, widespread poverty and inequality in developing countries, and insufficient food production, among others. Yet significant progress could be made in one of these areas without the development of a comprehensive plan to address all of these issues. For example, with support from the Rockefeller Foundation, Norman Borlaug sought to improve agricultural productivity by reducing plants' vulnerability to disease. Borlaug, trained in plant pathology at the University of Minnesota, played an important role in developing hybrid strains of wheat and rice that would greatly expand the yield per acre in countries around the world. He did not simply extend prevailing techniques but had to overturn several prevailing theories and practices in the area of plant breeding. The introduction of new varieties in turn led farmers to improve other facets of cultivation, further enhancing crop yields (Borlaug 1970).

Borlaug, who won the Nobel Peace Prize for his contributions in 1970, built on basic research in genetics dating back to Gregor Mendel in the nineteenth century and the development of chemical fertilizers in the early decades of the twentieth century. The green revolution was a cross-disciplinary applied effort, but it drew on specialized knowledge of plant breeding and plant pathology, and particular strains of wheat developed in Japan and in applied agriculture programs in land-grant universities in the United States (Borlaug 1983). Much of this research was advanced in research institutes located in Mexico and India. Later in his life, Borlaug saw genetic engineering and other forms of biotechnology as holding the potential to take the green revolution to the next level (Borlaug 2007).

This brief sketch underscores the value of distinguishing among disparate senses of the term "integration." The integration of ideas and techniques that takes place in the laboratory or even in the research group is different in kind from the integration of technical, social, and economic factors that takes place at the level of policy implementation. An integrated laboratory team and an integrated research program are quite different things. For most complex issues, it may not be clear in advance which areas of research will yield to breakthroughs or what aspects of a problem will be most amenable to solutions. For example, it is unlikely that an integrated AIDS research strategy developed in the early 1990s would have included circumcision as part of the research agenda, yet accumulated research indicates that it can make a big difference in reducing the spread of AIDS and other sexually transmitted diseases (Weiss, Quigley, and Hayes 2000).

In recent years, the widespread use of fertilizers and pesticides has led some to question central features of the green revolution. The call for an "evergreen" revolution is intended to promote sustainable agricultural practices that will nonetheless continue to enhance productivity (Swaminathan 2006). Some take these side effects of the green revolution as emblematic of the biased and incomplete knowledge produced by disciplinary divisions, and thus more evidence for the need for "integrated solutions." Whereas Bhaskar's approach might well lead to calls for a critical interdisciplinary approach to the problem of nourishing a hungry world, a successful path in promoting sustainable agriculture in the future is likely to resemble the one followed during the green revolution. Advances in understanding of particular issues, whether they might consist of hybrid plants, soil yields, or pesticide-free practices, will be developed, either in a basic-science laboratory, an agriculture research department, or by a multinational food conglomerate such as Monsanto. It may be that breakthroughs in economic incentives (such as microfinancing) or social arrangements (such as improving gender equality) will provide an important piece of the puzzle (United Nations 2011). Some potential solutions, such as the reduction of waste in the food supply chain (Cuéllar and Webber 2010) are easily visible to the naked eye and could be implemented today, while others, such as development at the nanoscale, can only be studied with elaborate equipment and may congeal into a solution only after years or even decades of research in the future (Busch 2008). Progress in one area will in all likelihood stimulate related developments, just as the introduction of hybridized strains of dwarf wheat prompted enhanced irrigation and a series of other agricultural improvements. Efforts to implement advances in one or more of these areas may be championed by prominent figures in the field of global development, including academics such as Jeffrey Sachs and philanthropists such as Bill Gates. Or perhaps more bottom-up, rather than "top-down," approaches will prevail (Sabatier 1986).

Integrated policy solutions thus are a very different matter than an integrated research program, which in turn needs to be distinguished from the integration of insights in a particular study. Policies draw on technologies that are currently available and lessons learned from previous efforts to implement reforms. The point is that knowledge needed for the development of effective public policies is different from the skills needed to succeed in the research lab. And the efforts to implement policy require yet another set of knowledge and skills.

Borlaug's research program was an integrated one that connected basic knowledge of plant diseases with a broad and vigorous approach to plant breeding. The results of these inquiries were rapidly integrated into agricultural policies first in Mexico and later in other countries. These reforms were in turn integrated to a lesser degree with other efforts to alleviate suffering and improve the standard of living in developing countries. Yet there was no need for all of the researchers on Borlaug's team to learn the fine points of population demography or the political economy of wealth and poverty.

Thus, sustainable agriculture will require neither a new epistemology nor a new mode of knowledge, and it will not require a reorganization of the disciplinary system of research. Instead, in all likelihood, it will emerge from the efforts of many different research programs conducted at universities and applied research labs around the globe along with the efforts of policy makers to disseminate what are currently understood as best policies and practices.

Similarly, despite the importance of promptly commencing efforts to inhibit climate change, it is important to recognize that effective measures are likely to evolve over time. Thus, at the level of active research, however valuable a concerted research strategy may appear to be, such programmatic efforts should not be allowed to completely crowd out other, competing research groups whose heretical ideas may eventually prove fruitful. Contributions will emerge in disparate pieces from the advances of diverse research groups working on a wide array of questions. These may one day be combined into a comprehensive strategy that will probably diverge in important respects from current plans.

A closely related proposition is that interdisciplinarity is necessary for the analysis of complex systems. If complex systems characterize the natural and social worlds, and understanding these systems depends on insights from disparate fields, then progress in all research domains will require an interdisciplinary approach. Newell maintains that the analysis of complex systems is the core mission of interdisciplinary studies: "the appropriate focus of interdisciplinary study is on specific complex systems and their behavior" (2001, 2). At its core, the complex systems perspective is a particular version of the more general argument for holism. In both cases, the premise is that disciplinary knowledge can only be partial and the reliance on a single disciplinary framework will make it impossible to develop accurate and informative system models.

Even if we grant the premise of the interconnectedness of all systems in the universe (and perhaps even multiple universes), scholarship over the last several centuries has shown that there is much to be learned by developing and gradually improving on simple and partial models. When the system in question is a biological one operating at the cellular level or a meteorological system operating on a planetary scale, specialists have made great strides by developing and gradually improving on simple models. Indeed, analysis at the level of complex systems may only be possible when various subsystems are understood.[3]

There is no doubt that interdisciplinary research can be valuable, but it should also be clear that interdisciplinarity per se is not a panacea. But what organizational form does it take? We now turn to question of the sustainability of interdisciplinarity as a distinct form of knowledge.

The Ballad of John and Yoko: An Interdisciplinary Fable

John, a successful humanist, and Yoko, an accomplished scientist, connect and make beautiful music together. In the terminology of interdisciplinarity, they combine their disparate insights, training, and imagination in a new transdisciplinary synthesis that we shall call "resonance." The world takes note. So far so good.

The question of interest here is what happens next. In one way that this story continues, resonance become a field of study. John and Yoko's students build on their insights, refine their techniques, organize conferences on resonance, and clamor for research funds. As resonance becomes a field of study, graduate students begin with a structured plan of study centered around foundational texts and exemplary research. They no longer need to recapitulate the training that the founders of the field pursued. In short, resonance forms its own field of study, with its own scholarly association, peer-reviewed journals, plan of graduate study, and claim on faculty positions. Over time, the course roster adds "resonance" to the list of offerings, and resonance scholars petition the dean for their own certificates, programs, and perhaps even their own departments. The more important the discovery, the more fertile the line of inquiry; the more rapid the growth of the field, the more likely the subsequent institutionalization of a program of research, and the more likely the new interdisciplinary field is added to the list of established fields of research. Thus, today's greatest interdisciplinary hits become tomorrow's conventional lines of inquiry. If its enduring successes themselves join the constellation of specialties and sometimes disciplines, interdisciplinarity becomes a self-limiting proposition, a valuable but transitional phase rather than an alternative approach to arranging academic life.

The fable sketched above is not mere speculation. New lines of inquiry regularly emerge for a variety of reasons, some congeal into a successful field, and some of these become part of the organizational landscape in higher education. As we have seen, few fields become full-fledged disciplines with their own academic departments and internal labor markets. Not even biochemistry has fully achieved this status. The more realistic question, then, is whether burgeoning fields such as neuroscience and nanotechnology will become established subfields in one or more disciplines, and whether in turn they will subdivide into a plethora of subspecialties.

We have seen evidence of this process in many settings. Applied fields spin off from academic disciplines and over time develop their own journals and their own research agendas, and they end up moving in the direction of a closed labor market, hiring mostly professors with credentials in the new field. Several examples of spin-offs from the field of sociology such as communications and criminology were outlined in chapter 3; many more examples of this pattern could be sketched. Scientific advances open vast new vistas for understanding the world, such as new insights into the functioning of the human brain gleaned from neuroscience or the prospect of new technologies developed through nanotechnology.

There is a strong possibility, then, that the latest wave of interdisciplinary advances will quickly settle into the broader university tableau. New units, new knowledge, new missions will compete with established fields and pre-professional programs for attention, students, space, and other resources. Rather than reverse the long trend toward ever greater specialization, the creation of the latest round of new fields only hastens its advance. In this vision, interdisciplinarity does not represent a fundamental break with the past but rather consists of a temporary transitional phase during which new fields become recognized in their own right.

Advocates of interdisciplinarity are aware of this possibility. For example, Peter Weingart writes, "After a period of emergence they [new interdisciplinary research fields] form into another specialized field" (2010, 12). While Weingart and a few others find this scenario likely and perhaps acceptable (Weingart 2010), many reformers seek to foster more fundamental changes. For example, Wolfgang Krohn (2010) suggests that instances of "interdisciplinary fusion" create new disciplines. The examples he gives are biochemistry, cognitive science, climate research, and public health. Rather than celebrate these cases, Krohn remarks that, from an interdisciplinary point of view, "newly fused disciplines leave observers where they started" (2010, 31). The next section explores how reformers have grappled with this scenario.

Stanley Fish: Is Interdisciplinarity Logically Impossible?

In a widely discussed essay published in 1989, Fish argued that interdisciplinarity was logically impossible. More specifically, Fish maintained that if interdisciplinarity is held up as a path to intellectual and political liberation, it will end in frustration. Many advocates of interdisciplinarity pursue it as a way of breaking through the limiting confines of disciplinary hierarchies. Fish argues, however, this approach founders on epistemological contradictions.

While some read Fish's arguments to be about interdisciplinarity in general, it should be understood that they target the self-contradictory goals of one particular strand of this reasoning. Interdisciplinarity, Fish maintains, "has acquired a new force and urgency" as it flows "naturally from the imperatives of left culturalist theory, that is, from deconstruction, Marxism, feminism, the radical version of neopragmatism, and the new historicism" (1989, 15). Fish suggests that these intellectual currents see interdisciplinarity as offering the promise of liberating scholars and their students from the narrow confines of particular disciplines. "By definition interdisciplinary studies do exactly that—refuse to respect the boundaries that disciplines want always to draw—and thus encourage a widening of perspectives that will make possible the fullness education is supposed to confer" (1989, 16).

A well-educated person, in this view, "would be 'full' in the sense that their intelligences would not be captured by any one point of view but would, rather, be engaged in exploring points of view other than those authorized by current orthodoxies" (1989, 16). Fish cites others who seek "a fullness of engagement, a mind and person that refuses to segregate its activities, to think, for example, that literary study is one thing, participation in the national political process quite another" (1989, 17).

Fish maintains that, however stirring this vision might be, "it is finally at odds with the epistemology that often accompanies it." Thus, Fish's philosophical arguments do not necessarily represent a challenge to all forms of interdisciplinarity for all purposes but rather whether the goal of liberation is a viable goal for the radical humanistic inquiry, given the philosophical assumptions of that perspective.

For Fish, interdisciplinarity offers the illusion of intellectual freedom because a new set of partial and incomplete understandings will inevitably replace the ones it succeeds in displacing.

> the interdisciplinary impulse finally does not liberate us from the narrow confines of academic ghettos to something more capacious; it merely redomiciles us in enclosures that do not advertise themselves as such. (1989, 18)

In other words, in Fish's view, the power of the deconstructionist perspective dismantles disciplinary standpoints, but in the process undermines any possible solid anchoring for an interdisciplinary critique. Fish extends the argument by suggesting that radical deconstruction will succeed neither in its academic nor in its political objectives. "The epistemological argument deprives the political argument of any possible force, because it leaves no room for a revolutionary project" (1989, 19).

So far Fish's argument would seem to pose a dilemma for a certain set of humanist scholars who pursue interdisciplinarity for particular goals and adhere to the philosophical premises of deconstruction. But Fish quickly leaps from this set of philosophical dilemmas to a broader set of conclusions. Fish makes a range of empirical claims that he asserts as logical necessities. In fact, as we will see, these may well have a kernel of truth, but they may also vary from scholar to scholar and discipline to discipline. Consequently, Fish jumbles together a well-argued skewering of interdisciplinarity based on deconstructionist principles with a broader critique of the practice of this approach in all settings and contexts, spanning interdisciplinarities designed to reach a wide variety of goals.

Fish steps from this philosophical conundrum to a set of real-world, practical issues: "Either . . . the announcement of an interdisciplinary program inaugurates the effort of some discipline to annex the territory of another, or 'interdisciplinary thought' is the name (whether acknowledged or not) of a new discipline" (1989, 19). This may be so, but it does not follow from the epistemological critique offered above.

Fish asks, "Can a practitioner of a given discipline practice that discipline and have some distance at the same time?" No, Fish concludes, on logical grounds: one is either practicing one's field or observing it. Can a discipline import ideas from other fields? No, "because the imported product will always have the forms of its appropriation rather than the form it exhibits 'at home'" (1989, 19). For Fish, ideas and techniques are themselves socially constructed and thus must remain alien to the field to which they are imported, or, alternatively, become corrupted once they arrive and are absorbed. Thus, in principle, Fish would hold that an economist using techniques developed by statisticians for use in a biological context cannot adopt them for his own purposes because they are foreign . . . or they will become part of economic practice and lose whatever properties made them distinctive in the first place. Perhaps, but such conclusions should be based on studies of the diffusion and reception of ideas rather than offering determinations based on extended reasoning alone. The evidence presented in chapters 5 and 6 strongly suggest that disciplines do indeed import ideas from other venues and these become part of the established frameworks in surprisingly rapid order. Fish's brief comments thus essentialize disciplines and do not acknowledge as a logical possibility the extensive intellectual hybridization that characterizes most fields.

Fish offers all of these assertions not as the empirical claims they are but rather as logical necessities that warrant no further inquiry. "The point is of course tautological," Fish asserts, in the context of practicing and observing one's field, rather than considering the possibility that some practitioners are more self-aware than others, and that the "practice" of research extends over months and years and thus provides abundant time to both practice and reflect.

> The impossibility of authentic critique is the impossibility of the interdisciplinary project, at least insofar as that project holds out the hope of releasing cognition from the fetters of thought and enlarging the minds of those who engage in it. (1989, 21)

Fish's logical conundrum assumes the goal of interdisciplinarity is liberation for faculty, students, and ultimately for society. As we have seen, the vision of universities as engines of economic growth discussed by Geiger and Sa (2009) does not start with this assumption, and they would likely view Fish's conundrum as having little relevance to their perspective. Fish raises a number of serious questions about the long-term trajectory of interdisciplinary movements, and thus deserves much credit, but we need to be clear on the aspects of his arguments that rest on logical premises and those that are empirical questions.

Alan Liu: Interdisciplinarity, the Sublime, and the Perpetual Revolution

Alan Liu is an accomplished literary scholar who has studied the romantic period as well as media culture in the contemporary period. His essay "The Interdisciplinary War Machine" was written in 1989–90 but was first published in English in 2008 as part of his collection of essays *Local Transcendence*.

Liu begins by suggesting the emergence of a consensus (circa 1990) on the roles that culture played in the French Revolution. This view developed in opposition to the emphasis on structural forces and long-term trajectories advanced by such scholars as Theda Skocpol in sociology and Fernand Braudel in history. If culture plays a key role in transformative historical episodes, then it quickly follows that the tools used to analyze cultural materials need to be assimilated by historians to decipher the rhetoric and symbols of the period. Thus, Lynn Hunt, a leading figure in this area, avers, "I propose to treat revolutionary rhetoric as a text in the manner of literary criticism" (Liu 2008, 168).

Thus, "historians have adventured into literary criticism" (2008, 170), while at the same time literary critics have "return[ed] to history" (2008, 172). Liu was a participant as well as observer of this intellectual scene, having studied the English romantic poet William Wordsworth, who toured France during the early years of the French Revolution.

An advocate of interdisciplinary could easily hold up this example as an interdisciplinary success story, as follows: The reality of human history is too broad and complex to fit into the narrow confines of disciplines, in this case literature and history, and eventually scholars from both fields come together in order to gain a fuller appreciation of the period. Not only do literary scholars and historians converge on a set of concerns, but a fuller understanding, an interdisciplinary synthesis, develops. This trend would seem to represent just the kind of success that would exemplify the transdisciplinarian agenda.

But Liu offers a different and more complex view. Even as he is presenting evidence of this new synthesis, Liu is alarmed by its rigidity. Liu presents "a parade of quotations," a parade he fears is "almost military in their basic uniformity" (2008, 168). The reader of Liu's essay need not wait long to find out what frightens him: an ideology of interdisciplinary freedom that yields "only a new tyranny" (2008, 174).

Liu embraces Stanley Fish's arguments on the logical impossibility of interdisciplinarity but seeks at the end of his essay a way to escape the traps that Fish sets out. Liu adheres to the very same liberationist goals of humanistic scholarship and teaching that Fish maintains are unattainable, and he feels the force of Fish's conundrum. For Liu, this is not simply a philosophical maze to escape but a real-life nightmare. The very success of cultural history in bringing textual analysis to bear on the French Revolution shows Liu the shallowness of the victory. He despairs that a new orthodoxy has replaced the old, and is appalled at the "quasi-military" discipline with which the new dogmas are enforced.

But in the end Liu turns away from despair in order to seek a way out. Liu's solution is a process rather than a result, including an emphasis on the value of the visual as well as the textual. In short, cognizance of limits leads to openness:

> The epistemology of interdisciplinarity is not a closed box because interdisciplinary knowledge is really a rhetoric, and the essence of that rhetoric is at last to arrive at an abject wordlessness that is NOT the same as closure. It is a striving to configure—refigure and re-envision—the forms of our closure so as to make it answerable to present urgencies. (2008, 185)

The goal of a complete understanding is replaced by a process of confronting new fields, new terrain that we realize we can never fully master, and, in the sublime moment of our realization of the limits of our knowledge, we become open to new understandings, new possibilities, new configurations.

Thus for Liu, interdisciplinarity is not an endpoint as much as a process, not a combination of history and literature in any particular form, but a yearning to combine history, literature, visual media, indeed, media in general, in new ways that challenge existing orthodoxies and power relations.

Once a new insight is gained, however, one must continue to reorder and rework it lest it become a new orthodoxy. Liu's approach may be viewed as a "permanent revolution," with reform holding the promise of presenting an continuing challenge to settled ideas rather than presenting a single "right" and enduring configuration.

There is a valuable insight in this view, since advancing scholarship always involves pursuing new terrain and reexamining untested assumptions. Scholarship is always seeking new frontiers and new approaches and will rarely be completely satisfied with current orthodoxy. Researchers working within disciplinary contexts already do this, and thus perpetual change is not unique to interdisciplinarity. But there is a central failing in Liu's view that is unfortunately shared by many writers in this area. Liu's vision is of individual scholars pursuing their own liberationist agendas without a disciplinary community and without any system for making authoritative judgments.

What is lacking in Liu's approach is any sense of authority, cumulative gains, and collective assessment of scholarship. Liu's individualist is off on his own, seeking the sublime experience without an explicit reference to whether the same ground had been previously explored. In looking for new terrain to till, how do we know we are not just rediscovering old chestnuts? Disciplines provide a community of scholars to make such assessments; they introduce novices to traditions of inquiry and provide guidance on those new frontiers that may most fruitfully be explored. Research and scholarship is a collective endeavor, even if many hours are spent in solitude and insights occur to individual investigators. The community of scholars in a field establishes understandings and contentions about what constitutes important questions and what constitutes good research. These are often contested because disciplines are so wide in their scope and diverse in their research approaches. Nonetheless, community evaluation of research is indispensable. Liu and others who seek to transcend disciplines seek to avoid the sanction of any community of scholars.

Thus, Fish's conclusion is correct but for very different reasons than he offers. There is no way to escape from the collective nature of scholarship. Individual thinkers of course chart new courses and directions, but the community plays a key role in determining whether to accept these insights, to make them part of the common core of established thinking. Sometimes insurgent groups coalesce in the form of a scientific/intellectual movement (SIM) to challenge accepted shibboleths (Frickel and Gross 2005). But, in the end, there is a collectivity of some sort that certifies certain views, ratifies some advances as established, accepts some approaches as valid, and denotes others as flawed and points in the direction of more promising lines of inquiry.

The challenges of evaluative judgments and research priorities would be problematic for Liu both within and across domains. Not only would a novice literary scholar lack guidance on the best topics to pursue, but without any boundaries there would be no clarity on whether her project is literary or historical, humanistic or scientific, since the point of the new approach is to erase such limiting distinctions. Thus, at the level of research areas, social organization is essential. The antidisciplinary position is thus not tenable. This is not a trivial point because so much writing and thinking in this area points in this direction.

The suggestion that critics espouse the "antidisciplinarian" perspective may seem a bit extreme, and perhaps even a caricature. Yet the term is increasingly used, and many who criticize disciplines maintain that they are essentially unredeemable. For example, Robert Frodeman, editor in chief of the *Oxford Handbook on Interdisciplinarity* (2010), calls for resistance against the pull of disciplinary structures for the field of interdisciplinary studies in particular and more broadly for academia in general.

> The power of knowledge to constantly overturn society . . . calls for a field of study, or an antidiscipline, devoted to the examination of knowledge in the largest possible compass. An antidiscipline, because it is crucial that such a study resist being once again drawn in by the gravitational pull of disciplinary approaches and standards . . . insofar as a field becomes disciplined it cannot offer the peculiar kind of insights that our times require. (2010, xxxi)

While some reformers seek to resist disciplines (and sometimes discipline as well), others see interdisciplinarity as coexisting, and sometimes even depending, on disciplines (Strober 2011). For example, Moran maintains that "as the composite nature of the term itself suggests, 'interdisciplinarity' assumes the existence and relative resilience of disciplines and modes of thought and institutional practices" (Moran 2010, 15). The alternative to antidisciplinarity sees value in the building of interdisciplinary bridges between disciplinary islands.

Here I am using the term "antidisciplinary" in a specific sense to refer to those who seek interdisciplinary arrangements that avoid the organizational structures that make disciplines work. In other words, antidisciplinarity represents the effort to keep interdisciplinary arrangements flexible and unstructured in order to keep them from "falling into the same traps" as disciplines. The question of whether and how disciplines might coexist with interdisciplinary arrangements in a "postdisciplinary university" is taken up in chapter 10.

Research Communities

Specialized fields of research represent a social as well as intellectual domain. Without a scholarly community functioning to at least a minimal degree, scientific advances would be more difficult to produce and even harder to identify. Robert Merton, from his early work on the religious roots of early English scientists to his studies of scientific priority disputes, viewed science as a social endeavor (1973). He and his followers (for example, Hagstrom 1975) emphasized the norms of the scientific community in an effort to distinguish science from nonscience.

Since Merton, the emphasis has increasingly been on scientific communities as a plural concept. The scholarly community is organized into a range of different types of communities with diverse social structures and varying levels of agreement. For example, Diana Crane's "invisible colleges" are small groups of researchers who share a focus on a particular set of problems. Crane's groups were smaller than disciplines and even smaller than the subspecialties discussed in chapter 3. These units, often working in far-flung institutions, converge around particular nodes of research and are central to both the creative energy of research and its evaluation. Even Thomas Gieryn (1983, 1999), whose research on boundary work continued Merton's concern with the border between science and nonscience, emphasized the diverse ways that claims to scientific authority were made in different disciplinary contexts.

Thomas Kuhn (1996 [1962]) also emphasized the commitments of diverse groups of scientists. Kuhn stressed the fact that problematic or negative results often do not lead scientists to abandon their theories. In Kuhn's terms, anomalous results are usually not sufficient to cause scientists to abandon their "paradigms"; indeed the everyday work of scientists was to resolve the puzzles such anomalous findings. Some of Kuhn's numerous readers mistook the term "normal science" to mean the pedestrian accumulation of facts, but Kuhn is quite clear that the tasks of solving puzzles and extending and refining theories is at the heart of the scientific enterprise. The key point is that the commitment of a group of researchers to a paradigm despite its imperfect account of the known and relevant facts is essential to the development of diverse areas of research. While Kuhn's framework has been challenged in many ways from many directions, the importance of groups of scientists working together, both as collaborators and competitors, on the frontiers of research remains an important touchstone for the social studies of science.[4]

A more recent generation of science studies has emphasized the social construction of scientific evidence. Detailed ethnographies of laboratory scientists in action indicate that findings do not simply reveal themselves but are painstakingly constructed. Karin Knorr-Cetina (1999) captures this plurality of scientific approaches with her term "epistemic cultures." She describes the divergent "epistemic cultures" of biology and high-energy physics. In the former, the lab group is key; in the latter, the collaborative group often involves hundreds of researchers spread out over institutes from multiple countries.

While a central message of these investigations is to raise questions about the privileged status of scientific inquiry, we should not lose site of the fact that these epistemic cultures are intensely social. The construction, execution, and solicitation of support for scientific research all depend on the ability of small groups, and sometimes large groups, of scientists to bring meaning to the streams of symbols and indicators produced by research. In other words, scientific "data" only become recognized and understood as data through the collective work of groups of researchers.

Departments represent one facet of the social world of academics, since this is where many face-to-face interactions occur and decisions regarding hiring and teaching are made. But the research unit typically differs from the department. In some contexts, the research unit is a laboratory group; in others, it is a shifting research team; in other cases, a university-based research center provides the setting. Some of the key communities essential for academic research, namely, Crane's "invisible colleges," are geographically disbursed. Some research tends to be more solitary in nature. But even without collaboration, the research community in one way or another plays a key role. Members comment on each other's papers, review each other's work, and hire each other's students. Scholarly research journals also represent a kind of community. Editors recruit editorial boards and solicit collective input into decisions. Journals are broader in scope than research nodes. Editorial boards agree (at least in general) on common research standards rather than sharing a commitment to a particular line of inquiry.

Thus the plural account of scientific communities is accurate, but this does not make science any less social. Community is needed for stimulation, support, evaluation, and training. From a certain point of view, disciplines represent an amalgamation of specialized scholarly communities.

Klein and Liu: Interdisciplinarity as Antidisciplinarity

Scholars are well aware of the self-limiting prospects of interdisciplinarity. Some feel that interdisciplinarity can avoid this trap by being perpetually innovative. Julie Thompson Klein at some points seems to take this position.

Unfortunately, Klein's prose, which is typically clear and direct, recedes into philosophical mists and eventually evaporates before resolving this matter. She quotes Alan Liu, who suggests that interdisciplinarity will lead to its own "closures" but will avoid the traps of the past because "ultimately, Liu proposes, interdisciplinary knowledge is a rhetoric, and the essence of that rhetoric is to reconfigure closures to make them answer to current urgencies" (Klein 2010a, 101). This formulation is unsatisfactory because it devalues the importance of cumulative growth of scholarly inquiry. If the virtue of interdisciplinarity is that it more rapidly adjusts to "current urgencies," one could reply that the virtue of disciplines is that they take into account both the long-term development of ideas as well as the short-term issues of the day. This is too weak an argument on which to base the reorganization of the modern university; stronger intellectual foundations would be needed. We would do better to endeavor to improve the remarkably successful system of disciplines we already have.

Let us be clear on what this approach entails. To return to the hypothetical new field sketched above, once resonance is established, the perpetual revolution approach would avoid the creation of a department of resonance. Those who have learned the basic insight would be encouraged to join with scholars from other fields to pursue new insights, new lines of inquiry, to explore exciting new and yet unexplored terrain. While this may appear compelling, it neglects to develop the unexplored potential of resonance. John and Yoko might have only scratched the surface, and decades more digging, refinement, and elaboration might be needed to flesh out the full potential that they imagined for resonance in the first place, yet the perpetual revolution approach would recommend seeking out new terrains for exploration.

Klein appears to endorse Liu's call for a permanent revolution: the problems of postrevolutionary society are "solved" by following the first revolution with a second and then a third. The period of reaction never settles in as it is indefinitely postponed. This seems entirely fanciful, and would preclude the practical accomplishments interdisciplinarity is held to offer. No new fields would become developed, established, and explored in depth. No established corpus of knowledge would be brought to bear on new challenges. Thus, to advocates of a permanent revolution, nanotechnology would be interesting, exciting, and fully interdisciplinary only as long it is in its infancy. Once it is established and scholars begin to dig deeper in order to mine the undiscovered gems beneath the surface of this terrain, it has simply another established field of inquiry and the truly adventurous interdisciplinarians need to move on.

As we have seen, the disciplinary system relies on communities of scholars.

Communities of like-minded researchers develop norms regarding evidence and interpretation, values regarding the importance of problems to be solved and issues to be addressed, hierarchies of reputation and reward—in short, disciplinary-like systems of social control. Either interdisciplinary recreates similar communities and Liu's freedom becomes limited, or chaos ensues: no community, no rules, no boundaries, no differentiating good from bad, typos from intended spellings, enduring insights from implausible suggestions.

Beyond the individual research specialty, there is a deeper level at which the disciplinary system is indispensable for sustained scholarly progress. Antidisciplinarity will not work for individual research groups but also not for the scholarly system. Systems of evaluation would become more difficult to construct, systems for employment more difficult to sustain. The accumulation of knowledge from the undergraduate to the graduate to the faculty level will be subject to an interdisciplinary blender. No doubt some interesting flavors will emerge but the likelihood of producing individuals capable of building on specialized knowledge will be reduced.

Institutionalizing Interdisciplinarity

The specific forms that interdisciplinary arrangements should take on campus is not often discussed by reformers. As we have seen, there is a tendency to celebrate a wide variety of interdisciplinary possibilities rather than to recommend a particular plan. And, as noted in chapter 2, prominent writers in this area view the spirit of interdisciplinarity as being the most important consideration.

One alternative is a distinct program and department for interdisciplinary studies. As we will see shortly, this organizational structure is currently quite rare. The notion of a separate department of interdisciplinary studies would seem self-contradictory and perhaps self-defeating, as it might lead to the creation of the very same organizational and intellectual barriers to interdisciplinarity that advocates seek to eradicate. One can find echoes of this theme in debates on the appropriate form of women's studies, an area of scholarship to which this author has devoted much of his research career. A number of advocates wanted women's studies to become integrated or "mainstreamed" into the general curriculum, rather than a separate unit that risked ghettoization in the university status system (Schmitz 1985; Boxer 1998; Guy-Sheftall 2009). In the end, Klein favors institutionalization not just as a program depending on faculty from various fields but as a separate department. In this way, her approach appears to be "both/and" rather than "either/or."

Klein has thought seriously about the many elements of a successful and enduring interdisciplinary program. Those about to embark down the road toward building new programs would do well to consult her *Creating Interdisciplinary Campus Cultures* (Klein 2010a). The elaborate processes and structures Klein recommends, however, resemble many of the same ones that make traditional discipline-based departments function.

There are two related points here. First, disciplines have been successful because they create a space for intellectual autonomy. Klein seeks to recreate this with interdisciplinary units, but doing so will be more difficult because of the more limited shared background, experiences, and intellectual tool kits of faculty with diverse backgrounds. Achieving disciplinary objectives is harder to do in the interdisciplinary context because there is inevitably less clarity regarding core intellectual commitments. As a result, interdisciplinary units will prioritize process over substance. Attempting to recreate this type of community in an interdisciplinary context posed a dilemma: it is harder to accomplish outside the context of an academic discipline, yet, if it is successful, it will end up recreating a system strikingly similar to disciplines. Second, disciplines have been successful because they create an intellectual community that supports their intellectual agendas. If these are the very strengths of departments, and subdisciplinary research units, and if these elements are recognized as such by reformers who realize their vital role, then perhaps disciplines are not quite as flawed as their critics claim.

Klein writes that "strong" interdisciplinary programs "have a core faculty with full-time appointments located entirely or partly within a program" (2010a, 106). These programs have a clear line to upper-level administration, including a voice in policy, budget, program evaluation, and personnel matters. This list sounds very much like the elements of a traditional academic department, specifically the autonomy and authority needed to manage the field's own affairs.

Klein sets out a list of how should interdisciplinary programs should be reviewed. Her criteria include:

1 how interdisciplinary the program is;
2 the presence of critical mass factors;
3 benchmarking versus counterparts;
4 balance in curricular offerings;
5 partnership, that is, strong ties to similar units in other schools.

With the exception of the first criterion, traditional disciplines and departments are routinely evaluated in these ways

Making reforms work is not just a matter of laying out a new set of principles or criteria. To make any system of evaluation work, there need to be shared norms, values, and understandings. In addition, one needs to know who writes reliable promotion letters, and who tends to be hypercritical. Sociologists refer to this informal knowledge as a type of "social capital." In short, one needs a community of scholars with shared experiences and reference points. Disciplines are often too broad to fully attain this sense of community, and thus the work of community building often occurs at the specialty or subspecialty level.

Klein to her credit again fully appreciates this. In her table 4.1, Klein lists eighteen elements that contribute to the critical mass needed for the sustainability of an interdisciplinary program (106). These include structural coherence, a shared intellectual agenda, a sense of community and shared experiences, proactive attention to integrative and collaborative processes, and adequate common space, among others. These are precisely the kinds of social dimensions that make traditional academic research departments work despite the internal challenges they face covering the broad intellectual terrain under their purview. The main difference is that Klein's interdisciplinary units would share far less intellectual substance, thus challenging the viability of the enterprise.

In the end, the shared community of interdisciplinary scholars that Klein lays out in delineating how best to institutionalize such programs is completely inimical to Liu's lone scholar pursuing a perpetual revolution. There is simply no way to build the shared understandings and goals that Klein rightly recognizes as central to any functioning academic unit while maintaining the antidisciplinary agenda that Liu and others call for and that Klein in some places appears to endorse.[5]

Interdisciplinary Research Programs in Practice

It is now time for these theoretical considerations to give way to a consideration of actual interdisciplinary training programs. Turning briefly to undergraduate programs, approximately 375 colleges and universities currently offer bachelor's degrees in interdisciplinary studies. This places interdisciplinarity ahead of classics and astronomy but behind anthropology, art history, and computer science in its prevalence. However, interdisciplinary studies per se rarely exists as a separate department.[6] In many schools, this means that there is an interdisciplinary coordinator who is responsible for responding to individual student requests for the creation of an individualized program of study. In other institutions, there is a list of fields that provide interdisciplinary training.[7]

The emphasis here will be on graduate training, since this represents a key determinant of disciplinary closure. Unless a field produces its own PhDs, it does not fully match the disciplinary criteria outlined in chapter 3. *The College Blue Book* lists thirty-two universities that offer PhD degrees in interdisciplinary studies (roughly the same number as offer American studies degrees). An examination of the websites of these institutions is revealing. Only a minority of these institutions offer systematically organized interdisciplinary doctoral degrees, and the most common of these programs are quite narrowly targeted.

In five schools, no information on interdisciplinary degrees could be found on the institution's website. Five other schools, including the University of Oklahoma; the University of Alaska, Fairbanks; and Marquette University, offer doctoral students the opportunity to create their own course of study, but do not list any specific interdisciplinary programs. This approach may be viewed as "individualized interdisciplinarity."

In ten other schools, a single program with an interdisciplinary component was responsible for the inclusion of the school on the *Blue Book* list. Thus, the University of Kansas offers an interdisciplinary doctoral degree in jazz studies, while Emory University offers an interdisciplinary degree in culture and society. This approach may be designated as "limited programmatic interdisciplinarity."

The remaining twelve schools offer an extensive array of interdisciplinary doctoral programs. For example, the University of Minnesota lists no less than fifty interdisciplinary graduate programs, while Boston University features fifty interdisciplinary centers, institutes, and programs. Among the leading research universities, Stanford's leads the way with forty interdisciplinary degree programs, but not all of these programs offer doctoral degrees.

In many cases, these doctoral programs represent graduate training in fields that are understood to be interdisciplinary. For example, the University of Minnesota offers doctoral degrees in American studies, bioinformatics, and toxicology, among others. These fields are viewed by some as inherently interdisciplinary because they draw on ideas and techniques from more than one discipline. In the framework presented in chapter 3, these fields are interdisciplinary because they do not possess separate departments that train doctoral students who in turn staff these departments.

In other cases, interdisciplinarity consists of dual-degree programs. These sometimes take the form of majoring in one field and minoring in a second. For example, the University of Arkansas offers five separate degree programs that link African American studies to fields such as history and sociology.

Thus, at Arkansas, African American studies doctoral programs are interdisciplinary not because the field is inherently interdisciplinary but because the doctoral degree program crosses fields.

Another way to put this is that students receiving their degree in this field are felt to be more effective scholars if their training includes concentrated study in one discipline in addition to African American studies.

Ohio State University had the most explicit rules about such arrangements, specifying the number of course hours required in the second field. In practice, then, in the schools that offer the greatest number of cross-field doctoral programs, interdisciplinarity means knowing two fields rather than one, or, more precisely, parts of two fields.

The proliferation of interdisciplinary doctoral programs is thus similar in many ways to that observed in new academic journals, as discussed in chapter 4. In practice, interdisciplinarity most frequently consists of the creation of new interdisciplinary niches at the border of two fields of research.

The common feature of these interdisciplinary setups is how much they resemble traditional graduate programs, with specific course requirements and qualifying exams. In other words, the proliferation of interdisciplinary fields expands the number of specialized degree offerings. These programs may well be worthy of support, but they generally add to the specialized landscape of academia rather than representing a new way of redirecting the proliferation of programs into broader units. Interdisciplinary integration in practice thus tends to represent the creation of new specialized niches of research and scholarship, leaving the structure of graduate training thus intact. In some cases, there may be extra coursework for the second field of study. However, in many disciplines, doctoral qualifying exams are already required in two or more specialties. The dual-department nature of interdisciplinary doctoral programs represents an extension of this notion, but it is only a small step beyond what already exists.

The list of interdisciplinary doctoral degree programs is incomplete in that it does not include every hybrid field. In other words, if we added up all of the neuroscience, bioinformatics, American studies, and other interdisciplinary degrees, the list of schools offering interdisciplinary degrees would be very long. But this fact just shows that labeling the degree with these specializations is seen as more informative than labeling the degree as interdisciplinary.

Will bioinformatics become its own field? There are currently twenty-three bioinformatics PhD programs, half of which are located in bioinformatics departments. If, over time, there are enough programs created for a closed labor market to emerge, that is, for doctoral recipients in bioinformatics to take the majority of new faculty positions in the field, then it will move in the direction of becoming its own discipline. The main stumbling block is that universities are slow to open departments in new fields. Bioinformatics is thus more likely to become like biochemistry than it is to become a separate discipline like computer science.

Neuroscience has moved further along the path to becoming its own field, with 117 neuroscience doctoral programs currently established. This field clearly become its own specialty, most likely based within psychology or biology departments, although some stand-alone neuroscience departments have already been created, including a number located within schools of medicine.

Conclusion

In this chapter the diverse meanings of the term "integration" were examined. The premise that solutions to complex problems require interdisciplinary research was interrogated with examples drawn from global warming and the green revolution in food production. The long-term trajectory of interdisciplinary fields has also been considered. While the goal of interdisciplinary communication may seem benign, the premise that disciplines are problematic and even negative units naturally leads their critiques to the quest for an alternative. In particular, the theme of antidisciplinarity has been considered.

The thrust of the argument is that an attempt to replace disciplines with an alternative, antidisciplinary system does not represent a viable alternative to the current arrangement of academic life. The rejection of disciplinary structures leads to a quest for a permanent revolution, a rejection of the intellectual constraints that form the basis for scholarly communities. While the freedom and dynamism suggested by such an image might seem attractive, a nondisciplinary or antidisciplinary system would quickly founder. Whatever insights and advances that might be generated by the rejection of disciplinary arrangements would quickly be lost without any evaluation system, without a way of knowing what to build on and what to discard.

More likely than the creation of a postdisciplinarity is the proliferation of specialties that happen to be at the border of present disciplines. These will represent valuable additions to academy but will not represent a fundamental challenge to the prevailing disciplinary system.

The social processes underlying scholarly advances are emphasized. While these may not be fully understood, there is clearly a need for shared knowledge, support, synergy, complementarity, and evaluation. Despite their weaknesses and shortcomings, disciplines as social systems represent efforts to address these needs. Thus, while interdisciplinary communication and collaboration may seem to represent an inherently desirable goals, the permanent replacement of disciplines with a system based on nondisciplinary or antidisciplinary principles seems risky at best and self-defeating at worst. The central issue, then, is the trajectory of fields of study over the long term.

In practice, the universities that offer interdisciplinary doctoral degrees typically do so in ways that closely resemble traditional doctoral programs. In some cases, these are simply degrees obtained in a single field that claims interdisciplinary influences. In other cases, these are dual-degree programs that train students at new research frontiers that happen to fall at the intersection of two established fields.

This theme will be addressed further by means of a case study. American studies has a history dating back to the late 1940s, and thus is well suited for examining the long-term trajectory of an area of inquiry. Despite many changes in organization, style, and substantive concerns over its history, the field of American studies has maintained a commitment to interdisciplinary inquiry. The question of whether it represents a model that should be emulated throughout the university is the subject of the next chapter.

American Studies: Interdisciplinarity
over Half a Century

This chapter reports on an extensive investigation into the field of American studies since its inception in the late 1940s.[1] This long time frame enables the consideration of many aspects of interdisciplinarity that fall beyond the purview of short-term evaluations of collaborations or programs. By considering not just the energy and excitement of a new field of study but also how it settles into the academic landscape over the long term, this analysis will help to put interdisciplinarity in a broader and deeper historical context.

American studies is an interesting case for considering both the promise and potential pitfalls of interdisciplinarity. American studies has been developed and promoted since the 1940s (its roots go back even further) explicitly to overcome the limitations of established academic fields, in particular the way literature and history were taught in traditional departments. The early leaders in this field sought to examine the unexamined spaces between literature and history and to develop a more integrated understanding of American society. As we will see, while the intellectual direction of American studies scholars shifted substantially over the decades, the drive to break down arbitrary academic barriers and to explore new intellectual frontiers is a thread that connects American studies scholarship over the decades.

A strong case can be made for American studies in terms of the vitality of its scholarship, yet in organizational terms, American studies can at best only be deemed a partial success. On the positive side of the ledger, the American Studies Association has endured, and even thrived; American studies programs have become established in fifty countries, and more than thirty American studies journals are published in twenty-eight countries. On the other hand, even at its peak of popularity in the early 1970s, a mere 0.2 percent of undergraduates obtained their degrees in American studies, and only a slightly higher fraction of doctorates were granted in this field. American studies programs are located in less than 10 percent of American colleges and universities.

From the perspective of disciplinary development, it is important to note that American studies never became a standard academic department with control of its own tenure lines in most colleges and universities in the United States. Consequently, American studies did not become a self-contained academic market, producing its own PhDs with a secure hold on faculty appointments in American studies departments, features that Abbott (2001), Turner (2000), and others take as the quintessential defining characteristics of an academic discipline, as we have seen in chapter 3. Indeed, most of the presidents of the American Studies Association over the last twenty years had their principal appointments in either English or history departments.

From the outside looking in, it is clear that American studies represents another province in the broad landscape of the humanities rather than a powerful force for the unification of humanistic scholarship. For all of the lofty rhetoric about the integration of the study of literature, history, and sometimes even the social sciences in an integrated account of American society, American studies never displaced the traditional departments of English and history. The connection with social science fields such as anthropology, economics, political science, and sociology has been tenuous throughout most of its sixty-year history. Nor did American studies ever achieve complete integration internally: Americanists are divided by their training largely into historians on the one hand and literary scholars on the other. American studies scholars are also divided along generational lines, by the period they study, and increasingly by a diverse array of research specialties.

This historical overview should not be misinterpreted to imply that American studies was a bad idea that should never have been pursued. Many doctoral candidates trained in American studies programs became accomplished scholars and authors, including the current president of Harvard University, Drew Gilpin Faust. American studies scholars also may have helped to encourage the transformation of English and history, which have changed substantially over the sixty-year period examined here.

The experience of American studies, however, also suggests that the simple moniker "interdisciplinary" is no panacea. American studies as a field has been subject to many of the same limitations as the established disciplinary fields it sought to displace. Scholarly endeavors undertaken by those with training in American studies typically are just as narrow and specialized as those pursued by their counterparts trained in English and history. The notion that "interdisciplinary" is equivalent to "broad," or "integrative" or "synthetic" is belied by much of the research undertaken in this area. The standards of contemporary scholarship appear to encourage a rather high degree of specialization even on the part of those who are committed to interdisciplinary scholarship.

What the American studies experience does suggest is that the efficacy in building enduring bridges between disciplines depends on many factors, including the currents percolating through adjacent disciplines, especially on the part of new entrants. Potential connections, such as the connection between American studies and anthropology, remained relatively dormant, despite the centrality of the notion of "culture" in both domains. It is hard to see how the type of intellectual ferment represented by American studies could be imposed from the dean's office. Individual academic entrepreneurs can see opportunities and linkages between fields, but establishing an enduring field of inquiry requires an intellectual vision powerful enough to secure the commitment of faculty, deans, grant-giving agencies and foundations, undergraduates, and prospective graduate students. Change is often easier to accomplish within an existing discipline rather than via the creation of an entirely new field.

The case of American studies also makes clear that the relationships between fields shift over time in response to developments on both sides of the fence. Thus, the emergence of social history as a powerful force in history departments and poststructuralism and multiculturalism in literature departments challenged the intellectual niche that American studies had developed. Ironically, given the lack of control over its own departmental appointments, American studies has depended on the presence of sympathetic scholars based in history and English departments, even as the field has continued to search for a distinctive approach.

American studies as an interdisciplinary program was followed in the 1970s by African American studies, women's studies, and subsequently by a host of other interdisciplinary endeavors. I examine whether American studies helped to create the intellectual climate for these programs by serving as an organizational model to be emulated by those that followed. The evidence suggests that interdisciplinarity fosters more interdisciplinarity. In other words, the establishment of American studies programs facilitated the subsequent adoption of African American and especially women's studies programs. On the one hand, American studies deserves credit for creating a template that other important cross-disciplinary programs have been able to emulate. On the other hand, this pattern suggests that an interdisciplinary university is more likely to differentiate into a large number of specialized interdisciplinarities than it is to consolidate into a small number of fields.

This chapter also sketches some of the main developments in American studies through several broad periods from the foundation of the field up to the present. In each interval, a review of the main intellectual currents is juxtaposed with trends in organizational developments, including the number of programs and the number of students receiving degrees in American studies. The case of American studies can be understood within the framework for the study of scientific and intellectual movements outlined by Frickel and Gross (2005).[2] This analysis drew on a wide range of data sources[3] and interviews.[4]

The Founding and Early Years of American Studies

One of the first goals of American studies scholars was putting the study of American civilization on the intellectual map. As strange as it may seem from the contemporary vantage point, during the 1950s American literature was given short shrift by many English departments. A related critique of literary scholars was an overemphasis (from the point of view of American studies) on scholarship geared to interpreting the accomplishments of a narrow set of canonical authors. Zenderland (2006) contrasts a view of culture that emphasized the great achievements of a small group of creators (writers, painters, composers, architects) with a broader, more anthropological view of culture. If the study of culture was restricted to canonical masterpieces, then America would continually fall in Europe's shadow. The cannon of literature in the English language would start with Shakespeare and the great British novelists, and only a handful of American authors would warrant inclusion. Americanists sought to make the case that the American culture was worth studying,[5] or, as Gene Wise would later write, "to free the study of American Literature from its role as an appendage to Anglo-Saxon literature" (1979, 304). While later scholars would seek to go beyond the study of Hawthorne, Melville, Twain, and Whitman, the task of the first generation of American studies scholars was to legitimate the study of American authors as worthy of the attention of American undergraduates.

The founders of American studies also sought to fill intellectual niches that were left unattended by other disciplines. In this way their rationale echoed Donald Campbell's argument for interdisciplinarity. As noted in chapter 2, Campbell (1969) maintained that traditional disciplines leave considerable terrain unplowed, that disciplinary boundaries unduly circumscribe legitimate areas of inquiry. The arguments advancing the need for the creation of a field of American studies were fully consistent with Campbell's approach. Advocates maintained that there were many aspects of literature that fell outside the confines of most traditional English departments, and, to a lesser extent, various aspects of cultural history that fell outside the confines of intellectual history as practiced in history departments at the time.

From this point of view, the evolution of American studies represents a case of "subject matter expansion" (Metzger 1987), as noted in chapter 5. In essence, Americanists were carving out a niche for themselves by laying out new territory for investigation, domains of inquiry that were not fully exploited by their colleagues in English and history.

This position is articulated in Henry Nash Smith's influential essay "Can 'American Studies' Develop a Method?" (1957). The "new criticism" approach, which dominated literary studies during the 1950s, was based on a close scrutiny of the texts by themselves, and tended to leave history and biography out of the picture. Smith complained that this approach was unduly limiting. "The New Criticism has made it extraordinarily difficult to relate literature to the culture within which it occurs and which it is indisputably a part" (1957, 202). Those interested in viewing literature in a broader cultural and historical context were among those drawn to American studies. Smith's complaints followed decades of debates within English departments about the emphasis on literature relative to philology, the role of generalists and general education, the place for writing, and various efforts to make the study of literature more scientific (Graff 1987).

On the history side of the ledger, the complaints were generally less pointed and specific, perhaps because intellectual terrain was somewhat different. While there was no shortage of courses devoted to American history, Americanists complained that too much historical scholarship was antiquarian and the discipline overly rigid (McDowell 1948). American studies scholars held that traditional history departments prioritized a limited set of political topics, from the biographies of presidents to military conflicts, and left out a great deal of American intellectual, cultural, and material history. The goal was not to do more "intellectual history" or "literary history" but to use the ideas and literature of the time to inform the understanding of American culture in a more synthetic or holistic manner (Spiller 1973; Tate 1973).

In addition to filling the intellectual gaps between literature and history, the founders of American studies sought to advance the cause of a general liberal education. The manifesto penned in 1948 by Tremaine McDowell of the University of Minnesota actually devotes slightly more space to the theme of general education than it does to the field of American studies per se. A number of accounts of the rise of the field point to the congruence between American studies and the broader movement toward general education (for example, see Walker 1958; Spiller 1976).

In addition to these intellectual currents, the end of World War II and the start of the Cold War gave additional impetus to the pursuit of a more unified exploration of American culture. The twin challenges of fascism and communism led many scholars to rise to the defense of freedom and democracy (Gleason 1984). Given the prominence of democracy in the founding documents of the United States, it was a short step from the promotion of democracy in general to the celebration of American culture as a cradle and bastion of democratic ideals. This theme was linked specifically to the notion of American exceptionalism and to national character studies (Zenderland 2006) more broadly.

During the 1950s, the scant attention to America as a civilization worthy of study seemed incongruous given the rise of the United States as a world power. In outlining the context for the creation of American studies programs in foreign countries, Robert Spiller wrote that "at the end of World War II, the United States suddenly found itself to be the major political and economic power of the west, whereas its culture had as yet almost no part in the curricula of most European countries" (1976, 4–5).

The Cold War also helped to provide financial as well as intellectual impetus for American studies. The Carnegie Corporation, the Rockefeller Foundation, and other foundations provided funding for American studies programs (Davis 1990; Wise 1979). US government funding played a particularly key role in the promotion of American studies programs in countries around the world (Davis 1990; Walker 1976; Rupp 1999). Government support was available for international conferences on American studies, and Fulbright grants facilitated the study in United States of international scholars while also promoting study abroad by American academics (Spiller 1976, 6).

During the 1950s and early 1960s, the "myth and symbol" approach emerged as emblematic of American studies scholarship. Among the exemplars of this approach were, Perry Miller, *The New England Mind* (1939, 1953); and Henry Nash Smith, *Virgin Land* (1950). Vernon Louis Parrington's *Main Currents in American Thought* (1927) was an important precursor. These scholars sought to identify currents in American intellectual and popular thought. The goal was to identify a unified conception of "the American Mind" as evident in the writing of prominent authors or as embodied in the landmarks such as the Brooklyn Bridge.

The goal of American studies scholars during the 1950s was to pursue a more integrated approach to culture. The reference point here was culture in the sense used by some of the leading cultural anthropologists, including Ruth Benedict, Margaret Mead, Franz Boas, and other (see Janssens 1999; and Zenderland 2006). It is ironic, then, that anthropologists played a relatively small role in American studies and anthropological methods remained relatively unusual for American studies scholars. Despite the active involvement of Margaret Mead in the early years of the *American Quarterly*, anthropologists remained scarce in the ranks of American studies scholars. This missed opportunity is discussed further below with respect to the relatively small part that the social sciences in general have played in American studies.

By the end of the 1930s, American studies programs were ensconced at several prominent research universities (Chicago, Harvard, and the University of Pennsylvania), and a smattering of liberal arts colleges, including Amherst and Smith. By the end of the 1940s, Yale and Minnesota had established programs as well, and McDowell could report that "more than sixty institutions offered the B.A. degree in American civilization, and approximately fifteen offered the M.A. degree or the Ph.D. degree or both" (McDowell 1948, 26). While most programs were named American studies, some (including Harvard and Penn) adopted the more impressive moniker of "American civilization." Debates over what name fit best continued into the 1990s (Radway 1999).[6]

The number of programs continued to expand gradually through the 1950s and into the 1960s. By 1957, a survey found seventy-two American studies programs, a figure that climbed to 150 by 1968 (Walker 1958).During this period, college enrollment soared due to higher rates of college attendance and the growing cohorts of baby boomers. This expansionary environment nourished the spread of American studies programs.[7]

However, it should be noted that during this founding period, American studies typically took the hybrid form of a cross-departmental program rather than a stand-alone department. Borrowing professors from history and English departments made sense initially since no scholars had been trained in an American studies department. But the next step, transforming programs into departments, was not taken at most schools. If the establishment of a separate academic department that offers undergraduate, master's, and doctoral degrees in a field is taken as a measure of institutionalization, then relatively few American studies departments became fully institutionalized.

The first volume of the journal *American Quarterly* was published in 1949. After being edited for its first year at the University of Minnesota, which featured one of the more active American studies programs, the journal moved to the University of Pennsylvania where it remained until the end of the 1980s. The American Studies Association (ASA) was established in 1951, several years after the creation of the journal, and it too found an organizational home at Penn.

Davis (1990) notes that American studies was slow in organizing a national meeting. During the 1950s and 1960s the model was regional meetings combined with American studies sessions sponsored at the national meetings of the American History Association and the Modern Languages Association. Davis suggests that this pattern followed the model of the Association of College Teachers of English, which was a federation of regional chapters. The first national meeting was not held until 1967.

American Studies as a Scientific/Intellectual Movement

As we saw in chapter 3, Frickel and Gross's (2005) notion of a "scientific/intellectual movement," or SIM, is a fruitful way of understanding changes in the intellectual landscape. While many of the examples they give involve insurgent movements within disciplines, the SIM concept is easy to apply to the case of American studies.

American studies benefited from the emergence of prominent intellectual leaders like Perry Miller at Harvard. The presence of American studies at leading institutions such as Harvard, Yale, Penn, and Minnesota helped to legitimize American studies as a distinct field of inquiry. By sponsoring these prominent programs, the Carnegie Foundation could foster the development of American studies as an enterprise, with the hope of seeing these successful examples replicated at other colleges and institutions. Thus, as the American studies model was subsequently adopted in dozens of institutions that did not receive foundation support, the impact of the original investment multiplied substantially.

Wise (1979) repeatedly refers to "our movement" in terms that fit neatly within Frickel and Gross's framework. While Wise's essay is organized around the contribution of several scholars, he nonetheless details many of the elements of successful SIMs that Frickel and Gross outline: the role of large foundation grants in supporting the staff of the American Studies Association, the key infrastructure contributions of Robert Spiller and others, and the tight network of scholars who ultimately elaborated the myth and symbol paradigm. The subsequent transformation of American studies fits the SIMs framework even more comfortably, since it represents a case of generational and intellectual insurgency.

1960s and 1970s: Transformation

In 1965, the field of American studies remained ascendant. Two notable books had just been published: Leo Marx's *The Machine in the Garden* (1964), and Alan Trachtenberg's *Brooklyn Bridge* (1965). The journal the *American*

Quarterly was well established. The number of American studies programs continued to expand in the United States and internationally. The first national meeting of the American Studies Association in the United States was still two years away.

Yet the institutionalization of American studies at this point should not be overstated. There were fewer than 150 such programs across the country, and most of these were programs rather than self-contained departments. This meant that American studies depended on the availability of sympathetic faculty tenured in traditional departments to staff courses. This was often a challenging proposition given the needs in faculty members' home departments. Moreover, debates over whether American studies was a distinctive field with a distinctive method or a multidisciplinary collection of scholars with broadly similar interests remained unresolved. And American studies scholars continued to debate the role of the social sciences in the field. These arguments aroused passionate opinions on all sides but did not dampen the spirit of optimism about the American studies project.

The political and intellectual climate, however, was about to shift. The Vietnam War shattered the consensus view of American history and American culture. A new generation of scholars entered the academy with new assumptions and passions. The myth and symbol approach so often associated with American studies scholarship lost its sway as a guide to new research. Opposition to the war along with a broader concern with what some saw as America's imperial role in international affairs burst into the corridors of the national meetings of the American Studies Association along with an interest in the experiences of minorities and women in American society and culture. In a short period of time, a new generation of scholars overturned the premises of the field (Wise 1979; Davis 1990; Zenderland 2006).

Academic revolutions, however, can take decades to work through the system. Given the long time frames for academic careers, the developments of the late 1960s were not fully felt until the 1980s ands 1990s. The struggles of graduate students and some younger faculty members under the banner of the "radical caucus" at the 1969 meeting of the American Studies Association (Sklar 1970) echo in the pages of ASA presidential addresses of the 1990s and 2000s (Davis 1990; Washington 1998; Kaplan 2004). As we will see, the organizational development of American studies continued on an upward trajectory for another two decades even as enrollments peaked and then declined.

The 1970s and early 1980s represented a transition period in several ways for American studies. Intellectually, as the myth and symbol approach from the 1950s began to ebb, scholarship turned to a diverse array of specialized topics. This period represented a halfway point between the unified notion

of culture from the 1950s and the emphasis on diversity and multiculturalism that would subsequently come to dominate American studies. In organizational terms, the trends were paradoxical: studies programs continued
to expand in numbers even in the face of sharp declines in undergraduate
enrollments.

Bruce Kuklick (1972) offered a trenchant critique of the myth and symbol
approach to American studies. Operating with philosophical precision, he
questioned the connection between popular literature and ordinary life, as
well as the assumption that a fixed conceptual schema identified by an author
has had enduring influence on behavior throughout American history. But
this approach was already losing its grip on the imagination of doctoral students by the time that Kuklick's essay was published.

While American studies scholars continued to endeavor to bridge the
divide between literature and history, during the 1970s they also sought to
shed light on a diverse array of topics that were not considered sufficiently
mainstream or legitimate in the traditional disciplines. Special issues of the
American Quarterly illustrate this pattern. While several issues were devoted
to topics that would not have been out of place in more traditional journals:
"Victorian Culture in America" (Winter 1975) and "The American Enlightenment" (Summer 1976), others would have had a harder time finding a comfortable home in either history or English journals. The Winter 1979 special
issue of the *American Quarterly*, "Film and American Studies," represents
just one example of a growing trend toward the study of cultural objects or
institutions that did not fit neatly within the confines of the traditional disciplines. Films were not "texts" in the literal sense, nor had they been considered topics for "serious" historians. The study of film caught on, and at
the 2008 American Studies Association meetings, no less than twenty-four
sessions were devoted to film. Similarly, the special issues on death (Winter
1974) and humor (Spring 1985) gave a priority to themes that had not been
treated as such by established journals in history and literature.

Under Kuklick's editorship (from 1974 through 1982), the *American Quarterly* did not embrace the radical turn of the new generation of American
studies students. The poststructuralist approach to literature and the interest
in multiculturalism in American history began to percolate through graduate
students' reading lists and dissertations but would not become predominant
in the journal until the 1980s and 1990s.

The intellectual currents in the 1970s remained vibrant, even if they represented a significant departure from the vision of the most prominent early
figures in the field. Trends in the social organization of American studies during this period, however, were mixed. After steady growth during the 1950s

and 1960s, the number of students earning bachelor's degrees in American studies peaked in 1974 at 1,844, and fell to 967 in 1986 (see figure 8.1). As a share of undergraduate degree recipients, American studies peaked in 1974 at just under 0.2 percent of degrees conferred in US colleges and universities (see figure 8.2).[8]

Ironically, programs continued a steady increase in numbers during the 1970s. The ASA count of programs increased from 219 in 1974 to more than three hundred during the early 1980s; and the number of programs offering masters nearly doubled during this period (from thirty-two to sixty) (see figure 8.3).

Was the decline in American studies degrees awarded due to the growth in popularity of women's studies and African American studies? While individual courses in these areas were no doubt popular, these programs were often fledgling operations too small to siphon off large numbers of degree recipients.

The enrollment trends for American studies partly reflected the stagnation in overall college enrollments. The baby boom cohort of the 1960s was giving way to the baby bust of the 1980s. The number of bachelor's degrees awarded in US colleges and universities peaked at 650,000 in 1974 and did not surpass this level until 1985. A decline in enrollments of men from an inflated Vietnam-era level (when young men enrolled in college to avoid the

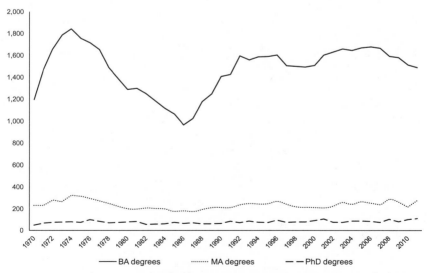

FIGURE 8.1. Trends in American studies degrees, 1970–2011. Source: US Department of Education, *Digest of Education Statistics*.

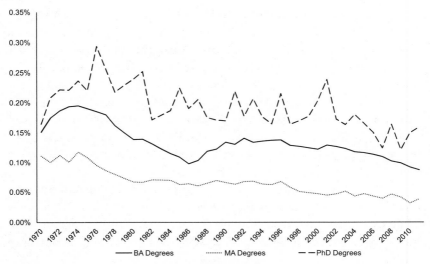

FIGURE 8.2. Trends in American studies degrees, as a percentage of degrees conferred, 1970–2011. Source: US Department of Education, *Digest of Education Statistics*.

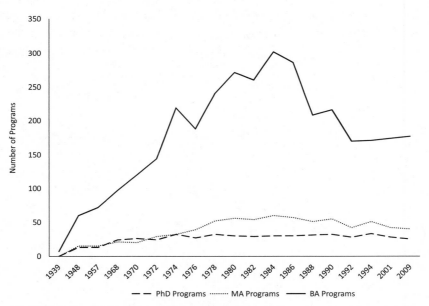

FIGURE 8.3. Trends in American studies degree-granting programs, 1970–2009. Source: American Studies Association.

military draft) was roughly offset by an increase in the enrollment of women, who matched men in the receipt of bachelor's degrees for the first time in 1982. The burgeoning ranks of women students should have helped to keep American studies classrooms full, since women have been disproportionately represented among students in the humanities.

The decline in American studies enrollments during this period, however, was primarily due to a broader shift of students away from the humanities. The small field of American studies was caught in a downdraft that enveloped even the larger and more established disciplines of English and history. Degrees awarded in English declined by half and those in history by over 60 percent between 1971 and 1984. The decline in American studies degrees reflected this trend (National Center for Education Statistics; Geiger 2006).

The loss of students from American studies was not to nascent fields such as women's studies and African American studies as much as it was to applied fields such as business, which doubled in degrees conferred between 1971 and 1984. The shift away from the humanities during this period reflected undergraduates' concerns about getting a good job following graduation. Economist Richard Freeman (1976) showed that the economic benefit to college enrollment ebbed during this period as the economy had difficulty absorbing the large number of recent college graduates.

The exodus from the humanities also reflected the growing materialism of undergraduates. As documented in large surveys, the proportion of freshman who reported that being "very well-off financially" was very important to them increased from 54.4 percent in 1974 to 75.6 percent in 1984. At the same time, developing a "meaningful philosophy of life" declined from 57.4 percent in 1974 to 44.0 percent in 1984 (Astin, Green, and Korn 1985). This shift in values probably contributed to the decline in enrollments in the humanities. (The theme of enrollment shifts is examined in more detail in the next chapter.) The expansion of higher education and the changing composition of the undergraduate student body also contributed to this trend.[9]

How did American studies programs continue to expand in number in the face of declining enrollments? It should be noted that the number of programs awarding doctoral degrees did not grow. Rather, programs continued to proliferate in smaller, liberal arts institutions that awarded only bachelor's degrees. This growth can be understood in terms of its modest cost on deans' budgets. After all, the creation of an American studies program did not mean a commitment of extra faculty positions or significant resources. These programs typically grew in smaller liberal arts colleges where the allegiance of faculty to disciplinary paradigms was often weaker than at larger institutions, and where opportunities to collaborate with colleagues were viewed as an opportunity rather than a burden. As we will see, the small size of many of these programs would later make them vulnerable.

Thus, the continued expansion of American studies during the 1970s in the face of declining enrollments seems to be more a matter of faculty mobilization rather than student demand. Student protests, which contributed to the creation of African American studies programs (Rojas 2007), did not play a role in the case of American studies.

Two complementary movements thus characterize the 1970s: a successful push to establish American studies in a much wider swath of institutions, and a broad-scale revisioning of the intellectual directions of the field. The former was no doubt led by more senior scholars even while fundamentally new intellectual directions were fomenting on the part of a new generation of graduate students and junior faculty.

1980s to the 2000s

By the late 1980s and certainly during the 1990s, the alternative approach to American studies that emerged in response to the Vietnam War came to fruition. This may seem like a long delay, but several factors need to be taken into account. In the humanities, taking nine or more years to complete a PhD is quite common, and thus there is a lag between events and when the faculty inspired by those events rise to positions of seniority. (See discussion of the duration of graduate training in chapter 4.) Moreover, American academia in the late 1970s experienced a drought in hiring, especially in the humanities, and this also contributed to the delay.

Evidence of the prevalence of gender and other forms of diversity in American studies research is not hard to find in this period. In 1988, the theme of the national meeting was "The Intersection of Race, Class, Gender and Ethnicity in American Culture." ASA President Linda Kerber delivered her presidential address entitled "Diversity and the Transformation of American Studies" (Kerber 1989). In 1993, a special issue of the *American Quarterly* was devoted to the topic of multiculturalism. By the 1990s multiculturalism had become established as a powerful force in American studies scholarship. The search for a method for the field preoccupied scholars for decades, but by the 1990s American studies scholars were more likely to complain about the need for more attention to diversity and to global concerns than they were to search for a unifying methodology.

Just how prominent multiculturalism became is apparent from a content analysis of dissertation abstracts in American studies. American studies dissertation abstracts from the period 1990 to 2000 were reviewed. In 1990,

30 percent of dissertations in American studies included some specific consideration of race or gender in the abstract (specifically, 21 percent addressed gender issues and 9 percent race, while none included both). By 2000, race and gender issues had become even more prominent, with 62 percent of dissertations mentioning either race or gender (45 percent of dissertations mentioned race, 31 percent gender, and 14 percent both) (author's analysis of Doctoral Dissertations in American Studies, 1989–90; Dissertation Abstracts, 1999–2000).

In addition to multiculturalism, the other major intellectual current was the rise of poststructuralism. Here again, the roots date back to the 1970s but did not fully flourish until the 1980s and 1990s. The French theorist Jacques Derrida and his American followers, including Paul de Man among others, sought to question the meaning imputed to canonical texts, and more generally to deconstruct authoritative interpretations of literature. This tendency represented something quite different from the 1950s goal of putting the literature back in its cultural context. The poststructuralist movement was powerful not only in American studies but in many literary fields represented in the Modern Language Association.

This approach to literature drew its share of critics, both internal and external. For example, Steven Watts, in his presidential address to the Mid-American American Studies Association in 1989, decried the "idiocy" of American studies. In addition to concerns over poststructuralism as a way of approaching literature, Watt's objections centered on the concern that it was difficult to use this approach to make sense of large periods of American history (Watts 1991; Shank 1992).

American studies dissertations often select specialized topics, as in "Landscape as Palimpsest: The Fugitive Images of Southeastern Colorado" and "Wards of the Nation: The Making of St. Elizabeth's Hospital, 1852–1920." While some endeavored to tackle somewhat broader themes, such as "Craven Images: Cowardice in American Literature from the Revolutionary to the Nuclear Era," it is fair to say that few if any in recent years seek to paint with as broad a brush as the authors of *The New England Mind* or *Virgin Land*.

This period also saw the increasing prominence of global themes in American studies scholarship. Where American civilization scholars of the early 1950s sought to underscore the America's distinctive commitment to liberal democracy, by the turn of the century American studies scholars were writing more critically of America's role as an imperial power (Kaplan 2004). While the very title "American studies" would seem to draw clear geographic boundaries around the subject matter, American studies scholars of this period sought to understand the global impact of American culture as well as international cultural transmission to the United States via immigration and other sources. Indeed, Rowe (2002) insists on comparative analysis as a central feature of the American studies project.

The transformation of the intellectual preoccupations of American studies coincided with the decline in influence of male professors at leading institutions. The *American Quarterly* had been edited at the University of Pennsylvania from 1950 through 1987. In 1988, the journal moved to the Smithsonian Institution under the editorship of Gary Kulik, before it moved again in 1994 to Georgetown University, where Lucy Maddox served as editor for a decade. After Lois Banner served as the first female ASA president from 1986 to 1987, ten of the next twelve ASA presidents were women.[10]

In organizational terms, national meetings of the American Studies Association began in 1967 and have been held annually since 1987. The national ASA meetings have thrived since the decision was made to switch to an annual meeting. The number of program participants roughly tripled between 1991 and 2006, although the number of institutional members has been essentially unchanged. For example, the 2008 meeting held in Albuquerque featured approximately 1,200 presenters in more than 250 sessions spanning four days, plus dozens of business meetings and receptions.

Funding for national scholarly organizations such as the American Studies Association begins with a base of journal subscriptions and membership dues. The *American Quarterly* has over two thousand library subscriptions that provide a reliable financial base for the association.

Other organizational trends, however, were not as positive. The receipt of bachelor's degrees in American studies finally bottomed out during the 1980s and began a modest rebound. The number of bachelor's degree recipients dipped slightly under one thousand in 1986 and climbed back toward 1,700 by 2006 along with other fields in the humanities. However, this figure has yet to surpass the high-water mark of 1,844 reached in 1974.[11] While enrollments have rebounded from their low point during the mid-1980s, American studies programs declined in number sharply during the 1980s and have yet to fully recoup these losses.[12]

American studies has endured for over sixty years, although many of today's prominent themes would surprise and perhaps disappoint its founders. But before trying to say more about the intellectual trajectory of American studies, let us turn to a more sustained consideration of the organizational dimensions of American studies. This discussion will include not only its closest neighbors, history and English, but also the social sciences and other the interdisciplinary programs such as African American and women's studies.

Organizational Strengths and Weaknesses

Most reviews of American studies naturally focus on the intellectual trajectory of the field and largely take the organizational structure for granted. What does American studies look like viewed from an organization lens rather than a close reading of the field's paradigmatic texts? As we have seen, the current picture is mixed. On the one hand, American studies has a thriving and secure national organization with well-attended national meetings, and a wide international scope. On the other hand, in the United States, American studies awards degrees to only the smallest sliver of students and has secured departmental status in only a handful of universities.

As of 2009, American studies has not succeeded in becoming an academic department in most institutions of higher education in the United States. This review has identified only ten universities with graduate departments in American studies, only seven of which offer a PhD degree.[13]

In 2009, a total of forty colleges and universities offered a master's degree in American studies, while twenty-five offered a PhD.[14] These academic programs typically do not have dedicated faculty positions and are dependent on appointments from established departments in the humanities and occasionally the social sciences.

In only six universities (Brown, Hawaii, Indiana, Minnesota, New Mexico, and Texas) are American studies departments fully established, that is, with their own faculty lines and ability to offer a doctoral degree.[15] These departments averaged just over ten core faculty members. This level of institutionalization must be judged to be quite low given that there are over 2,500 four-year colleges and universities in United States. Even if the 250 PhD-granting institutions is taken as the relevant universe, American studies is represented in only about 10 percent of these institutions. Thus, of universities with doctoral programs about one in ten offer a doctoral degree in American studies while 200 out of 2,500, or less than one undergraduate institution out of ten, has an American studies program.

Since academic departments continue to represent a basic unit of American higher education, especially in terms of control over hiring decisions, the extremely limited number of American studies departments must be taken as a central indication of the partial success of the field as a scientific/intellectual movement to achieve a universal degree of institutional acceptance. In this sense, American studies has not joined the small list of liberal arts disciplines discussed in chapter 3.

In terms of PhD recipients, American studies doctorates topped one hundred per year only twice, in 1976 and 2001 (see figure 8.1). The number of new PhDs in American studies has averaged seventy-six since 1970, representing just under 0.2 percent of new PhDs. Another way to understand the relatively small size of American studies as a field is to compare it to its two principal neighbors, history and English. In 2011, there were nearly eight times as many doctoral degrees granted in history as in American studies, and nearly twelve times as many doctoral degrees in English.

If there are fewer than one dozen American studies departments with control over faculty hiring, many of which would not need any new faculty in a given year, there would seem to be a mismatch between degree production and hiring potential. Why would anyone spend six or more years pursuing a doctoral degree in a field that has so few openings? This disparity leads to the question of what becomes of American studies graduates.

During the late 1990s and early 2000s, the ASA surveyed recent graduates of American studies PhD programs (American Studies Association Survey of Doctoral Recipients, various years). While respondents often reported that they desired tenure-track positions in American studies programs, only a small fraction reported realizing this goal. About one in five of those American studies doctorates responding to the ASA surveys reported employment in American studies. History, English, and "other field" were each more likely destinations than was American studies.[16]

A final aspect of the organizational picture of American studies must be added, namely, the international dimension. American studies is not solely the province of academics based in the United States. From an international perspective, America is a topic of considerable interest. Given the worldwide influence of America since World War II, it is not surprising that observers in many countries are anxious to understand American history, culture, and politics. As a result, American studies programs are active in quite a number of countries. By 2008, the American Studies Association website listed thirty-two journals in twenty-one countries outside the United States, including journals from Brazil, France, Germany, Hungary, Italy, Japan, Poland, Scandinavia, South Africa, Taiwan, and Turkey.[17] This list probably focuses on the countries with the most active programs, since maintaining a journal represents a considerable amount of effort and requires a critical mass of scholars. The ASA website notes that there are "nearly fifty" American studies associations around the world that sponsor conferences and publications. American studies may be thought of as a kind of "area study" localized to a single country (see Stevens and Miller-Idriss [2009], for a discussion of area-studies programs).

Just as other countries have a natural interest in understanding the United

States, the US government has sought to promote a favorable understanding of the United States. American studies in foreign countries is often supported by funds from the US government. While the main vehicle for this has been the Fulbright Program, there has also been direct support for American studies programs. For example, the Institute of International Education is a nonprofit organization that supports American studies programs in countries around the world. The US Information Agency and the US Department of Education also support American studies programs. Rupp (1999) views US government support for American studies programs in foreign countries as a form of "cultural diplomacy."

Program Durability

In addition to the lack of control over hiring, among the chief worries of those who run interdisciplinary programs is that the program will be eliminated by the next dean or the next financial tsunami. The rate of survival of American studies programs depends on the type of program and the size of the college or university in which it is located. The most deeply rooted, and most enduring, have been PhD programs located at major research universities, while the most vulnerable have been programs located in smaller, liberal arts colleges that offered no degrees in American studies.[18]

While several programs offering PhDs in American studies have closed over the years, the survival rate is actually quite high. The ten-year survival rate for American studies doctoral programs is 93 percent. Programs located in smaller institutions appear to be somewhat less durable. Between 1970 and 1980, in a period of dramatic growth in the number of programs, approximately 15 percent of American studies programs closed. Most of the programs that closed were located in small colleges rather than large universities.[19]

Programs that offered a bachelor's degree in American studies were more vulnerable to closure than were PhD programs. In particular, a substantial decline in the number of schools offering bachelor's degrees in American studies occurred during the late 1980s and early 1990s, after which there has been a slight rebound during the 2000s (see figure 8.3).[20] About one-third of American studies programs were closed during the late 1980s. These programs often did not offer a degree and were located in smaller institutions, typically liberal arts colleges.

This episode reflected a long drought in humanities hiring. In other words, shorthanded faculty could only be stretched in so many directions for so long. In a way, this period of decline represented a delayed reaction to trends in enrollments and hiring that had been in place since the early

1970s. However, these closures were premature, or ironic, in that humanities enrollments began to climb again in the late 1980s just as these programs were beginning to shut their doors. This increase clearly would have been somewhat greater had not so many American studies programs closed their doors during this period.

Specialized Studies Programs: Competition or Complementarity?

As we have seen, during the 1970s, American studies programs continued to proliferate even as the number of students who sought degrees in the field declined. This decade also saw the birth of two additional interdisciplinary studies programs, namely, African American studies and women's studies.

Did American studies help to pave the way for the creation of women's studies and African American studies programs? An intellectual case could be made for these connections. While few women appeared in the classic works of the myth and symbol era, by the 1960s American studies was beginning to be more open to diverse scholarship. Griffin and Tempenis (2002) show that the race, gender, and other multicultural themes were present in the pages of *American Quarterly* during the 1960s and spiked after 1970.

In addition to intellectual contributions, it is interesting to consider the organizational linkages between American studies and other specialized studies programs. In order to make the comparison as systematic as possible, these data are drawn from a common source, *The College Blue Book*. These data have several valuable features: there is a single, common metric for comparing across programs; the measures are consistent over time; and the data are gathered systematically from colleges and universities across the country (see figure 8.4).[21]

The 1970s was a fertile time for the proliferation of specialized programs. African American studies grew quite rapidly after the campus demonstrations of the late 1960s. Women's studies followed suit shortly thereafter, but it was not until later in the 1970s that programs offering bachelor's degrees in women's studies became established. Given the expansion in the number of these alternative programs, the continued growth of American studies during the 1970s is quite notable. The decade of the 2000s is another period in which all three fields experienced growth, especially women's studies. The trend during this period in all likelihood represents the acquisition of degree status of programs already in existence to a greater extent than the creation of new programs.

These data also suggest that the rise of African American and women's studies did not substitute for American studies as an organizational arrange-

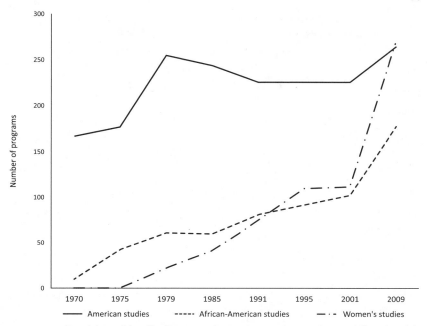

FIGURE 8.4. Trends in special studies degree-granting programs, 1970–2009. Source: *College Blue Book.*.

ment. All three grew at the same time. Moreover, the declines of late 1980s in American studies was unique to this field and was not reflected in declines in other specialized studies programs. So in terms of general trends throughout higher education, African American and women's studies appear to be complements to, rather than substitutes for, American studies programs.

American studies was neither necessary nor sufficient for the emergence[22] of African American studies. For example, fifteen newly formed African American studies programs in existence in 1970 overlapped with American studies, while eighteen did not. Nonetheless, American studies programs are disproportionately present in schools that subsequently created African American studies programs.

Table 8.1 displays the association (odds ratios) between American studies, African American studies, and women's studies.[23] The data indicate sizable relationships between these programs. In other words, these three sets of special studies programs were not distributed in US colleges and universities at random but tended to overlap in the same institutions. The strongest connections are between African American and women's studies.

The results of statistical connections presented in table 8.1 point to a relationship among these special studies programs. Since American studies pro-

TABLE 8.1. Relationship between American studies, African American studies, and women's studies programs

Year	American studies/ Af-Am studies odds ratio	American studies/ women's studies odds ratio	African American studies / women's studies odds ratio
1970	7.65		
1976	3.84		
1981	5.07		
1986	5.7	5.46	10.42
1991	7.18	11.04	32.92
1996	6.11	6.55	17.24
2001	5.1	7.22	13.29
2006	4.24	6.91	18.7

Source Data: IPEDS data file on nearly three thousand colleges and universities, compiled by Steven Brint and Kristopher Proctor.

grams were established first, it seems plausible to suggest that any causal relationship would run in the direction of African American studies. However, these results do not necessarily prove a causal relationship because (a) the associations are cross-sectional, and (b) there is the possibility that other factors (such as school size) may be responsible for promoting each type of program.

A series of multivariate analyses were conducted to ascertain whether the presence of one interdisciplinary program contributed to the subsequent creation of others. To illustrate this approach, the presence of an American studies or African American studies program in any year before 2001 was used to predict the presence on the same campus of a women's studies program in 2006.[24]

With no controls included in the model, the odds of having a women's studies program are seven times greater if the school had an American studies program five years earlier; the presence of an African American studies program five years earlier increases the odds by fourteen-fold. Taking both types of programs into account simultaneously brings these odds down to five-fold and ten-fold, respectively. Adding other controls to the model, such as school size and institutional selectivity, further reduces but does not eliminate these effects. In the final model, American studies increases the chances of women's studies by three-fold, and African American studies does so by five-fold. Sizeable effects, to be sure.[25]

This analysis was repeated with African American studies as the outcome of interest. The impact of American studies on African American studies was weaker, which makes sense given the unique history of African American studies programs. In the final model, the coefficient is not statistically significant. This result matches the finding reported by Rojas (2007).

In a second analysis, these effects were estimated at five-year intervals over the period 1976–2006 for African American studies and 1986–2006 for women's studies to see if the initial "chartering" impact was large but weakened over time as these programs diffused according to their own logics. The results (summarized in table 8.2) provide some evidence for this dilution process in the case of African American studies, but in the case of women's studies, the coefficients grow in strength over time. A possible explanation is that American studies faculty on campus helped to support the institutionalization of women's studies in terms of practical, political, and personal assistance, rather than through the more general process of legitimation that would be most relevant in the early years of women's studies.

If the results presented in these analyses can be generalized to other fields of inquiry, then efforts to introduce one set of interdisciplinary programs will result in the proliferation of additional interdisciplinary programs. As a consequence, an interdisciplinary-based university will offer more programs based in many more units than is currently the case.

What other factors influence the institutionalization of women's studies and African American studies programs on campus? Resources matter. Larger schools and richer schools are more likely to feature these programs than are smaller schools with fewer resources per student. It is also the case

TABLE 8.2. Trends in the chartering effect of interdisciplinary studies programs

	1976	1981	1986	1991	1996	2001	2006
			Logistic	*Regression*	*Coefficients*		
A. Predicting women's studies							
American studies (lagged)			1.807	2.148*	2.354***	2.643***	3.108***
African American studies (lagged)			4.935***	8.270***	5.428***	4.662***	5.099***
B. Predicting African American studies							
American studies (lagged)	2.269**	2.348**	2.151*	2.164*	2.911***	1.955**	1.461(ns)

Source data: IPEDS data file on nearly three thousand colleges and universities, compiled by Steven Brint and Kristopher Proctor.

Note: The control variables included in the analysis include total student enrollment, the percentage of international students; the percentage of nonwhite students, the per-student operating budget (logged), Baron's Imputed Selectivity Score, and the presence of masters and PhD programs.

* $p < .05$; ** $p < .01$; *** $p < .001$

that more selective institutions are more likely to feature these special-studies programs. It may be that less selective schools are more focused on applied programs of study and thus are less inclined to develop these less-applied and more academically oriented programs.

Student demographics also matter. Women's studies programs are more prevalent in schools with a larger fraction of female students, and African American studies programs are more common in schools with above-average shares of minority students. While members of the faculty like to feel that the power of their ideas will be sufficient to carry the day, the broader patterns of institutional diffusion suggest that some colleges and universities offer a more hospitable landscape for the development and institutionalization of special-studies programs such as American studies, women's studies, and African American studies.

In addition to the many accomplishments of American studies faculty, scholars who helped to promote and institutionalize this field of scholarship may well be able to take credit for contributing to the subsequent rise and institutionalization of African American and women's studies.

American Studies and the Social Sciences

The interdisciplinary agenda of American studies has at times included the social sciences, and some scholars have continued to build bridges between the largely humanistic ASA and the social sciences. Indeed, at the 2008 ASA meetings there were a number of social science sessions: three anthropology sessions, four sociology sessions, and five sessions focused on ethnography. Nonetheless, American studies has remained firmly rooted in the humanities. Griffin and Gross (1999) document the scarcity of references to social science scholarship in the pages of the leading American studies journals. Janssens (1999) suggests that many area studies programs have stronger ties to the social sciences than do American studies programs, but he does not provide systematic evidence to support this hypothesis.

Why has it proven so difficult to forge strong links between American studies and the social sciences? In part this reflected the rejection by Americanists of the quantitative methods employed by many social scientists.

Henry Nash Smith (1957) criticized the quantitative focus of his social science contemporaries. This line of critique would presumably have been equally applicable to public opinion polls in political science and quantitative models in economics. To this day, Americanists rarely cite social surveys, polling data, economic analyses, studies of social mobility, and other quantitative indicators of American society. After documenting a gap based on ISI citation data, Dubrow (2011) stresses the methodological distance as the main reason for the gulf between American studies and American sociology.

Over the 1960s and 1970s the intellectual trends in sociology largely militated against connections with American studies. In the 1950s, broad-gauged scholars like David Riesman and Robert Merton could easily connect with concerns regarding Americanists' interest in American exceptionalism and national character than would those that followed them a decade or two later. Indeed, Riesman served on the editorial board of the *American Quarterly*. By the 1970s, multivariate regression analyses dominated the leading journals in sociology, especially elaborate studies of intergenerational social mobility. Interest in humanistic and multicultural approaches would resurface in sociology somewhat later. The strongest connection today between sociology and American studies operates through mutual interest in race and ethnic studies and gender issues.

The early intellectual connections to anthropology were quite evident, as the anthropologists' notion of culture held considerable appeal to founding American studies scholars (Janssens 1999; Zenderland 2006).[26] However, the connections remained stronger via common intellectual referents rather than in terms of contemporary practitioners. In the 1950s and 1960s relatively few anthropologists focused on the United States. During that period, anthropologists earned their stripes by learning a native language and conducting their dissertation research in a non-Western community. Thus, although Margaret Mead was active in the early years of the *American Quarterly*, few of her anthropological compatriots followed her lead.

In part the difficulty was a numbers game. In other words, the small size of American studies meant that all but the very largest programs could include only a handful of social scientists. This meant that it was hard to cover much of social science, it was hard to do so in a particularly integrative or distinctive way, and it was hard to have much impact on how fellow social scientists approached social research.

Penn's American civilization department represents a good example. The long-time department chair Murray Murphey viewed the social sciences as an important part of the interdisciplinary mix of the field. During his tenure as editor of the *American Quarterly*, several papers advocating tighter linkages between the social sciences and humanities were published. Murphey was committed to including social scientists on the faculty, but he could not really advance this agenda very far.

The American civilization program at Penn achieved the status of its own department, and was thus more firmly institutionalized than at most universities. Even at Penn, however, American civilization had only six or seven dedicated faculty members during the 1970s.[27] There was thus room on the faculty for perhaps two or at most three social scientists. This representation of the social sciences in American studies did not reach the critical mass needed to sustain itself, or to provide for innovative synergy with other social scientists.

During the 1970s and 1980s, perhaps the most compelling explanation for the modest presence of social science in American studies can be found in the activities of a competing movement. The rise of social science history was a more powerful magnet for historically oriented social scientists than was American studies. Even historical sociologists who were qualitative in their approach were more likely to connect with social science history because of a shared interest in explanation over interpretation.

Here again there is a Penn connection: Penn's Lee Benson was a prime mover in the development of the Social Science History Association (SSHA) and served as its first president (Benson 1972, 1978; Bogue 1987; see also Graff 2001). Prominent sociologists (not at Penn), such as Charles Tilly and Theda Skocpol, and economic historians, including Robert Fogel and Stanley Engerman, were also active in the SSHA.

Indeed, it is interesting to contrast the course of social science history with the American studies movement. While both were ostensibly interdisciplinary, American studies sought to create its own programs and its own departments. In contrast, social science history endeavored to include economists, political scientists, sociologists, and others, but did not seek to create departments of social history. Historians working within this framework labored largely within the confines of history departments rather than seeking a new set of institutional structures.

The tremendous popularity (among researchers) of quantitative social history during the 1970s spawned a backlash in the discipline of history and provoked a resurgence of interest in cultural themes (Sewell 2005). This flowering of more culturally oriented history may well have contributed to the resurgence of American studies during 1990s and 2000s.

The multicultural turn in late 1970s and 1980s actually brought American studies intellectually closer to sociology. Sociologists had become increasingly interested in culture, and interest in race, class, and gender was shared by sociologists and Americanists. Anthropologists now study American society as well as tribal experiences in postcolonial contexts, and thus anthropologists and ethnographers are now represented at American studies conferences. So once again there are intellectual opportunities for connections, especially among social scientists involved in Ethnic studies, African American studies, or gender studies. However, to date, the social science connections remain

secondary. Griffin and Tempenis (2002), for example, have shown that traditional concerns of sociologists such as social class remain at the margins of
American studies scholarship even as multicultural themes have become very
prominent.

The remaining gaps appear to be more a matter of method than of substantive interests. Few Americanists have been trained as ethnographers,
while relatively few sociologists and anthropologists do primary research in
archives as historians or use texts as principal sources. There is also little push
toward American studies from the social scientists' side. There is plenty of
room for ethnographic or humanistic approaches in the social sciences, at
least in anthropology, sociology, and political science. In sociology, the advent of interest in comparative social history has led to stronger connections
with social history located in history departments rather than to the cultural
history based in American studies programs.

The disconnect between the social sciences and American studies persists,
but the reasons for this disconnect shift over time. The explanation offered
here points to evolving intellectual trajectories, missed opportunities, and
more successful competitors as well as demographic constraints. To build
enduring linkages, there needs to be a shared substantive interest, shared
techniques, and a complementarity among a critical mass that gives those
engaging in interdisciplinary work a clear and compelling advantage over
those who work in their disciplinary contexts. The social science linkages
with American studies have not yielded this type of comparative advantage,
and thus this interdisciplinary frontier remains underdeveloped.

Divisions within American Studies:
Interdisciplinarity and Internal Differentiation

Thus, despite its commitment to interdisciplinarity, American studies established some cross-field ties more effectively than others, with ties to the social
sciences being notably weak. Now it is time to reverse the question in order to
consider the degree of integration and communication within the field.

Advocates of interdisciplinarity caricature established disciplines as hermetically sealed enclaves, closed silos that are all but impervious to intellectual trends in other fields. In contrast to this dismal state of academic bal-
kanization, true interdisciplinarity is held up as a fully integrated alternative
where barriers to communication across specialties have been shattered.

By assessing how far American studies has traveled in the direction of
complete academic integration via an examination of the reception of American studies research, it can be determined whether its impact has been

broadly felt throughout the humanities or whether it has been confined to its own narrow niche. The citation patterns of articles published in the *American Historical Review*, the *Journal of American History, American Literature*, and *American Literary History* served as baselines for comparison with *American Quarterly*, the leading American studies journal. In other words, the issue is identifying where *American Quarterly* (*AQ*) papers are visible, and also how this pattern compares to papers published in established disciplinary journals.[28]

Overall, citations to articles in *American Quarterly* appear in journals spanning a wide range of disciplines (see table 8.3). Nearly one-third of *AQ* articles were cited in history journals (31.3 percent), somewhat more than journals in literature and American literature, which combine to just under one in five (10.6 + 8.5 = 19.1 percent). The next ranking area is interdisciplinary journals in the humanities. (Roughly 45 percent of these citations appear in other articles published in *AQ* itself, and well over half are found in various American studies journals.) Other fields citing *AQ* articles include sociology, law, religion, and women's studies.

Thus, there is support for the claim that the *American Quarterly* is interdisciplinary to a large extent. There is variability, however, among *AQ* articles: some are based on archival and other historical methods and are consequently of greater interest to historians, while others are based on literary analysis and are more likely to appear to literary scholars. The next question,

TABLE 8.3. Citations to articles in *American Quarterly*, by subject area of citing journal

Subject category of citing journal	*American Quarterly All articles* *Percent of citations*
American history	22.6
American literature	10.0
Literature	11.6
Humanities, interdisciplinary	10.6
Sociology	6.2
Law	5.2
Geography	4.8
Women's studies	4.0
Anthropology	3.2
History of social sciences	3.2
Other fields	19.6
Total	100.0

Source: Author's analysis of Web of Knowledge data.

TABLE 8.4. Citations to articles in *American Quarterly* and three comparison journals, by subject area of citing journal

Subject category of citing journal	All articles (%)	Historical articles (%)	Literary articles (%)	Theory/ social science (%)
Source journal: *American Quarterly*				
	All	Historical	Literary	Theory/ SS
American history	22.6	47.3	23.1	12.1
American literature	10.0	6.3	26.9	8.1
Literature (other)	11.6	4.8	19.2	12.9
Humanities (general)	10.6	14.0	15.4	19.4
Comparison source journals				
	American Quarterly	American Historical Review	American Literature	American Literary History
American history	22.6	53.0	4.4	4.8
American literature	10.0	2.6	34.4	28.0
Literature (other)	11.6	3.2	37.0	34.6
Humanities (general)	10.6	7.4	10.0	11.2

Source: Author's analysis of Web of Knowledge data.

then, is the diversity in the reception of papers published in *AQ*. In order to address this question, all of the papers with fifteen or more citations were coded into one of three categories: historical, literary, or theoretical/social themes (see table 8.4).

The contrast between the literary and historical papers published in *AQ* is clear. The audiences for these two groups of papers are roughly mirror images of one another. Roughly half of historical papers are cited in historical journals, while only about one in ten citations appears in literature journals. In contrast, among the *AQ* articles devoted to literature, just under half are cited in literature journals, while about one in five are cited in historical journals. Thus, when taken as a whole, the readership of *AQ* appears to be remarkably diverse, but when its papers are analyzed along disciplinary lines, it is clear that the audience remains substantially divided.[29]

Another way to get insights into the reception of papers published in *AQ* is to compare them to journals specializing in history and literature. As we have seen, historically oriented papers published in *AQ* are more likely to be visible and influential in history journals. For this group, 47.3 percent of the references appear in history journals. How does this compare to articles published in history journals? Using the *American Historical Review* as a point of comparison, the results indicate that 53.0 percent of citations to *AHR* articles appear in history journals. Thus, the reception of historically orientated papers in *AQ* is only slightly less concentrated among historians (47 percent versus 53 percent) than are those published in a journal firmly rooted in the discipline of history. Articles published in the *Journal of American History* have a somewhat stronger disciplinary audience. Sixty percent of the citations are in history journals, while the rest are distributed across the social sciences and humanities. The fact that 40 percent or more of the references to these history journals come from fields outside of history is itself notable: the audience for historical research is hardly confined to a single field. This does not fit with the picture of isolated disciplinary silos advanced by advocates of interdisciplinarity.

The picture of disciplinary closure is somewhat more evident in literature. The citations to articles in the journal *American Literature* overwhelmingly appear in literary journals: 71.4 percent of the references appear in either literature or American literature journals. These results were replicated with another journal, *American Literary History*, with largely the same results. In contrast, the *AQ* literature papers appear much more broadly directed. Just under half (46.1 percent) of the citations to literary-oriented *AQ* articles appear in literary journals, compared with more than two-thirds in *American Literature*. This finding suggests that the interdisciplinary increment or "bounce" for literary scholars of publishing in *AQ* is substantial, and is somewhat greater for literary than for historical papers.

The final category of *AQ* articles may be referred to as "theory/social issues." For example, these are papers that explore the nature of multiculturalism, or seek to "redefine suburbia." Where are these hybrid papers cited?

These papers have a remarkably diverse audience. About one in five are cited in literature journals and another one in five were cited in interdisciplinary humanities journals, while roughly one in ten are cited in journals in the social sciences and history, with references in anthropology and urban studies journals not uncommon. There is, then, a category of broadly oriented papers with a potentially broad audience.

In considering the citation patterns of the *American Quarterly*, Barbara Welter's piece deserves its own mention. Welter's 1966 paper "The Cult of True Womanhood" has been cited over five hundred times in academic journal articles, while no other paper in the history of *AQ* has been cited more than one hundred times. This paper has been cited far more than any paper in the four established disciplinary journals discussed above. The impact was as diverse as it was powerful: 29.4 percent of the citations appear in history journals, 14.8 percent in literature journals, 11.8 percent in multidisciplinary humanities journals, and 7.8 percent in women's studies journals. Welter's paper has also been widely cited in journals in sociology, the history of social sciences, education, law, religion, and many other fields. Mary Kelley (1999) notes that much of Welter's analysis has been challenged by subsequent research, yet it is clear that Welter's study was paradigmatic for a generation of feminist scholarship.

Would "The Cult of True Womanhood" have made as many waves had it been published in the *American Historical Review*? Of course there is no way to give a definitive answer to this counterfactual question. But Welter's piece was not published in *AHR*, and perhaps for a reason. During this era, little that could be described as feminist scholarship appeared in *AHR*, and thus *AQ* likely performed a valuable service in providing a prominent alternative outlet for research that was not considered serious enough or mainstream enough to be published in the disciplinary outlets. I could find no articles in *AHR* that focused on women or women's issues after 1960 until Edward Shorter's 1973 study of birth control. It really is not until Jane Abray's 1975 paper that a self-consciously feminist paper is published in *AHR*. In the *Journal of American History*, only a few papers on women's topics appeared before the paper coauthored by Caroll Smith-Rosenberg and Charles Rosenberg (1973) on medical and biological views of women during the nineteenth century.[30] On the other hand, both of these leading history journals were more receptive to research on topics of race than gender during this particular period. As noted above, Griffin and Tempenis (2002) document the prominence of studies of race and gender in the pages of *AQ* during the 1960s.

While *AQ* served an important role as an alternative outlet for innovative research, it is not necessary that a journal take an interdisciplinary form to achieve this result. Thus, *Gender and Society* appeared as a feminist journal in sociology in 1986 and *Feminist Economics* in 1994 as an alternative outlet in the discipline of economics.

These findings from a citation analysis of *AQ* suggest that American studies has been somewhat successful in breaking down academic boundaries. Articles are more widely cited if published in *AQ* than in disciplinary journals. Just to be clear: publication in *AQ* does not necessarily mean more visibility, influence, or citations, but rather citations by a more diverse audience than is typical in disciplinary journals. In relative terms, this is most true of literary articles, which rarely find a broad external audience when published in journals such as *American Literature*. Historical articles in *AQ* were more broadly cited than papers published in *AHR*, but only by a modest amount, since roughly half of *AHR* citations appear in journals outside of history. The papers with the most diverse audience were those focused on broad themes such as the nature of multiculturalism. Yet *AQ* audiences remain somewhat divided internally, with papers more likely to find an audience in a cognate discipline than elsewhere. Historically oriented papers are thus more likely to be cited in historical journals, and literary articles are more likely to be cited in literature journals.

While the early scholars of American studies sought a unified, overarching understanding of American culture modeled on an anthropological approach to culture, subsequent generations of scholarship have become increasingly fragmented by topic even as they seek a synthetic or holistic understanding of their issue.

A recent (2008) program of the meetings of the American Studies Association reveals the remarkable scope and specialization of researchers attending the conference. Papers were organized by period (early American studies, nineteenth century, twentieth century), by ethnicity (African American studies, Asian American studies, Chicano studies, Native American studies, Pacific Islander studies), and by place (border studies, cultural geography, and landscape and the built environment). The conference included a variety of approaches to gender issues (gender and sexuality, queer studies, transgender studies), and global perspectives (global, transnational, cross-cultural, postcolonial studies, and studies of US colonialism). The study of culture extended beyond a narrow set of canonical authors to include popular culture, print culture, material culture, foodways, music, film, television, media, performance, and visual cultural studies.

While considerable vitality and dynamism is evident in this list, these diverse topics are not unified by a single or even a small set of theoretical perspectives. Moreover, in addition to these topical divisions, a deeper divide runs between those scholars focused principally on literature, or using literature as a primary source material, and those starting with archival or other source material. Thus, a session on "Eco-Criticism from Melville to Yamashita" examines environmental themes in literature, while another entitled "Environmental History and Policy-Making in the United States and Mexico" included papers that marshal historical evidence on environmental politics. The citation data discussed above indicate that the audience for these papers is likely to differ.

This pattern suggests that interdisciplinarity is not synonymous with integration. The field of American studies is not likely to draw together under a unified theoretical banner any time soon. While this type of differentiation is by no means unique to American studies, the diversity of topics and frameworks is probably viewed by Americanists more as a source for celebration and less as a cause for concern than in other fields. Indeed, if a unified conception of culture were to emerge, the current generation of American studies scholars would probably be among the first to rebel against this common framework.

Conclusion: American Studies and Interdisciplinarity

As we saw in chapter 2, advocates of interdisciplinarity seek to go beyond merely drawing on disparate influences to achieve a new, transdisciplinary syntheses. They lament the fact that many efforts at interdisciplinarity fall short of this goal (for example, Klein 2005a). What light does the history of American studies shed on the prospects for a transdisciplinary intellectual synthesis?

American studies during the 1950s did in fact achieve an original synthesis. The myth and symbol approach to American culture drew on diverse sources but represented a distinctive perspective developed largely by American studies scholars. This was a collective achievement, the result of a group of scholars who interacted with one another and who built on each other's contributions. In this way, it is exemplary of what an interdisciplinary intellectual movement (or SIM) can achieve. But this synthesis did not survive the fractured political landscape of the late 1960s and early 1970s. In other words, achieving a real synthesis of ideas and methods across disciplines is really just the beginning. For the emerging paradigm to endure, it must continue to generate a dynamic research agenda that elicits commitment from succeeding generations of scholars. In the case of American studies, a unique and powerful synthesis was successful for a time but was ultimately replaced by a broad, diverse, and evolving set of agendas. In short, the original American studies SIM was displaced by new, insurgent intellectual movements largely internal to the field but with many links to broader intellectual currents.

The evolution of American studies and related fields and disciplines suggests that the intellectual landscape can fruitfully be organized in many ways. American studies is one interdisciplinary approach that puts American culture but usually not the American economy or institutions at the center of its intellectual agenda. Global studies, as was also the case for an earlier approach, modernization theory, is interdisciplinary as well but takes globalization rather than America as its main focal point. African American studies gives priority to the African American experience while Africana studies places Africans and the African Diaspora center stage. Each of these fields represents its own intellectual movement; each is interdisciplinary; each of these has carved out a niche in American academia, but none has become fully institutionalized as a replacement or as an alternative to the established disciplines.

In its efforts to transcend disciplinary boundaries, a fully interdisciplinary approach to academia would create a dizzying array of alternative maps of the intellectual terrain. The history of American studies suggests that these alternative studies could themselves morph over time in ways that would surprise, confound, and sometimes dishearten the founders of these intellectual movements.[31]

In retrospect, it seems reasonable to speculate that the best window for the creation of American studies departments would have been the late 1950s and early 1960s: at this time there was a strong intellectual paradigm and universities were experiencing rapid growth. By the end of the 1970s that window had closed: shrinking enrollments, a fractured paradigm, new competition in the form of African American and women's studies, and the acceptance of program status rather than department status as the standard university home for American studies.

A final lesson to be learned from the history of American studies is that successful interdisciplinary endeavors are not simply a matter of individual scholars making ties between fields, or even organized efforts to promote communication across disciplinary boundaries. Enduring interdisciplinary ties like those formed by American studies scholars take years to develop and depend upon the efforts of a large and committed group of researchers. They must be powerful enough to draw in substantial numbers of scholars, to develop journals, to host conferences, and to create national associations. These intellectual currents do not arise every day, and do not fit the efforts of most individual scholars seeking to develop particular connections between fields. For all of its limitations, American studies has proven to be a far more dynamic and enduring interdisciplinary force than most small-scale efforts to promote interdisciplinarity by university administrators or individual researchers.

American studies has survived for decades as a program-based field. The organizational and intellectual implications of this arrangement should be noted. American studies depends on history, English, and other humanities departments for the placement of its graduate students. Consequently, the field needs to be open to currents coursing through literary studies and historical research. In other words, if there were too much intellectual distance between American studies and these companion fields, it would become more difficult to recruit historians and literary scholars to participate in American studies programs, and it would become harder to arrange for placement of

new PhDs. The dependency of American studies on related academic departments thus forces it, to some degree, to connect personally, substantively,
and methodologically with the established disciplines. Thus, its status as a
program dependent on traditional disciplines for positions and support represents a powerful force that has helped to keep Americanists open to the
ideas of its intellectual neighbors. But the other side of the dilemma should
also be clear: the more American studies is open to these fields, the harder it
is to claim a distinctive vision and voice.

As we have seen, American studies arose in part as an effort to reform
undergraduate education more broadly. In the next chapter, the role of undergraduates in the current disciplinary system takes center stage.

Integrative Undergraduate Education

The question of how the education of undergraduates should be organized is just as large and just as complex as the issues pertaining to research that have preoccupied us thus far. There are many important issues here in their own right that also have significant bearing on the organization of research. Reformers often highlight the neglect of undergraduates in making their case for change. Academics write minutely specialized treatises that no one reads, indeed, that few are even capable of reading, while their students, hungry for wisdom and guidance, are ignored as soon as the lecture ends. Furthermore, disciplinary fragmentation makes it difficult if not impossible for undergraduates to pursue a genuinely integrated educational experience. In the context of expensive higher education that often leaves students with mountains of debt, the critique of disciplines often takes the form of an aggravating offense: not only is higher education too expensive, but it does not provide the fully rounded education it promises.

In some ways, the enhancement of undergraduate education is included among the more compelling of the arguments for interdisciplinarity. Yet, in other ways, the thorny issues in undergraduate education place in bold relief some of the central conceptual weaknesses in the entire interdisciplinary framework. The central tenet—integrative education—is an especially elusive concept with a number of divergent meanings. And the challenges in designing and implementing a truly integrated undergraduate experience remain daunting.

As with most of the focus on interdisciplinarity, applied and preprofessional education is usually not the focus of debate. As we will see, applied programs tend to be more integrated but at the cost of being narrower in scope. This paradoxical pattern points to the ambiguities and complexities in the meaning of the term "integrative education." The thrust of the conclusion offered here is that the liberal arts are not the problem but rather the best hope for a broad and demanding education in a world that increasingly depends on educated citizens and open-minded professionals.

This chapter begins with an examination of the meaning of integrated learning in the context of undergraduate education. There are many facets of a holistic education, which sometimes includes the development of moral and even spiritual goals. Subsequently, the ironies of integrated learning are examined. Specifically, the trade-off between integration and breadth is developed. Data on interdisciplinary coursework suggest that cross-departmental connections are surprisingly prevalent. While these courses may not make the undergraduate experience fully integrated, an assessment of the extent of current offerings is a necessary but often overlooked part the discussion. Evidence on the share of students who choose to major in more than one field is also reviewed.

How big is the demand for integrative education? When the yardstick employed is the number of degrees conferred, the data indicate that applied and preprofessional fields are far bigger and have grown more quickly than interdisciplinary education.

The chapter proceeds to consider the relationship between liberal arts disciplines and their preprofessional counterparts. Ironically, liberal arts fields have helped to provide the intellectual underpinnings of many applied fields, which in turn tend to offer specialized degrees to a much greater extent than is evident in liberal arts fields. Thus, the growth of applied fields has provided opportunities for those seeking an integrated education focused on a particular set of objectives, while the liberal arts continue to emphasize breadth and critical thinking. Finally, the value of interdisciplinary experiences is examined with the limited data currently available. The results place interdisciplinary majors in a favorable light, both in terms of self-selection and educational gains.

Integration Overcoming Fragmentation

In their overview of integrative education, Mary Taylor Huber and Pat Hutchings view integration as the centerpiece of efforts to reform undergraduate education.

> One of the great challenges in higher education is to foster students' abilities to integrate their learning over time. Learning that helps develop integrative capacities is important because it develops habits of mind that prepare stu-

dents to make informed judgments in the conduct of personal, professional and civic life. (2004, 1)

Integration becomes ever more vital with the advent of the information age. As globalization and the Internet make unprecedented volumes of data accessible, the ability to make connections becomes more vital than the ability to memorize a set of facts. This view maintains that integrative education is necessary for navigating an increasingly interconnected and complex world, for being a good citizen, for connecting theory and practice, and for truly inspiring students.

At certain points, the benefits of integrated learning seem almost too good to be true. Huber and Hutchings maintain this type of learning is "greater than the sum of its parts. . . . The promise that 'integrative learning' leads to personal liberation and social empowerment inspires and challenges higher education to this day (Association of American Colleges and Universities 1998)" (Huber and Hutchings 2004, 2). Integration makes students into "intentional learners" who become lifelong learners after graduation.

It is fair to ask how integrated learning relates to critical reasoning based on diverse perspectives. These two goals are not necessarily identical. It may be easiest to illustrate this point with reference to social diversity on campus. The value of a diverse student body does not rest on students' ability to distill the commonalities of this diversity but rather to appreciate the range of experiences and perspectives that a diverse group of students brings to campus (Gurin et al. 2002). Similarly, exposure to broad theories and varying perspectives in the liberal arts context gives students the capacity to see the world from different vantage points (Nussbaum 1997).

Of course aspirations and the reality need to be distinguished. The premise that college should inculcate diverse perspectives leads to the establishment of distribution requirements. Many students, however, seek the easiest possible way out of the requirements that they are least comfortable with. For many, this means finding the easiest possible courses that fulfill the mathematics, science, or language requirements; for others, the challenge is to get through the humanities, or world culture, requirements. Consequently, laudable efforts to insure that undergraduates receive a broad education have the unintended consequence of making courses a hurdle to be circumvented or overcome. In this way, requiring a broad education may ironically make it less personally meaningful and thus less integrated with a student's personal interests.

The equation of "integrated" with "interdisciplinary" seems natural enough but closer consideration raises questions about this assumption.[1]

For example, many college language instructors do their utmost to integrate language instruction in its cultural context. Similarly, mathematics teachers, especially those who teach large service courses that fulfill the students' quantitative reasoning requirement, often strive valiantly to connect mathematic principles and insights to everyday experiences. These examples suggest that integration may be as much a matter of how a topic is approached rather than the number of disciplines that are included.

The example of mathematics raises an additional question regarding different meanings of the term integration. One sense emphasizes the connections between mathematics and other disciplines, while another stresses connections with daily life. The answer here could be "both/and" rather than "either/or," but as a practical matter there is only so much instructional time available. And there are many integrative goals in mathematics instruction: connecting disparate fields within mathematics, situating mathematical advances in their historical context, and so on (Czerniak, Webber, Sandmann, and Ahern 1999).

Integrated education is designed to overcome the balkanized knowledge on offer in contemporary colleges and universities.

> The fragmentation of the curriculum into a collection of independently "owned" courses is itself an impediment to student accomplishment, because the different courses students take, even on the same campus, are not expected to engage or build on one another. (Association of American Colleges and Universities 2002, x)

Echoes of the "silo" critique of disciplines can be found in discussions of undergraduate education.[2]

> The organization of universities and college around disciplinary departments also hardened in a simpler time. In too many institutions, faculty members feel the strongest attachments to their disciplines, the weakest to the institution as a whole. The departmental structure reinforces the atomization of the curriculum by dividing knowledge into distinct fields, even though scholarship, learning and life have no such artificial boundaries. (Association of American Colleges and Universities 2002, 16)

There is, no doubt, at least a kernel of truth in these points, as is the case with all of the criticisms of disciplines. Yet the suggestion that disciplines per se "atomize" the curriculum seems to go too far. The scope of knowledge requires some division of material into subjects. Once students reach high school, and even middle school, teachers with specialized knowledge are needed to teach mathematics, the sciences, foreign languages, English, history, and other topics. Surely the more specialized instruction at the college level also requires a division of labor. The question should not be whether specialized courses should be taught, but how they should be taught so that graduates have received an education that includes both breadth and depth.

As we saw in chapter 7, the goal of achieving "integration" is more complex and elusive than it might initially appear. In the instructional context, integration can refer to connectivity between intellectual domains, but it can also refer to the ties between the subject matter and students' individual interests. When they wrote of the exuberance and empowerment of an integrated education, Huber and Hutchings were referencing personalized connections with each student. This is an important goal but one which is especially difficult given that college students are often trying to figure out who they are and who they would like to become. In this context, personalized education may be as much a matter of effective advising as it is the structure of courses. Having guidance in orchestrating the college experience is probably more important in making the college years meaningful than is the number of interdisciplinary courses that are offered. Cutbacks in higher education, particularly at large public campuses, will in all likelihood reduce the informal personal connections between students, faculty, and advisors, and thus will make this type of individualized college experience harder to come by.

Education for the Heart and Soul

Integration takes many forms, including efforts to connect learning to moral, philosophical, and even spiritual goals. In their book *The Heart of Higher Education* (2010), Parker Palmer and Arthur Zajonc promote a vision of integrative education that connects mind, heart, and spirituality. This book reflects discussion of hundreds of educators at a 2007 conference on integrative education as well as decades of Parker and Zajonc's own experiences and advocacy of such issues. College, they write, should be a time when students are able to search for "meaning and purpose." The undergraduate experience loses its way when it focuses on subject matter education to the exclusion of the student as a multifaceted individual. "Something essential has gone missing, something that brought coherence and true purpose to our colleges and universities" (2010, 3). They suggest that the world is confronting daunting challenges that require leadership "whole people."

Surveys of undergraduates concur that college is often a time during which young individuals explore the fundamental questions of meaning and purpose. Yet this goal competes with other important objectives during the college years and appears to have declined over time as material values advanced.

A series of large national surveys of college freshmen has included a question on developing a meaningful philosophy of life since 1967 (Higher Education Research Institute, various years). In 2009, just under half (48.0 percent) of college freshmen in four-year schools reported that this objective is essential or very important to them, down from over five in six (85.8 percent) in 1967.

On the other hand, meaning and purpose are by no means the only or even the principal objective students are pursuing. Since the late 1960s, college students have become substantially more focused on material goals and the financial rewards of college. Over three out of four freshmen (78.0 percent) in 2009 indicated that being very well off financially was an essential or very important goal, compared with only two in five who admitted as much in 1967.[3]

Figure 9.1 shows the steady advance of pecuniary objectives for college freshman during the 1970s and 1980s, against the steady decline of philosophical goals. The presentation of these data is not meant to downplay the importance of the pursuit of meaning among undergraduates but rather to suggest that this is not the only matter on students' minds, and that the group that places a very high priority on this objective, while still very large, no longer compromises the vast majority that it had been a generation earlier. Financial

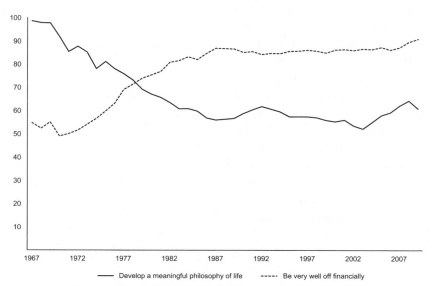

FIGURE 9.1. Trends in freshman student priorities, 1967–2009. Source: Higher Education Research Institute (HERI) data on college freshmen.

considerations are certainly understandable given the high cost of college and the heavy debt loads that graduates accumulate (Kantrowitz 2010).

While Parker and Zajonc argue that the college experience is more fragmented than ever, there have been powerful trends operating in just the opposite direction. Ironically, colleges increasingly attend to the whole student, but they do so one specialized program at a time, mostly outside the confines of the lecture hall. Academic programs are just one, albeit the most prominent, of a broad range of student-oriented programs and activities organized and sponsored at today's residential universities. Residential colleges attend to many needs of students. Students have access to academic counseling that is normally centered in the office of the dean of students. As electronic access to information has become an increasingly central part of the college experience, colleges routinely provide computer support and Internet access to students. The office of student life provides support for a wide variety of clubs and activities, from the chess club to fraternities and sororities. The performing arts on many campuses offer choral, theatrical, and instrumental performances, not to mention both intercollegiate and intramural athletics. Colleges also provide health care and psychological counseling to students. Many schools offer support services targeted to special groups, such as women's centers. Career placement, summer internship support, study abroad—a student with questions in any of these areas will find an office on campus piled high with brochures, an elaborate website filled with links, and a staff ready to help. In this way, universities serve as a "total institution" for students, a term developed by sociologist Erving Goffman (1961) to suggest a setting in which all of the needs of an individual are addressed by the institution in one way or another.

Overall, college spending on student support services is increasing sharply, much more rapidly than spending on instruction, especially at private four-year institutions (Desrochers and Wellman 2011). Yet these diverse programs colleges offer to address each set of student needs are themselves segmented into a broad array of specialized units and departments. In short, the modern university does increasingly address the whole student, but it does so via a series of segmented programs and services. Integrating these experiences, just like integrating the curriculum, would represent an organizational challenge beyond what most schools have considered.

Integration, Breadth, and Focus

As a practical matter, trying to provide a fully integrated intellectual curriculum for today's liberal arts undergraduates would seem to be an unattainable goal. Paradoxically, integration is more practical the narrower the task and subject of instruction.

Consider first the notion that integrating ideas in the research context is a far easier task than providing an integrated undergraduate experience. For example, if a sociologist incorporates into her research some ideas from psychology, political science, and perhaps economics, we may judge the result as interdisciplinary, and perhaps even transdisciplinary. If a good number of scholars at the same institution also endeavor to cross disciplinary boundaries, we might reach the conclusion that this school is a hotbed of interdisciplinarity. But achieving an integrated undergraduate experience at this institution requires much more. It requires not just that there are some faculty who are building intellectual bridges between fields but that they are building the same bridges, that is, working toward the same apex from both ends. To continue the example from sociology, there are innumerable theoretical ways to connect sociology to political science and related fields, and any number of substantive topics where these connections might be made. Helping undergraduates to see these connections in a clear and compelling way in a limited number of courses would be no mean feat. But that would just be the beginning, because the connections to philosophy, statistics, history, and countless other fields would be needed as well.

As we saw in chapter 4, in the context of connections between research journals, the number of ties required to link all nodes in a system is surprisingly large. A few simple of calculations reveals how daunting it would be to integrate instruction across all fields of study. Let's say that our goal is to knit knowledge together across 12 disciplines by having faculty in each field learn enough about other domains in order to lecture on the nature of these cross-field connections. If we endeavored to build bridges between each pair of fields, a total of 66 links would be needed. Taking the ideal of integration one step further to encompass all three-field connections, the number of ties needed soars to 220. It is hard to imagine how faculty members would find the time necessary to learn the material required for this type of integrated instruction. And the class time necessary to lay out all of the connections between fields would quickly crowd out time needed to introduce the subject matter.

As the number of fields we seek to integrate climbs, the number of bridges required quickly skyrockets. Moreover, these conservative estimates assume a single tie between fields would suffice. Since the broad arts and science disciplines all contain a considerable number of specialties, the number of bridges needed to connect all of these research domains to each other is astronomical. Taking into account the order in which students take classes in different fields shifts the calculation from combinations to permutations, which sharply increases the number of possible arrangements. Alternatively, making all two-way ties between individual classes offered during a given semester would require over 120,000 connections (assuming a roster of 500 courses). Furthermore, these calculations assume that knowledge in each field is static. Full connectivity in a dynamic university thus seems out of reach, especially given the constraints of a four-year undergraduate course of study.

And, to this litany of intellectual connections, we would have to add connections to the real world, to volunteerism, to diversity, in short, to the many other important objectives we would like to promote among undergraduates.

The point here is that, in most practical contexts, the term "integration" must be seen as a relative term. As we saw as well in the research context discussed in chapter 7, it is usually not possible to connect everything that can possibly be connected. Building a solid bridge or two between related disciplines usually represents a major intellectual achievement, but for most undergraduates this would represent only a single strand of connection among many that would be needed to weave together the web of an integrated undergraduate experience.[4] Therefore, an educational experience that develops an in-depth knowledge of one discipline can represent an integrated experience for students.

To approach this issue from another vantage point, consider what is involved in teaching a teenager how to drive a car. One can design a holistic, integrated approach to inculcating this set of skills. Practical experience behind the wheel would be combined with some insights from research on perception and reaction times so that the new driver understands how much distance will be covered before the car can come to a complete stop. The basic features of the car are explained along with the steps to be taken when warning lights appear, when tires become flat, and when routine maintenance is required. The student would be made to understand the serious risks and dangers inherent in operating a motor vehicle, and ideally would be taught some perspective on using the vehicle safely and wisely. In the case of driving, simply teaching driving theory or the history of the automobile might seem silly, and teaching technique without an emphasis on safety would seem foolhardy. A holistic and integrated approach would seem not only advisable but essential.

Learning to drive a car is far narrower, simpler, and more clearly delineated task than any subject that warrants a college degree. Nonetheless, the example is instructive in making the point that the more limited the task, the more likely it is amenable to a thorough, complete, and even holistic educational treatment.

In short, there are many instances in which a specific set of skills can be taught in a comprehensive manner. Indeed, as a general proposition, the more specific the educational goal, the easier it is to design an integrated educational program. Taking this reasoning a step further, applied subjects are at once narrower and more amenable to a holistic treatment than are the broad and diffuse basic disciplines. This pattern is compounded by the pattern, documented later in this chapter, that applied fields tend to splinter into many finely delineated subfields. As we have seen, reformers typically define the term "integrated" as synonymous with broad, but, ironically, education that is holistic, integrated, effectively combining theoretical and applied dimensions, experiential, and classroom-based knowledge, is more likely the more highly circumscribed the topic and setting.

To pursue this contrast in the college context, it may well be easier to design an integrated program of study for a criminal justice major than it is for a sociology major. Students in the former area can observe police in action, perhaps study prisoners or parolees, combine theories of criminal behavior with real-world internships or service learning opportunities. A capstone course could be used to distill the insights garnered from criminological theory, empirical research, statistical studies, ethnographic investigations, and personal experience.

Criminal justice raises a wide swath of fascinating and challenging issues, including the history of penal policy, the interconnections between drugs and crime, the politics of hate crime legislation, race and ethnic profiling, domestic violence, and countless other issues. If criminal justice is a relatively circumscribed field, it is only by comparison with the much wider tableau of sociology or history.

Sociology, in contrast, offers a broader view of society and correspondingly less opportunity to fully integrate its disparate elements. Sociology ranges from social history to laboratory experiments in social psychology, from survey research to network models, from ethnographic investigation of schools to critical analyses of gender and culture. Fieldwork and service learning can complement classroom instruction in social theory and research methods, but the whole is less likely to come into an integrated focus for the sociology major than it would for the student of criminal justice. Sociology is a liberal arts field that may be harder to sum up succinctly, yet it has a broader reach, and connects to many more intellectual and applied issues than does criminal justice.

Building on the comparison of sociology and criminal justice, the problem with liberal arts majors is not their narrowness but rather their very breadth. Integrated learning is indeed possible, but the liberal arts setting makes this goal particularly challenging. The staggering range of possibilities in a modern full-service university makes designing a fully integrated curriculum a daunting task.

Undergraduate Enrollment Trends

How likely is an undergraduate to encounter interdisciplinary instruction? In answering this questions it is important to distinguish between courses and majors. While most bachelor's degrees are awarded in specific fields of study, interdisciplinary courses are surprisingly common.

The fact of the matter is that a surprising number of professors report offering interdisciplinary classes. In the most recently available UCLA national faculty survey, conducted in 2007–8, 41.0 percent of full-time faculty teaching in four-year schools reported that they had taught an interdisciplinary course within the past two years (Higher Education Research Institute, various years). This finding has been remarkably consistent in the five waves of this survey administered since the 1995–96 academic year. Team teaching is also not uncommon, with nearly one-third of faculty reporting offering a team-taught class within the last two years. Many of these courses may not be as fully synthetic as some reformers recommend, and the transdisciplinary synthesis they seek is probably the exception rather than the rule. Yet these data suggest that the current disciplinary system coexists with a remarkable degree of boundary crossing. The isolated silos that critics maintain dominate contemporary universities are crisscrossed with far more connections and linkages than is usually recognized.[5]

Most courses are offered by departments, but sometimes courses are "cross-listed." This practice in part reflects local rules in various schools about apportioning enrollment credits to one unit or another. Nonetheless, cross-listing is one indication of the degree of openness or connectedness. For example, a review of sociology courses taught during the Spring 2012 semester at the University of Pennsylvania revealed that 80 percent were cross-listed. This high rate reflects sociology's connections to many related fields, especially interdisciplinary programs such as African American studies; gender, women's, and sexuality studies; health and society; and urban studies, among others.

Overall, 35 percent of the courses offered in the School of Arts and Sciences at Penn were cross-listed. While this fact by itself does not prove that these courses are necessarily broad or fully integrative, this pattern does suggest that the intellectual isolation of instruction by discipline and department may well be overstated.

Turning our attention to the issue of majors, an important question is whether student interest contributed to the growth of interdisciplinary fields of study. The case of American studies suggests that the expansion of programs had more to do with faculty interest than undergraduate demand. The decade of the 1970s saw the greatest expansion in the number of American studies programs, with an increase from 120 in 1970 to over three hundred by 1980. During the same period, however, the number of students obtaining a degree America studies began a 55 percent decline that bottomed out in the mid-1980s. This pattern was part of a larger decline in enrollments in the humanities during the 1970s. During this period, a sluggish economy combined with a burgeoning pool of new graduates depressed the economic payoff to higher education, resulting in a flight to more applied fields of study.

In order to address whether the experience of American studies is typical, trends in degrees received since 1970 were categorized into three groups: the traditional liberal arts disciplines, applied and preprofessional majors, and interdisciplinary fields of study. This last group includes area studies, ethnic studies, cultural studies, general studies, gender and women's studies, and multi/interdisciplinary studies. It also includes those whose degrees were classified as "liberal arts and humanities" without a specific field of study being listed. It does not include students who majored in one field and minored in another, as well as those who double majored (see more on this issue below).

Table 9.1 indicates that the traditional liberal arts majors garnered just under 40 percent of degree recipients in 2011.[6] The main alternative to the liberal arts disciplines is preprofessional education, which accounts for over half (56 percent) of undergraduate degrees. The traditional academic disciplines do not comprise a majority of student enrollments, and have not for many decades.

Figure 9.2 traces the share of bachelor's degrees awarded from 1971 through 2011. These data indicate that the 1970s represented the major transition period. During that decade, the share of degrees in the liberal arts fell from just under half to just over one-third of degrees before rebounding to just under 40 percent. Most of the share was lost to preprofessional fields, although interdisciplinary fields grew by a few percentage points. Enrollment-wise, interdisciplinary fields account for roughly 6 percent of bachelor's degrees. This represents a substantial increase since 1970 but remains a modest total compared with preprofessional education.

Business's share of degrees rose from 14 percent in 1970 to 24 percent in

TABLE 9.1. Bachelor's degrees received in disciplinary and applied fields of study, 2011

Disciplinary fields of study

Biology	90,003			
Computer science	43,072			
English	52,744			
History	34,999			
Foreign languages	21,706			
Mathematics and statistics	17,182			
Philosophy	12,836			
Physical sciences	24,712			
Chemistry		12,194		
Physics		4,955		
Psychology	100,893			
Social sciences	142,145			
Anthropology		9,677		
Economics		27,207		
Political science		39,123		
Sociology		29,271		
Theology	9,074			
Visual and performing arts	93,956			
Disciplinary total			643,322	37.5%

Interdisciplinary or multidisciplinary fields

Area, ethnic, cultural, or gender studies	9,100			
Liberal arts, general studies	46,727			
Multidisciplinary, interdisciplinary studies	42,228			
Interdisciplinary total			98,055	5.7%

Applied fields of study

Agriculture	28,623			
Architecture	9,832			
Business	365,093			
Communications	88,132			
Education	103,992			
Engineering	93,117			
Family and consumer science	22,444			
Health sciences	143,430			
Legal studies	4,429			
Library science	96			
Military studies	64			
Parks and recreation	35,942			
Public administration	26,774			
Homeland security and law enforcement	47,602			
Transportation	4,941			
Other (precision production)	43	37		
Applied fields of study total			974,536	56.8%
	1,715,913		1,715,913	100.0%

Source: US Department of Education, data on degrees conferred, 1970–2012.

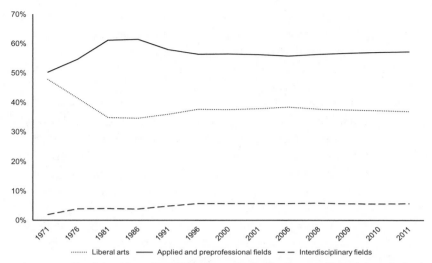

FIGURE 9.2. Trends in undergraduate degrees, 1971–2011, for liberal arts, applied and preprofessional, and interdisciplinary fields. Source: US Department of Education, data on degrees conferred, 1970–2012.

1986, and has settled back down in 21 percent in 2011. As we saw in the last chapter, a variety of applied fields, from criminology to communications to various health-related specialties, have grown since 1970 as the curriculum at many institutions has diversified.[7]

At present, the competition for students between the liberal arts and interdisciplinary majors is limited because these programs typically remain under the rubric of schools of arts and sciences. For example, a history professor might teach a course in American studies, but continue to have a tenured position in history. In contrast, the growth of a criminal justice degree program in a separate school of criminal justice or public administration would represent a loss to the number of tenure lines in the arts and sciences, unless the criminal justice majors were required to take a certain number of liberal arts classes as part of their degree requirements. Thus, preprofessional education at present is a more powerful competitor for resources than are interdisciplinary programs based in the arts and sciences. This could change if truly fundamental interdisciplinary reforms in undergraduate education are enacted.

Reformers might argue that the relative scarcity of interdisciplinary programs limits their enrollment. If such programs were larger, more robust, and more prevalent, their enrollments would likely be higher. Perhaps, but the enrollment levels at current interdisciplinary programs may provide a guide. The average American studies program graduates ten students per year. The average African American studies and women's studies program graduates only six students per year.[8] In these cases, it is not the lack of availability but rather limited interest that seems to be the constraining factor.

It may be that there is a great thirst for more integrated education, but other factors constrain the choice of an interdisciplinary field as a major. A graduate's field of study helps to signal to prospective employers what skills are likely to have been acquired. The financial prospects of students vary to a considerable extent with their major (Arcidiacono 2004; Robst 2007). In this context, degrees in interdisciplinary studies are less likely to convey what a student has learned. In short, the limited practical value of a degree in interdisciplinary studies may deter students from selecting this as their major, despite their underlying interests.[9]

The economic crisis that began in 2008 has yet to divert enrollments away from the arts and sciences. While it is still too soon to see its impact in degree data, the HERI Freshmen Surveys can serve an early warning system. While interest in particular fields has varied, such as an increase in biology and a small decline in the humanities, overall the share of freshmen planning to study the liberal arts has actually grown slightly since 2007. There has been more of a shift among applied fields—more interest in engineering, less in education and business—rather than a shift away from the liberal arts. While the long-term impact of the great recession remains uncertain, thus far the effects do not appear to be great.

In this context, it is interesting to consider the types of fields pursued by students on line. For-profit institutions emphasize applied fields much more than they do the liberal arts. The University of Phoenix, for example, offers bachelors degrees in many applied and preprofessional areas, but only offers degrees in two fields (education and psychology) that would be classified here under the rubric of arts and sciences. Interdisciplinary program have not been prominently featured in these on-line degree programs.

Massively open online courses (MOOCs), represent the latest in a series of innovative application of information technology to higher education. Thus far, MOOCs have offered open access, nondegree courses via the Internet in partnership with leading universities. Enrollments in such classes can reach into the thousands. Three of the most largest and most important MOOC programs are Coursera, Udacity, and edX. A survey of the courses offered by these sites conducted in late 2012 revealed the predominance of practical subjects. The forty-six courses offered by Udacity and edX combined focus almost exclusively on applied topics, such as computer programming, although basic courses in the physical sciences and mathematics are also available. Coursera currently offers by far the broadest spectrum of courses, but only 47 of the 313 courses (15 percent) offered thus far are explicitly interdisciplinary in nature. Most of these courses are in the social sciences, or are explorations of a particular topic or issue such as global warming or AIDS.

Experiential and Service Learning

One notable form of integrative learning stresses the connection between classroom and other forms of learning. Experiential learning is based on the premise that students absorb and retain only a small fraction of the materials presented in lectures (Fink 2003). Students are less likely to learn by listening and more likely to learn by doing. Even a cursory acquaintance with campus life makes it clear that what goes on in the classroom represents just one small part of the college experience.

Academically based service learning, an important version of experiential learning, combines public-service activities with reading assignments and classroom-based lectures and discussion. Evaluations of service learning programs are often quite favorable. Astin and his colleagues (2000) report gains on eleven outcome measures, including academic performance, writing, leadership, and plans to pursue public service after graduation. These gains, which were measured in a panel design, were greater than those for students who performed community service outside the rubric of a class.

Service learning thus has considerable promise, but it is hard to do well. Finding the right placements can be very time consuming, and extensive supervision and feedback are needed to bring out the most in the experience. One can certainly make the case that service learning helps to integrate the curriculum in some areas like social work and education, but it is hard to see how this type of experience would fully integrate liberal arts. While hands-on instruction has long been a staple of the curriculum in lab-based classes in biology and chemistry, it can be much harder to build learning by doing into other parts of the curriculum. Whether the topic is medieval history, or metaphysics, some subjects do not lend themselves as well as others to experiential learning. Reformers would like to see excellent advising, extensive service learning opportunities, and the opportunity to receive detailed feedback on a senior honors thesis that connects theory to a students' question. These are all valuable components of an undergraduate education, but they are expensive. The real challenge facing integrative education going forward will be the fact that cost-cutting efforts in an era of expensive higher education will make his type of personalized educational experience increasingly difficult to provide to students in many educational settings.

Specialization within Applied Fields

The story of academic specialization has one further twist: applied fields are prone to a high degree of splintering, that is, a tendency to subdivide internally.

While the arts and science disciplines may lead the way in research specialization, the applied fields take the lead in specialized degree offerings. In fact, applied fields such as education, communications, and business generate highly specialized degree programs. Thus, the promise of applied fields of study as an integrative force for undergraduate education is illusory. Nor do such fields typically have the scholarly scope to offer any realistic promise of broad intellectual synthesis.

American higher education offers a mind-boggling array of degrees. In 2008, the *Digest of Education Statistics* listed over one thousand different degrees that could be obtained at the bachelor's, master's, or PhD level. This list does not include professional degrees such as law and medicine, and also does not include all of the specialized fields that lead to degrees at the associate's level (i.e., two-year colleges).

These degrees are reported under 30 major headings (see table 9.2). In perusing this list of degrees, it quickly becomes apparent that some fields are followed by a long list of specialized entries while other fields have few subdivisions. Thus, there are ninety-four separate degrees offered in the field of education, with specializations ranging from art, languages, math, and music to special education and early childhood education. Similarly, business school students can specialize in some eighty-nine fields, ranging from accounting, finance, and human resources, to marketing. The classification "health professions and related clinical sciences" includes a list of 169 specialties that includes many types of nursing majors, but also a dazzling array of specialties including occupational therapists, dieticians, laboratory technicians, and so on. The visual and performing arts also represents a catch-all area with fifty-four specialties, including design, drama, theater, art history, ceramics, and music management.

Some of these entries no doubt represent the overzealous classification efforts of the statisticians in the Department of Education, and in all likelihood no single school offers the full array of choices. Nonetheless, a review of contemporary degree statistics leaves no doubt that applied fields routinely differentiate into a remarkably broad array of subspecialties.

The contrast with the liberal arts and sciences fields is striking. Few of these fields feature a large number of subspecialties, and most of the specialization that does occur is found only among graduate students. For example, there are seventy-eight specializations listed under "biological and biomedical

TABLE 9.2. Number of specialized degree offerings for disciplines and applied fields, 2011

	Number of specialties
	1,184
Applied fields	
Health professions and related clinical sciences	182
Education	96
Business, management, marketing, and related support services	86
Visual and performing arts	64
Agriculture, agriculture operations, and related sciences	50
Engineering technologies/technicians	56
Engineering	52
Family and consumer sciences/human sciences	28
Natural resources and conservation	22
Communication, journalism, and related programs	23
Legal professions and studies	20
Security and protective services	23
Communications technologies/technicians and support services	13
Theology and religious vocations	17
Mechanic and repair technologies/technicians	10
Transportation and materials moving	8
Architecture and related services	11
Public administration and social service professions	11
Parks, recreation, leisure, and fitness studies	12
Science technologies/technicians	5
Construction trades	6
Precision production	2
Library science	2
Military technologies	3
Arts and science disciplines	
Biological and biomedical sciences	84
Foreign languages, literatures, and linguistics	50
Area, ethnic, cultural, and gender studies	38
Multi/interdisciplinary studies	31
Social sciences	30
Psychology	27
Computer and information sciences and support services	26
Physical sciences	47
Philosophy and religious studies	12
Mathematics and statistics	13
English language and literature/letters	12
History	8
Liberal arts and sciences, general studies, and humanities	4

Source: US Department of Education, Digest of Education Statistics, 2010.

sciences", but fully three-quarters of undergraduates major in only two of these fields—general biology and biochemistry. Nearly all psychology undergraduates earn their degrees in "general psychology," and nearly all economics undergraduates obtain a general degree in economics. Area studies and foreign language represent the main exceptions, since the diverse content of these degrees makes them difficult to substitute for one another.

Thus, the liberal arts and science fields, regularly castigated for their silo-like isolation by critics, typically provides a much broader degree program for undergraduates than do the applied fields that ostensibly endeavor to integrate learning around a set of substantive concerns.

The specialization of applied and preprofessional fields should come as no surprise. In a vocational context, offering more specialized credentials can enhance students' employment opportunities, which in turn can help to increase the attractiveness of the program. Thus, a business major can master a set of skills and increase her marketability by specializing in finance or accounting. The tighter link to the labor market of applied fields leads to the proliferation of specialized degree programs.

The process is quite different in the liberal arts. For example, among English majors, there is no clear advantage in employability that follows from specializing in early American literature versus British poetry. Consequently, there is little pressure stemming from concerns about employability to fuel the creation of specialized degrees within liberal arts disciplines.

The quest to stand out leads liberal arts students to pursue double majors rather than garnering a specific marketable credential. National data (from the US Department of Education's IPEDS data series) indicate that roughly 12 percent of bachelor's degree recipients receive their degrees in two fields. This figure in all likelihood does not fully capture the number of students who major in one subject and minor in another. Moreover, the choice of double majoring is more common at more selective institutions. For example, over 25 percent at the University of Pennsylvania and Vanderbilt University graduate with more than one major.[10] Students' concerns over the marketability of their degrees thus lead liberal arts students to greater breadth, while, for students in applied fields, the same concern prompts greater specialization.

Learning and Selectivity in Interdisciplinary Programs

Reformers sometimes recite stories about the exceptionally gifted undergraduate who arrives in the faculty member's office with a set of deep questions that transcend disciplinary boundaries. Today's universities, we are told, will fail these remarkable students, who will be forced into narrow channels, their intellectual curiosity stunted, their profound questions unanswered. While these stories are undoubtedly true, as they are told so vividly, the broader question is whether current patterns of enrollment in interdisciplinary fields of study fit this picture (Taylor 2010).

Here data collected by Richard Arum and Josipa Roska are pertinent. A national sample of students was tested in order to assess how much they learned during their college years. The test employed was designed to tap critical reasoning and problem-solving skills; in other words, it was geared to the kinds of goals we would like to see colleges advance.[11] Arum and Roska's sample includes a small number of interdisciplinary students, but enough to provide some preliminary evidence. In the parlance of social science, students in interdisciplinary majors are self- selected. While they entered college trailing students in the natural sciences and math in test scores, but they match others

TABLE 9.3. Test score performance for interdisciplinary students
Regression models (adjusted for clustering of students within schools)

	Predicting 2007 CLA		Predicting 2009 CLA	
Controlling for	2005 CLA	2005 CLA and SAT	2005 CLA	2005 CLA and SAT
Major [reference: business]				
Interdisciplinary	94.173**	42.439	62.261	34.769
	(31.658)	(30.080)	(40.272)	(28.547)
Social science/humanities	69.266**	41.621*	56.088*	26.947
	(19.780)	(18.466)	(20.480)	(16.154)
Natural science/math	77.346**	44.760*	57.792*	14.586
	(27.073)	(19.875)	(26.916)	(18.650)
Health	25.016	36.269**	6.412	15.516
	(13.853)	(9.039)	(14.803)	(14.624)
Education/social services	4.444	31.297	−0.043	12.634
	(23.165)	(15.508)	(23.680)	(25.381)
Engineering/computer science	35.429	26.348	16.143	5.263
	(17.437)	(17.016)	(20.102)	(18.514)
Communication	25.394	35.963*	2.094	8.418
	(17.264)	(16.851)	(16.674)	(17.921)
Other	22.893	17.211	−4.734	−7.204
	(18.711)	(16.722)	(23.261)	(20.481)
SAT (mean centered)		0.450**		0.446**
		(0.057)		(0.049)
cla05 (mean centered)	0.476**	0.245**	0.420**	0.210**
	(0.045)	(0.032)	(0.035)	(0.033)
Intercept	1,122.616**	1,134.909**	1,191.861**	1,211.052**
	(15.699)	(14.293)	(14.079)	(13.482)
N	2,322	2,322	1,666	1,666

* $p < .05$; ** $p < .01$; *** $p < .001$

Soure: CLA (Collegiate Learning Assessment) data provided by Arum and Roska.

in the social sciences and humanities, and surpass students in applied fields such as business, communications, and education (see table 9.3). Students who major in interdisciplinary fields also learned more than many of their peers even when entering test scores are controlled in the analysis. Learning gains were similar to social sciences and natural sciences, and surpassed those in applied fields such as communications and education. They scored slightly higher than did students in the social sciences, but this difference was not statistically significant.

These findings suggest that today's interdisciplinary students are often above average and learn comparable amounts to students in other arts and sciences fields. Students in interdisciplinary majors do not represent the bottom of the barrel—quite the contrary—but we cannot say that interdisciplinary education represents a discernible improvement over the traditional disciplinary fields.

Conclusion

While integrated learning may seem to be an appealing objective, on closer scrutiny this goal becomes rather elusive. The number of connections between diverse research specialties are too numerous to count, and clearly surpass what can be squeezed into a four-year undergraduate curriculum.

Turning from theoretical desiderata to empirical patterns, the degree of cross-field connectivity in the undergraduate curriculum is far greater than might be expected. Data suggest that interdisciplinary courses, cross-listed classes and dual majors are surprisingly common. There is more to be learned with regard to the effectiveness of these programs in meeting various educational objectives.

Moving beyond the curriculum and the classroom, a brief review reveals that much is being done to attend to the whole student. Colleges and universities spend a great deal on the college experience outside the classroom, from exercise facilities to counseling and support service to assistance in career placement. Service learning provides an attractive alternative to large lecture-based courses, but such programs are very labor intensive and require close faculty supervision to be effective.

The equation of interdisciplinary, broad, and integrated evaporates when applied fields are compared with the arts and sciences. Ironically, the liberal arts are difficult to integrate precisely because they are so broad. An integrated program is more feasible instead within the confines of an applied course of study. Liberal arts now attract only a minority of undergraduate majors, as applied and preprofessional fields have become far more appealing to undergraduates than either discipline-based majors or interdisciplinary programs. Ironically, these applied fields tend to divide into many specialties in order to make their graduates attractive on the job market.

The case for a liberal arts education rests on its contribution to a broad understanding of our world and for its advantage in developing critical learning skills. These lofty goals are more realistic and achievable than the goal of fully integrated learning. Of course if students experience courses as scattered at random with little or no connection between them, then the curriculum will not fully succeed in promoting breadth, critical reasoning, or any other goal.

It may be best to think about integration as a matter of degree. It is not possible to integrate all knowledge, and it is not possible to devise a fully integrated curriculum that will be engaging and compelling to all students at the same time. Consequently, those who are interested in improving the undergraduate experience might do well to focus on taking steps in the direction of integration rather than to attempt the creation of a fully integrated curriculum.

For example, some programs and some majors no doubt do a better job of providing a more coherent learning experience than do others. Learning more about these programs, while maintaining a dynamic and diverse curriculum, would be a worthwhile goal. Coherence and integration are more likely to occur within the confines of a major than they are in the elective part of the curriculum. Learning more about possible trade-offs between breadth and exposure to a wide spectrum of subjects and approaches, on the one hand, and more cumulative, integrated experiences on the other, is an area that warrants further inquiry.

Thus far, over the course of this book, the vitality of disciplines, communication across domains of scholarship, the long-term trajectory of interdisciplinary fields, and some of the vexing issues pertaining to undergraduate education have been considered. It is now time to turn to an assessment of specific interdisciplinary initiatives that are actively under consideration.

Implementing Interdisciplinarity

It is time to consider specific proposals designed to promote interdisciplinarity, setting aside the temptation of antidisciplinarity as an unattractive and unsustainable option. A principal concern about each of these plans is the centralization of decision making and a declining role of faculty power and influence in the university. An interdisciplinary system will be vulnerable to more frequent programmatic reorganizations, and it will be more difficult for faculty to make an effective case for a longer-term view.

In terms of specific approaches to implementing interdisciplinarity, I consider four principle strategies: joint appointments, cluster appointments, imposing an interdisciplinary structure, and eliminating undergraduate majors. The chapter includes a discussion of ways to promote interdisciplinary communication, and ways to strengthen the liberal arts in the context of a university increasingly dominated by applied fields. A summary of the main themes and empirical findings presented in this book is offered as a conclusion.

The Centralization of Decision Making

Interdisciplinarity seems likely to result in a shift of power away from faculty toward the central administration of the university, a trend that some have suggested is already quite advanced (Ginsberg 2008). Interdisciplinary programs and projects by their very nature take place beyond the confines of departments, and thus they reduce the opportunity for, and utility of, faculty input. Faculty members are able to participate in departmental decisions in a way that is natural and informed. Whereas faculty are in an excellent position to have a say regarding their department's strengths and needs, they are in a weaker and less informed position to contribute to decisions taking place beyond the realm of their departments.

Although university administrators are typically very smart individuals who are devoted to their institutions (see Tuchman [2009] for a less glowing account), there are nonetheless good reasons to believe that the quality of decision making improves when it is decentralized and declines when it is overly centralized. First, deans often have shorter time frame than do faculty members. Deans and university presidents come and go, but academics make investments with a much longer time frame. In recent years, college presidents have served an average of 8.5 years, which is an increase from the low of 6.6 years reached in 2001 (American Council on Education 2007). The most commonly cited figure for deans is an average tenure of five years (Kardashian 2011; University of Missouri, Kansas City 2011), although I was unable to locate an authoritative source for this statistic. Deans will thus often be tempted to pursue initiatives that yield tangible results during their tenure in the dean's office.

The time horizon of scholars, especially tenured professors, can be quite long. Techniques take years to master; the payoff in terms of lines of inquiry may take many years or even decades to become clear, and the practical results of research are often highly uncertain. Doctoral degrees take five to ten years to complete: by the time one has obtained one's degree, a graduate student may well have survived one or two new deans and a new university president. While six or seven years of training may seem like forever for a graduate student, from the faculty's point of view, creating an effective training program is an even longer-term proposition. Training cohorts of graduate students takes years, and seeing these graduates established in the careers even longer. An important asset of discipline-based scholarship, then, is a long time horizon. While the content of disciplines evolves over time, disciplines provide an intellectual and employment context in which scholars can plan to devote their careers.

Even without the intervention of deans and presidents, interdisciplinary programs change their focus and scope more frequently than disciplines do. Consider the evolution of women's studies. When these programs were first launched during the 1970s and early 1980s, a principal goal was to uncover the hidden contributions that women had made in many fields. However, over time these programs often evolved to encompass gender issues more broadly as research began to consider the nature of masculinity as well as femininity. The next step for women's studies was to encompass sexuality, as scholars delved into questions involving gay and transgendered experiences. The result is that many women's studies programs became gender studies

programs, or women's and gender studies programs, and then women's, gender and sexuality studies programs. Each of these changes involved intense
and lengthy discussions and debates (Boxer 1998).

The evolution of women's studies programs typically occurred without
control over faculty lines. In other words, scholars pursued the evolution of
ideas and research without having to debate how many positions should be
allocated to women's issues, how many to gender issues, how many to sexuality issues. There were few if any positions to begin with, and women's studies
programs succeeded because of outreach to various departments and centers
where like-minded scholars could be found. But imagine the conflicts that
would arise if women's studies were a department that sought to change its
name every few years, and along with a change in name sought a change in
faculty appointments. Surely this would be a recipe for extraordinarily con-
tentious academic politics.

Scholarship within departments evolves as well, but because the intellectual rubrics tend to be broader, there is no need to change the name of the
discipline. Thus, sociologists have led many of the shifts in women's, gender,
and sexuality studies without having to change the name of their discipline.
This programmatic stability, accompanied by intellectual dynamism, is valuable. It allows for greater certainty, longer time horizons, and greater faculty investments in long-term research ventures. In short, disciplines create
a zone of academic freedom that is essential for the vitality of critical inquiry,
research, and scholarship. A degree of faculty input, both based in local institutions and national professional associations, has been instrumental in
making American research universities great. An interdisciplinary university
would ironically and inadvertently threaten to undermine faculty voices.

Then there is the level of engagement by deans and presidents. Not only
are interdisciplinary fields evolving at the ground level, but deans and presidents are likely to have their own reasons for suggesting, and perhaps even
imposing, change. A dean who is less than enamored of African American
studies may be inclined to fold it into a broader, interdisciplinary ethnic
and cultural studies program. Financial arguments might be the grounds for
combining mathematics, statistics, and computer science into one department. A unit focused on global health issues might be shifted from the School
of Public Health to the School of Sustainability to the School of Global Studies for good reasons, bad reasons, or even no apparent reason.

It is thus safe to predict that programmatic reorganizations would be en-
demic to an interdisciplinary system. Each of these changes would preoccupy
tremendous amounts of faculty time and interest, since each new configura-

tion could shift the social ties and power relations in the unit. More important, each department restructuring would affect decisions about long-term investments in scholarship. As we have seen, successful research programs require a long time horizon. Each reorganization thus will raise questions about these long-term commitments, and will in general shorten the time horizon that researchers employ in pursuing their research. Tenure becomes less meaningful when it is linked to programs that themselves do not have tenure.

In our current disciplinary system, faculties have a degree of power to resist wholesale reorganizations. When a French department is threatened with closure, colleagues from all fields within the affected school, and Francophone faculty from across the disciplines, rally to support the program. Sometimes such efforts fail, as in the case of the University of Albany's closure of its French department. Sometimes faculty resistance prevails, as in the case of the efforts to close the Yale University sociology department during the 1990s.

Faculty will likely be in a much weaker position to resist departmental reorganization in an interdisciplinary system because interdisciplinary decisions by their nature take place outside the confines of departmental expertise, and thus the playing field shifts markedly toward executive authority. It is also the case that the scarcity of similar departments in other institutions weakens the faculty's hand.

Take the case of a school of sustainability. There are a small number of such arrangements across American universities, and perhaps they represent a rising tide. But let's say that a dean decided that the unifying theme should be climate change rather than sustainability. Or that certain divisions should be shifted to a school of environmental sciences while others were combined in a school of global studies. At present, there would be relatively few national voices to object to such a change. In an interdisciplinary university, this pattern would be even more common: centralized decision making with fewer national, discipline-based faculty voices to object to arbitrary and capricious reorganizations.

The main concern is that disciplines and programs will become elements in a portfolio rather than academic disciplines that need careful and long-term nurturing. The risk is that deans will pursue short-term strategic opportunities over the long-term cultivation of particular departments; that organizational innovation will become an end itself; that the importance of the slow and steady building of departments and disciplines will take a backseat to a myriad of other short-term priorities.

Imposing an Interdisciplinary Blueprint

Let us now consider particular strategies for implementing interdisciplinarity. While joint appointments and cluster hires may have a substantial cumulative effect if consistently applied over a long period of time, another approach to interdisciplinarity is to create an interdisciplinary structure all at once. Under the leadership of President Michael Crow, Arizona State University has pursued a complete restructuring along interdisciplinary lines. In other words, ASU has not simply sought to promote an interdisciplinary major here and a joint appointment there, but has restructured schools, research centers, and programs along broad thematic axes. For example, ASU has established a School of Evolution and Social Change that brings together anthropologists, social scientists, and applied mathematicians focused on issues of the evolution, the environment, and global health. ASU has also established a School of Sustainability, which seeks real-world solutions to environmental, economic, and social challenges, as well as a College of Technology and Innovation and a New College of Interdisciplinary Arts and Sciences.

In some cases, this new structure produces new degree fields. For example, a PhD in sustainability is the culmination of required coursework, solutions workshops, electives, and dissertation research. Yet in many other areas, the new structure is a reorganization of familiar degree programs. Overall, *The College Blue Book* lists 154 degree programs at ASU, including over eighty in the School of Arts and Sciences. Alongside such staple fields as history, English, engineering, and business, ASU offers degrees in animal behavior and ethnology, building science, communication disorders, English as a second language, graphic design, Italian language and literature, molecular biology, radio and television, real estate, statistics, and theater. In short, ASU continues to be a full-service university that provides specialized training in a dazzling array of subject matter. Thus, if the problem with disciplines is the existence of many different departments and degree programs, then the ASU model has not overcome these divisions. On the other hand, if the concern is the demise of specialization, then it appears to be unfounded thus far.

Given the wide range of offerings, it is difficult if not impossible for any particular arrangement of fields within schools or programs to be fully coherent. Not all relevant programs will be housed under one rubric, and not all offerings in a given division will necessarily produce the desired synergies. Thus, the ASU College of Technology and Innovation is separate from the business school and the engineering school, even though business and engineering might well seem central to issues of technology and innovation. This school includes programs as diverse as air traffic management, food industry management, and technological entrepreneurship and management, not all fields that necessarily fit together or that one might associate with technology and innovation. Yet ASU's entrepreneurship certificate programs are located in the business school, and the graduate program in civil, environmental, and sustainable engineering is located in engineering, not in the School of Sustainability.

In some cases, ASU's reorganization resulted in the division of departments. For example, the sociology department was disbanded after sociologists were divided into one group focused on family studies, now located in the School of Social and Family Dynamics, and another focused on environmental sociology located in the School of Evolution and Social Change. Sociology bachelor's degrees continue to be offered, and sociology was among a minority of departments to be divided in this way.

One principal concern for new interdisciplinary programs has to do with the presence of employment opportunities in peer institutions. For example, there will be questions about the employability of newly minted PhDs in the field of sustainability if other schools do not have parallel programs. The implications of this disjuncture were evident in the case of American studies. A PhD in American studies makes sense if the field is not that different from history and English, which would enable American studies PhDs to seek positions in history or English departments. Similarly, sustainability doctoral programs may well work to the extent that they are somewhat similar to other established fields of research, whether these are in biologically related fields such as plant ecology or social science fields such as the economics of development. For the employment dimension of graduate training to operate smoothly, one of two possibilities will have to occur. Either new fields spread rapidly, as computer science did during the 1970s, or new entrants into the academic marketplace need to align their degree recipients with those in established programs that have openings.

A major concern with the ASU model is the centralization of decision making. Interdisciplinarians often rail against the ways that disciplines undermine intellectual freedom. The heartfelt complaint is that a relatively small number of intellectual figures at leading institutions set the agenda for researchers throughout the discipline, thus unduly constraining creativity and scholarly advances. Yet central administrations are less likely to support the level of faculty autonomy and authority of interdisciplinary clusters that discipline-based departments have secured.

By all accounts, President Michael Crow has been instrumental in devising and implementing the new interdisciplinary structure at ASU. More generally, faculty are likely to attain a degree of input when decisions concern local matters—the content of requirements, the timing of graduate examinations, decisions regarding new faculty appointments. As decisions move from departmental initiatives to decisions occurring at a university-wide level, faculty's information advantage will decline and their ability to influence decisions will shrink.

More frequent programmatic reorganizations will make faculty less secure and tenure less meaningful. For example, the field of sustainability may be a sensible way of organizing a program, but the commitment of the central administration to this area of inquiry may itself not be sustainable. What happens when the next president decides to divide the School of Sustainability into a School of Global Health, a School of Environmental Sciences and Climate Change, and a School of Global Studies? Each way of arranging the deck chairs has implications for the structure and identity of programs and faculty. The durability of disciplines is an important strength even as the content of individual fields continues to evolve.

Geiger and Sa note that of the thirteen interdisciplinary projects begun at Duke University in 2001, only two were on the list of centrally supported programs five years later (2009, 167). This winnowing might be seen as evidence of effective management, but the implications of this type of rapid turnover on educational programs need to be considered. The rise and fall of research centers is one thing, but educational programs require a longer time frame is needed. A five-year window is hardly enough time to hire a small group of faculty members, to recruit cohorts of graduate students, and to establish a nascent program. Within five years, some programs would be barely up and running, and few graduates would have earned their degrees. Few assistant professors who were hired would have had the chance to be considered for tenured appointments. If a program were terminated five years after being created, most of the faculty and students in the program would be placed in limbo. The present arrangement, with enduring discipline-based degree programs and more flexible research centers that can be expanded and contracted as needs and funding permit, seems a much more appropriate approach.

Joint Appointments

A much more gradual approach would involve a slow and cumulative effort to change the nature of faculty appointments. Appointing professors to two departments instead of one would seem to be a simple and straightforward way of breaking down disciplinary "silos." While short term impact of such a strategy would be limited, the cumulative effect could ultimately undermine disciplines.

Suppose that a university seeks to hire a professor who spans the fields of education and philosophy. The logic is to build bridges between these two fields, to stimulate conversations, and to help undergraduates obtain a more integrated intellectual experience. The first issue for a jointly appointed candidate would be whether the two departments can agree on the selection. Consider the search process step by step until a faculty appointment is made. At each step of the way, there is a certain degree of slippage or attrition. Not all searches produce faculty hires.[1] It may well be the case that there is a fine candidate with a background in philosophy who is not acceptable to the educational scholars on the committee, or vice versa. So in all likelihood the pace of hiring will slow while particular search committees come up empty. Over time, however, departments may get used to interdisciplinary hiring.

The variety of expectations across fields should not be underestimated. In some fields, such as experimental physics, having one hundred coauthors on a paper is considered routine, while in many humanities fields, coauthorship remains the exception. Even within the sciences, in some fields, researchers require two or three postdoctoral fellowships before becoming effective candidates for assistant professor positions, while a single postdoc or even no postdoc suffices in others. More broadly, the cultural assumptions of scholars in different fields are not always easily reconciled (Lamont 2009; Knorr-Cetina 1999; Strober 2011).

After agreeing on a recruit, the next challenge is to attract him or her to campus. One issue is whether the candidate has a department-based offer in one university and an interdisciplinary offer from a second. A tenure-track prospect may well prefer to be hired in a single department in order to reduce the complexities of obtaining tenure. A joint-appointment hiring strategy thus may be costly in terms of the efficacy of searches and the quality of the candidates recruited.

Assuming an interesting candidate in education and philosophy is selected and brought to campus, the first effect of his hire would be to strengthen the specialty of educational philosophy, a venerable field dating back to Jean-Jacques Rousseau and perhaps further. This is an established niche, and in the short term there is little reason to believe that this scholar's presence on campus would affect most of the scholarship in either department. As we have seen in reviewing newly creating journals, many interdisciplinary entries can be thought of as filling particular niches as much if not more than building new bridges. On a campus the size of the University of Pennsylvania, with nearly five hundred faculty members in the School of Arts and Sciences, one could appoint quite a large number of joint faculty members and still have few or none in most departments. These joint appointments would mostly represent additional scholarly specialties, and the extent to which scholarship writ large would be "integrated" as a result of their presence is an open question.

Another practical consideration regarding joint appointments is where the scholar spends the majority of his or her time. While in principle the idea of spanning departments may be attractive to some, as a practical matter departmental membership involves a number of time-consuming responsibilities. Departments ask members to serve on search committees, run graduate and undergraduate programs and take on many other important responsibilities. Jointly appointed faculty are thus vulnerable to the possibility of doubling administrative duties, not to mention the obligation to attend two sets of departmental meetings and two sets of colloquia. On the other hand, some jointly appointed faculty members are clever enough to use their dual set of responsibilities as a way to avoid all administrative tasks by complaining of overload to both departmental chairs.

The stage at which the recruit is ready to be considered for promotion to tenure has received the most attention. The question is whether a candidate can be fairly evaluated if her scholarship falls outside the boundaries of traditional disciplines. In the case of joint appointments, the issue would be convincing two sets of colleagues that one has met or exceeded the standards for tenure. It is possible to create a system that is designed to address the need to have an appropriate set of evaluators. In this vein, the University of Southern California has designed tenure criteria for scholars whose research spans more than one discipline (Berrett 2012). But as a practical matter, it seems clear that earning tenure twice, convincing two sets of colleagues of one's merits, will be more difficult than earning tenure once. Perhaps this is why some efforts to promote joint appointments, such as those at the University of Pennsylvania, have focused on senior-level faculty recruitment. Star professors with established reputations can be recruited without having to traverse the grueling tenure process in two departments (Popp 2008).

The cumulative impact of joint appointments over time has not been given serious consideration. How many joint appointments is a good number? Should all appointments going forward be made involving at least two departments? It is clear that, over the long run, the cumulative effect of a systematic joint appointment strategy would be the undermining of disciplinary coherence. In the case of sociology, for example, joint appointments could be made with any number of fields—women's studies, African American studies, and health and society programs, not to mention related fields such as political science, anthropology, social work, criminal justice, and education. Thus, sociology would not be paired with any single field but would become connected with any number of fields. Over time the core group of faculty dedicated to sociology as a discipline would most likely erode, and the ability of the department to advance sociological inquiry would be undermined.

Cluster Hires

Cluster hiring is a clever idea that avoids many of the thorniest aspects of joint appointments.[2] This approach involves a commitment to hire several faculty members with a particular focus spread across several departments. For example, a cluster might be devoted to research on questions of diversity. Scholars in this area would be targeted by a search committee, perhaps all at once, perhaps spread out over several years. One year the hire might be in sociology, the next year in education, the following year in history. The result would not only be the addition of a valued group on campus, but the school would be creating a latent interdisciplinary group. The problem with building some interdisciplinary bridges is that there are not always the right colleagues at either end of the span who share the same interests. Cluster hiring is designed to seed neighboring departments in such a way as to promote the likelihood of such interdisciplinary connections. Furthermore, it may be argued that cluster hires improve faculty quality because a successful candidate must beat out competition from several disciplines in order to garner an appointment.

Cluster hiring avoids many of the pitfalls of joint appointments. Both departments in question do not need to agree on a candidate: the search committee simply brings its top candidates to the attention of a particular department. Junior scholars do not need to earn tenure in two departments; recruits do not need to serve on two sets of committees. There is a lot to be said on behalf of cluster hiring. Yet in the end, the cumulative effect of such efforts is likely to lead to the same erosion of disciplinary and departmental coherence that would result from a systematic policy of joint hiring. In the context of a steady state or declining faculty roster, the growth in the numbers of faculty members whose principal commitments lie in the cluster rather than in the department would likely make department politics, which can be tricky in the best of times, even more complex.

Eliminating Departments and Majors

The surest way to eliminate liberal arts disciplines would be to disband (or dramatically curtail) major fields of study and to eliminate the conferring of degrees in disciplinary areas. This might seem like an odd proposition: surely the status of physics rests on theoretical breakthroughs from Newton and Einstein forward; surely the double helix has cemented the vital role of the life sciences, and so forth. Yet we have seen that undergraduate majors play an indispensable role in sustaining the liberal arts disciplines. Even venerable fields such as astronomy have established only a modest foothold in contemporary universities because they have failed to sustain sufficient undergraduate enrollments.

Majors, along with course requirements, generate enrollments that enable departments to make the case for faculty appointments. This is the main reason that the entrepreneurial university has its limits. While opportunities to develop new drugs via research in the life sciences and new products via research in nanotechnology and many other fields continue to grow, student enrollments in the physical sciences remain low and have inched up only slowly in the life sciences.[3] In the end, continued enrollments in history courses will justify the appointment of a certain number of history professors, language requirements will still justify a certain number of foreign language professors, and course enrollments in the social sciences will sustain a number of faculty appointments in these fields. Thus, entrepreneurialism in the university context will most likely continue to be confined to a limited number of fields with the most promising commercial prospects.

Without any majors, however, the employment stability that has been a vital element of the academic disciplines would be undermined. Deans would be free to create a variety of programs and centers focused on one apparently compelling idea or another without disciplinary-based faculty playing an essential decision-making role. Faculty members who have invested decades in training and scholarship in a particular line of inquiry would be vulnerable when the next dean decides to reorganize yet again or the next financial crisis requires cutbacks. Disciplines, departments, and majors do indeed insulate faculty from such pressures to a certain extent.

Is there a way to structure undergraduate education without majors? The "great books" approach is one. One could also imagine a service learning/integrated learning approach that would eliminate or greatly reduce the role of majors. Imagine two years of required coursework with a heavy emphasis on service learning followed by a year of study abroad. Senior year might focus on an interdisciplinary project that would serve as a capstone learning experience. Whatever the plusses or minuses for the undergraduates that such a system might yield, the cost in terms of the damage to disciplines could be significant.

Thus, an undergraduate college program could be designed with minimal differentiation by specialty and minimal departmental structure. This organizational approach, however, is not at all feasible in the context of graduate education. Graduate degrees of all sorts, from computer engineering to special education teaching to urban and regional planning, require mastery of a certain body of knowledge and a set of techniques. In each of these areas, employers will want to know whether the graduate in question has the background and training that is appropriate for the position under consideration.

Moran (2010), along with Repko (2008) and many others, maintains that interdisciplinarity presumes disciplines. He also notes that disciplines have proven resilient in the UK context. But the suggestion that disciplines are politically powerful and empirically resilient is not exactly an argument for disciplines. As Lattuca notes, "Observers of interdisciplinarity typically have framed the disciplines as negative influences on interdisciplinary scholarship" (2001, 253). A stronger case for disciplines would entail an explanation of their value of disciplines, such as that offered here in chapter 3, along with a recognition that once an interdisciplinary research program becomes successful, it will be most likely to thrive within the organizational arrangements of established disciplines.

The sharp reduction or elimination of degrees, departments, and majors in nonresearch institutions would thus not eliminate disciplines, but would dramatically reduce their scope. These institutions represent a substantial part of the market for scholars with specialized degrees. In other words, if research universities produced PhDs only for other research universities, their doctoral programs would be much smaller than they are today.

Proliferation versus Integration: Disciplines Plus

At present, the wholesale elimination of departments, disciplines, majors, and specialized degrees would be a nonstarter. Resistance from faculty would be too great. Whereas faculty may not be strong enough to reinstate a French department closed during a budget crisis, they are probably strong enough — especially at elite institutions — to defend against the closing of all departments across the board. The only way to eliminate departments would be to first weaken them via a sustained period of attrition and erosion. After fifteen or twenty years of joint appointments, investments in interdisciplinary programs, and the blurring of disciplinary lines, the position of department-based faculty might be sufficiently weakened that the wholesale replacement of the disciplinary system could be considered.

For the moment, the way forward for interdisciplinarity is to add a layer of cross-field programs on top of the current disciplinary system. This approach might be called a "disciplines plus" strategy. It should be noted that the present organizational structure of research universities already accommodates a substantial number of interdisciplinary research institutes and centers. As was noted in chapter 5, such centers are far more numerous than are established disciplines. Expanding the number of research centers does not represent a change in this organizational arrangement. The reform being considered here adds a set of interdisciplinary degree programs to the set of mostly discipline-based degrees. Again, interdisciplinary programs already exist on most campuses. For this to represent a fundamental reform, the number of interdisciplinary divisions would have to expand substantially.

In the short run, an interdisciplinary university that adds new degree programs without reducing the established departments and programs will have far more nodes than currently populate the university's organizational charts. As we saw in chapter 5, the leading research universities have already gone down this path via the proliferation of research centers. If even a small number of these research centers are converted into departments or programs, then the number of partitions on campus is almost certain to grow. Unfortunately, there is no reason to think that this new set of units will integrate knowledge in any meaningful sense of the term.

The proliferation of interdisciplinary programs would in all likelihood be self-reinforcing. In other words, there is every reason to believe that interdisciplinary programs would continue to multiply. As we saw in the case of American studies, interdisciplinary programs appear to beget more interdisciplinary programs. In this case, a field intended by its supporters to be holistic helped to pave the way for the creation of a series of other special studies programs.

The temptation to create programs in response to funding opportunities will result in a multitude of forms. Returning to the case discussed in chapter 5, no less than twenty-one research centers that emerged at Penn State to address homeland security. Notable in its absence from this list is criminal justice, a fine program at Penn State. The twenty-one homeland security centers at Penn State thus do not begin to tap all the possible angles on this single issue. And there are countless other topics that could easily generate as many subdivisions as homeland security.

The current university system has the flexibility to add new programs that take the form of research centers and institutes. However, once we begin to think of these as interdisciplinary departments or programs with teaching as well as research functions, the cost of this organizational proliferation will increase. Because training programs necessarily require a long-term commitment of resources, the proliferation of interdisciplinary training programs will make the university less nimble and flexible than it would be with new centers and institutes.

Reformers might argue that this type of university will integrate knowledge by creating a new set of bridging structures that will serve to connect isolated disciplinary islands. But the islands are not isolated; as we saw in chapters 5 and 6, there is already a steady flow of traffic between them. Moreover, interdisciplinary undertakings quite often represent another set of specialized niches in the academic landscape rather than broad-gauged forces that fully integrate disparate fields of research.

There is nothing wrong with adding new interdisciplinary programs as long as there is a clear-eyed understanding that these should have the same standing as established fields and programs. In other words, interdisciplinary programs are often quite narrowly targeted in scope and thus are similar in their likely impact to the addition of new disciplinary programs. Of course, at some point, the carrying capacity of even the largest universities will be stretched to its limits. The current economic challenges facing higher education have probably slowed the proliferation of new interdisciplinary programs.

Among the concerns about postdisciplinarity is that disciplinary boundaries are not the only lines to be crossed, not the only barriers to be overcome. The lines between knowledge and action (Wickson, Carew, and Russell 2006), between university and community, and between scholarship and performance (Case 2001) are among the many targets of reformers who seek to break down disciplinary boundaries. The effort to reshape American higher education around interdisciplinary principles is thus fraught with risks. It is hard to see how interdisciplinary arrangements could succeed without the complex organizational structures that have made the current system so creative and dynamic. Consequently, instead of trying to devise a new form of interdisciplinary university, the project should be how do we build on and strengthen the best elements of our current system.

Promoting Communication, Strengthening Disciplines

Interdisciplinarity is not an end itself, although many are beginning to think in these terms. Advancing knowledge is an end; interdisciplinarity may be a means in some circumstances. There are many simple steps that departments can take in order to make it easier to keep up with the relentless advance of knowledge. One way is to encourage disciplines to invite colleagues from related departments to present an overview of recent research in their field. This could encourage cross-disciplinary communication. While it will never be possible to keep up with everything, simple steps along these lines can help. Deans can advance such initiatives with a small amount of financial support.

In my ideal university, central administrations would leave the system of discipline-based departments alone. Exciting new intellectual opportunities, whether these take an interdisciplinary form or not, can be fostered under the rubric of centers and institutes. These are flexible organizational arrangements that can respond to new opportunities without constantly reorganizing departments and disciplinary training programs. If an interdisciplinary area comes to need its own appointments, this is most likely to occur within the rubric of an existing department. In rare instances in which a genuinely new field emerges, such as the emergence of computer science as its own field, it will become its own department.

Given the current and apparently enduring financial challenges facing higher education in the United States, disciplines will be under pressure as colleagues are asked to do more with less, yet the best way to promote interdisciplinarity is to give faculty more time to explore. The main obstacle to interdisciplinary communication and innovation is the shortage of faculty time. If the current economic crisis endures and continues to put faculty programs throughout higher education under pressure, the prospects for creative exploration across disciplinary lines will be more limited than one might hope.

Similarly, the best way to enrich the undergraduate experience is to lower class sizes in order to give more students more opportunity to know and engage with faculty. Integrated learning experiences are those in which faculty help individual students make connections that are meaningful to them.

Disciplines are not bad; they are good. They are not isolated silos but rather nodes in a remarkably vibrant web of scholarship. At major research universities, disciplines are connected by an extensive network of interdisciplinary research programs, centers, and institutes. Disciplines are broad, not narrow; they are dynamic, not static.

Liberal arts disciplines are uniquely valuable because they take the long-term as well as the short-term view. Paradoxically, they are useful in part because they do not focus exclusively on immediate utility. Disciplines create the intellectual space for scholars and researchers to ask deep questions, to take the longer view, and to make extensive investments in learning that pay off not in months or years but over the course of careers.

Over time, the liberal arts have become a smaller slice of the university pie. The push toward interdisciplinarity fails to appreciate the fact that the main challenge to intellectual breadth comes from the proliferation of applied programs on campus. The threat to the academic vitality of the American university does not come from the persistence of English, history, biology, and political science as separate fields: it comes from the proliferation of applied programs with more targeted missions, less intellectual breadth, less faculty autonomy, and less focus on the long term. Interdisciplinary reforms generally target the arts and sciences, but perhaps the focus of reform should be the accounting department, the school of dentistry, and the forest management program.

The key question, then, is whether there is a way to maintain and strengthen the arts and sciences. The case for the arts and sciences should begin by ceasing to refer to those fields as silos. This critique is misplaced and inaccurate. Disciplines are indispensable and vital; liberal arts education produces a broader understanding of the world, with broader and clearer thinking, than do alternative programs on campus.

One practical way to strengthen the liberal arts is to require more liberal arts courses for applied programs. In essence, this is an agenda of "re-disciplining" the academy and reestablishing the arts and sciences as the vital center of the university. Ironically, this would be a way to promote more interdisciplinary learning at the undergraduate level, not by reducing the role of the disciplines but by strengthening them.

This chapter began with a not-so-gentle critique of the role of central university administrations, but of course there is an important role for them to play. Central administrations should nurture disciplines rather than treat them as elements of an academic portfolio. There needs to be an emphasis on the value of the long view as well as solving immediate social challenges. Disciplines must do what they can to show their utility in the short run, but they must not only focus on the short run. Doing so would be shortsighted and would undermine their rationale and the organizational structure that has made them so successful.

Conclusion

Over the course of this book, a number of empirical findings have been advanced and several reconceptualizations of the debates over interdisciplinarity have been offered. The notion of academic disciplines as isolated silos uninterested in external developments has been debunked. On the contrary, ideas flow quite frequently between fields. Statistical innovations are adopted far and wide as they prove useful; conceptual innovations make their way across the frontiers between disciplines. And, if the case of educational research is at all representative, there is relatively little delay between the production of ideas in one discipline and the reception of these innovations in neighboring fields. Nor do discipline-based scholars shun the vexing issues of the day. Thousands of researchers over the years have flocked to study society's challenges, from poverty to health care.

The challenges of communicating effectively given the high volume of specialized research are serious. With twenty-eight thousand active peer-reviewed academic journals, it is clear that no single individual or even research team can stay abreast of intellectual developments in all fields. The growth in the number of journals shows no sign of coming to a close, especially with the advent of open-access outlets and the growth of journals outside the United States. An intellectual division of labor of one form or another seems unavoidable.

Approximately one-quarter of newly established journals have donned the mantle of interdisciplinarity, but many of these are highly specialized. The empirical examination of these new outlets challenges the notion that interdisciplinary is equivalent to broad. Moreover, there are good reasons to question the viability of a system in which research findings are spread out over thousands of interdisciplinary journals. If such a journal system comes to pass, the role of journals is likely to decline in favor of search engines that scan the web for research on particular topics.

If interdisciplinarity is not always broad, disciplines are far from narrow. Indeed, I suggest that their very breadth was essential in their widespread adoption across colleges and institutions. Broad disciplines attain departmental status, while narrow fields remain specialized niches that are most often found only in the largest research universities.

Broad disciplines are dynamic because specialties within these fields are constantly jockeying for position, resources, and recognition. Competition occurs at several levels—among individual researchers, among specialties within a discipline, and between disciplines. The resulting system has enough stability to justify extensive investments on the part of individual scholars but enough dynamism and vitality to regularly produce intellectual ferment and advances in field after field. And disciplines cooperate as well as compete: the university context provides opportunities for faculty in different fields to work together, from the ubiquitous interdisciplinary research centers to school-wide and campus-wide committees and programs.

Over the long haul, some interdisciplinary endeavors become part of the landscape of academia. A case study of the field of American studies is revealing. The field has many intellectual accomplishments to its credit, and it has endured for over half century, with an energetic national association, a number of research journals, and active programs in dozens of countries around the world. However, American studies has not succeeded in attaining departmental status, and consequently does not control the hiring of its own faculty. American studies graduates must seek positions in neighboring fields, such as history, English, and diverse special studies programs, including race and ethnic studies, film studies, and cultural studies. Its dependence on other fields for employment opportunities means that American studies cannot stray too far from the norms, standards, and expectations of these receiving fields. To do so would jeopardize the employment prospects of its graduates.

American studies scholars have sought a more holistic understanding of American society and culture than they felt was available in the context of individual disciplines. Yet American studies itself becomes highly specialized, and in turn contributes to the proliferation of other interdisciplinary fields. American studies programs are entitled to credit for laying the groundwork for the subsequent adoption of interdisciplinary programs such as women's studies.

The proliferation of specialized fields occurs not just in research journals but on campus as well. Ironically, liberal arts disciplines themselves helped to develop the knowledge base that helped to launch many of the applied programs that have come to represent the majority of campus life. Applied programs, in turn, tend to proliferate large numbers of very specialized degree offerings. These are designed to secure employment advantages for their graduates, yet the accumulated effect of the growth of such specialized programs is to balkanize the university landscape. The intellectual splintering of American higher education is thus more the result of the creation of hundreds of narrow applied programs rather than the existence of a small number of broad and dynamic liberal arts disciplines.

The challenge of providing undergraduates with an integrated educational experience is filled with a number of unexpected findings. If faculty surveys are to be believed, interdisciplinary courses are remarkably common in American colleges and universities. Yet the promise of integrated learning seems most achievable in the context of narrow prevocational programs precisely because these programs do not attempt to cover the broad scope of ideas addressed by the liberal arts. The liberal arts seems best suited to promoting critical reasoning, even if a fully integrated curriculum seems difficult to craft.

Interdisciplinarity seems appealing to many scholars as a way of getting past the artificial barriers and constraints of life in their discipline and department, but this is a case of the grass seeming greener on the other side of the fence. Antidisciplinarity is not a viable way of organizing intellectual life. It is hard to discern how scholarship could build on previous work in a cumulative manner if all efforts are focused on upsetting the applecart. As serious inquiries are made into what it would take to make interdisciplinarity sustainable, it becomes clear that something closely resembling contemporary academic disciplines is needed.

And substituting interdisciplines for disciplines is unfortunately not just a matter of pouring old wine into new glasses. The system of disciplines has emerged in such a way as to develop a certain degree of autonomy and authority for faculty. An interdisciplinary system is likely to be one in which central administrations play a much larger role in academic decision making. Ironically, the efforts to liberate faculty from the strictures of arbitrary disciplinary constraints will most likely end up recreating the same departmental structures that interdisciplinarians seek to avoid, but without the departmental autonomy that has played such a central role in making the liberal arts the center for critical thinking and sustained intellectual advances.

Over the last sixty years, the liberal arts have made many valuable contributions to the nation's well being, in no small part because they have not exclusively focused on immediate utility. This system of disciplines has been based on a structure of stable employment and training that starts with undergraduate majors, proceeds to master's and doctoral degrees and culminates in department-based faculty appointments. This system, which enables faculty to invest in long-term lines of inquiry with uncertain payoffs, has produced remarkable advances in field after field. This system is being challenged in many ways and will surely have to adapt to the pressures it is facing. Nonetheless, the US research university has continued to be the model that is most often emulated around the world. If this enviable position is to be maintained, the arts and sciences disciplines will have to remain as the vital and vibrant core of the twenty-first century university.

Appendix: Data Sources

The research presented in this book draws on many sources. While in some cases, I cite the findings of others; more often, I sought out untapped data sources to address previously unanswered questions. The strategy was to examine in detail some of the many questions underlying the case for a more interdisciplinary university. I summarize these data below in order to provide sufficient detail about these investigations without unduly distracting from the flow of the text.

1. Citations. Citation data speak to the question of the extent of communication between disciplines. In chapter 5, I draw on citation data from the Web of Knowledge as reported by the National Science Foundation. I also conducted subject matter queries to estimate the volume of research directed at various social issues. Searches of article titles tend to understate the extent of research on a topic, since the precise words may not appear in an article title. On the other hand, keyword searching may overstate the prevalence of research because the terms may refer of a variety of issues beyond those of interest. I employ both these methods to obtain low-end and high-end estimates. I also conducted similar searches in Google Scholar, which also provides useful citation data. Google Scholar results tend to be significantly higher, typically by a factor of two. The principal virtue of the Web of Knowledge data for our purposes is that a large number of journals are classified by field in a consistent manner. In contrast, Google Scholar does not neatly classify citations into detailed subject matter areas. In chapter 6, I analyzed Web of Knowledge data in more detail by utilizing their subject classification system. By comparing the timing of citations in education versus neighboring fields of research, I can address questions of whether research is significantly delayed when it crosses the boundaries between fields.

2. Research Centers. The Cengage Learning (2012) compiles information on organizations. I queried this database for research centers based in educational settings. These data allow me to estimate the number of research centers in American higher education based on a consistent definition, and to report the number based in each of the top twenty-five research universities. In order to check the validity of the data, I conducted my own investigation of university-based research centers based on information gleaned from a school's website. These figures match the results obtained from the Gale data quite closely. This evidence is pertinent to the analysis in this volume because the vast majority of these research centers are interdisciplinary in orientation.

3. New Peer-Reviewed Journals. Journal data from Ulrich is examined in chapter 4. Ulrich compiles information on journals, including the date when it was established, whether it is peer reviewed, the country of publication, and other useful data. While it may not be completely comprehensive with respect to new journals published in foreign countries, such as China, it nonetheless is the most comprehensive database of academic journals of which I am aware. The analysis in chapter 4 focuses on 740 new peer-reviewed journals established in 2008.

4. Degrees and Programs. I examined several different types of data on degrees. While the Department of Education provides information on the number of students receiving degrees, these data are not always the best source for obtaining the number of schools offering degree programs in particular areas. Specifically, the national tables reported in the *Digest of Education Statistics* provide a wealth of detail on particular degree offerings, but the data sets that allow for analysis of degrees offered in particular institutions are more highly aggregated. Consequently, I compiled data on degree offerings from individual schools from *The College Blue Book*.

   Chapter 3 relies heavily on data from *The College Blue Book*. The *Blue Book* is a rich source of data on degree offerings by particular schools. Its coverage is quite systematic dating back to the late 1960s. This continuity helps in terms of examining growth of applied programs.

   In chapter 3, I also draw on data from a series of reports entitled *American Universities and Colleges* published by the American Council on Education (1928–36). In the first three editions, published in 1928, 1932, and 1936, data on the number of faculty by department and rank are reported. I included data on full, associate, and assistant professors, but not instructors. The 1936 volume included data on 514 colleges and universities (teachers' colleges and normal schools are not included in this analysis of liberal arts departments). Of these, twenty-one, including Harvard and Penn, did not list the number of faculty in individual departments.

5. Department Structure. While the *Blue Book* data identify degree programs, they do not report on department structure. Thus, these data indicate the

presence of a degree in French language and literature, but they do not indicate whether this is awarded by a French department, a Romance language department, a foreign language department, or some other type of entity. For this level of detail, I examined several selected fields of study across 383 colleges and universities. The sampling frame was drawn from Brint's Institutional Database. Brint and his colleagues had already identified a representative sample of institutions that was manageable in size, and so it seemed opportune to take advantage of this sample of schools. The fields of study were selected because of their substantive interest.

6. Trends in the Field of Sociology. The discussion of trends in the size of the field of sociology are based on data obtained from the American Sociological Association. The name changed from American Sociological Society to American Sociological Association during the 1950s. I use the current name throughout for consistency. I calculated department size in 1950 by tabulating ASA membership by department (American Sociological Society 1950). This technique probably understates department size to some degree, because not all faculty members would have been members of the association. The 1950 membership directory lists faculty in 438 US colleges and universities.

7. Faculty Hiring Patterns. I examined data on faculty hiring patterns by discipline from the National Survey of Post-Secondary Faculty (National Center for Education Statistics 2011).

8. American Studies. Chapter 6 draws on a wide range of data pertaining to the field of American studies. Estimates of the number of American studies programs are based on the American Studies Association's (ASA) annual surveys (conducted from the 1960s through the 1980s), as well as data from *The College Blue Book* and estimates from Brint's databases. Data on participation in annual meetings, data on American studies dissertations, and other material are also obtained from the American Studies Association website.

9. Student Values and Learning. Data from UCLA's Higher Education Research Institution on freshman norms is examined to shine some light on trends in student values and intended majors. Richard Arum and Josipa Roska, generously provided analyses of their data on college student learning. These results speak to the selectivity of interdisciplinary students and the learning gains of those enrolled in interdisciplinary programs.

Notes

Chapter One

1. As used throughout this book, a "discipline" is an established field of study that is institutionalized as a degree-granting department in a large number of colleges and universities. An extended discussion of this definition can be found in chapter 3. Interdisciplinarity is used here in a general way to refer to cross-disciplinary connections. This term is contrasted with related concepts such as multdisciplinarity and transdiciplinarity in chapter 5.

2. Writing over a decade ago, Peter Weingart and Nico Stehr suggested that "interdisciplinarity has become almost synonymous with creativity and progress" (2000, xi). Since then, support for interdisciplinarity has grown considerably.

3. In the preface to Philip Altbach's study, Kapil Sibal, the minister of human resource development of India, writes: "Whether the institutional structure of the modern university is flexible enough to accommodate learning across disciplines and to harmonize education with the needs of society is yet to be tested. The world today is ripe for another tectonic shift in our understanding of the university as an institution" (Sibal 2011, xiv).

4. Several dozen formal interviews and many informal conversations were conducted. The greatest concentration of interviews were with leaders in the field of American studies, and to a lesser extent the field of education research. These interviewers are rarely cited directly but rather are used to better understand the context from the point of view of participants.

5. The terms "interdisciplinarians," "critics," "advocates of reform" and "reformers" are used interchangeably here, even though in some cases "revolutionaries" might be more appropriate than "reformers" because the suggestions for change could fundamentally reorganize higher education.

Chapter Two

1. Andrew Abbott (2001) and Roberta Frank (1988) note that the call for interdisciplinarity began almost as soon as disciplines were established. The emphasis here is on the reformers' appraisal of disciplines. A consideration of the diverse goals of interdisciplinary scholarship can be found in chapter 7.

2. When writers seek to provide a supporting reference for the notion of academic tribes, they often cite Tony Becher's study of British higher education. However, Becher's view of aca-

demic disciplines is actually quite benign. Becher's goal was to show the relationship between academics and their subject matter, the cultural connections between tribes and their territories, not to paint academics as objects of amusement by comparing them to natives wearing grass skirts. Moreover, the second edition of Becher's book notes the many changes throughout the British system of higher education. In their preface to the second edition, Becher and Paul Trowler are at pains to emphasize the evolution toward a more porous and open system (Becher and Trowler 2001; see also Trowler 2011).

3. There has probably been more rhetorical evolution in the ends of interdisciplinarity than in the critique of disciplines. This topic is discussed further in chapter 7.

4. Klein devotes an entire chapter to the topic of "borrowing," that is, the use of ideas from one field by another. Thus, she acknowledges the "openness" of the field of psychology to ideas and techniques from physics, physiology, and mathematics (1990, 105); see also Lattuca (2001, 253). Unfortunately, she treats these cases as exceptions and stresses the risks in this area—misunderstandings and miscommunication—rather than the many important ways that disciplines learn from one another. Furthermore, Klein suggests that discipline-based scholars borrow ideas with the wrong spirit. They do so without the right commitment to dialog, without a real commitment to synthesis and problem solving. To be more useful and successful, cross-field borrowing must be more "symbiotic"; less "asymmetrical" and more "reciprocal" (1990, 93–94). The extent to which information and ideas flow between disciplines is addressed empirically in chapters 5 and 6.

5. A review of the product development literature suggests that researchers in this area emphasize multifunctional arrangements much more often than they do multidisciplinary ties in the sense of researchers with diverse technical skills.

6. University of California Commission on General Education in the 21st Century 2007, 14. The commission, chaired by two distinguished sociologists, Michael Schudson and Neil Smelser, did not advocate sweeping reforms in line with the interdisciplinary agenda.

7. Diverse meanings of the term "integration" are discussed in chapter 7 and again in chapter 9. The integration of academics with students' lived experiences is quite different from efforts to promote scholarly integration, such as efforts to tie economics, philosophy, and politics together into a more integrated study of public policy.

8. Strober (2011) emphasizes the lack of a common culture as a key rationale for interdisciplinarity, although she examined faculty seminars rather than the undergraduate experience. See the University of California report (2007) for an informative discussion of why colleges have moved away from a common core set of course requirements to a system more geared to students' choices.

Chapter Three

1. The discussion emphasizes a national market for scholars in a field, yet in some fields the employment pool is international in scope, with foreign researchers comprising a considerable share of employment (Franzoni, Scellato, and Stephan 2012). The global scope of disciplines in many fields is evident from international scholarly associations and journals. While a fuller account would incorporate the international dimension of scholarship, this pattern does not alter the main points developed here with respect to discipline-specific employment.

2. Repko (2008) attempts to map disciplines in terms of their discrete subject domains. While a certain degree of simplification may be attributed to the fact that this book is intended as a text for undergraduates, unfortunately the framework is at odds with the realities of research. For example, in recent decades, economists have advanced analyses of political decision mak-

ing (Arrow 1963), legal rules (Posner 1972), and the family (Becker 1991). Thus, Repko's outline simply does not comport with the evolution of disciplinary boundaries.

3. The attribute approach to the professions has been superseded by perspectives that emphasize the boundaries between professions. The discussion here owes a great deal to Magali Sarfatti Larson's (1977, 1993) and Andrew Abbott's (1988) analyses of the professions.

4. This discussion could have built on Abbott (2001, chapter 5), as he includes many of the elements included here. For purposes of exposition, however, Turner seemed preferable as a starting point, since a proper discussion of Abbott would require a beginning with consideration of his complex theory of fractal change in the course of disciplinary development.

5. The fact that disciplines provide employment opportunities for those trained in the field does not mean that getting a job is the main motivation of researchers and scholars. Academics have similar motivations to those in other fields: they seek financial security, collegiality, status, and fame, among many goals. Some scholars are interested in ideas for their own sake, while others are more oriented to the solution to social problems. Yet employment is a prerequisite for accomplishing any of these goals, and stable employment allows researchers to pursue deep questions that may take many years to answer.

6. What Turner is hinting at here is that scholarship depends on a long time horizon, to induce scholars to make substantial investments early in their careers and to give research enough time to yield fruit. The internal labor markets of disciplines provide a degree of shelter from demands for immediate productivity in ways that are more difficult if not impossible with other organizational arrangements. If interdisciplinary units were to be reorganized and relabeled as frequently as divisions within large corporations, this would pose serious challenges to the viability of long-term lines of inquiry, not to mention the stresses it would place on the disciplines' employment and political systems. I develop this idea further in discussing the costs and risks of interdisciplinarity in chapter 10.

7. The data discussed here are drawn from the 2010 *College Blue Book*, a reference guide to degree programs offered in US colleges and universities. The *Blue Book* includes Canadian institutions, but only those degrees offered in the United States are included in the figures presented here. See the appendix for more detail on data sources utilized in this study.

8. The analysis of disciplines presented here focuses on disciplines in the US college and university system. Turner (2000) touches on several research specialties whose employment base is located in other settings. The focus here is on the unique relationship between majors, departments, and disciplines in the university context.

9. Specifics about these plans can be found at the Institute for Translational Medicine and Therapeutics, University of Pennsylvania 2011; and the Philadelphia Business Journal 2011.

10. Turner (2000) suggests that the availability of considerable financial support before the 1970s enabled physics faculty to pursue pure-science questions without a great deal of concern for practical utility. The effect of the trend Turner describes was a narrowing of the base of undergraduate majors to those interested in esoteric topics. When the availability of large grants declined, physics was left with limited funding and relatively few majors, although physics courses remained a requirement for students in many fields.

11. Abbott includes this in his perspective on disciplines when he distinguishes between "immediate" and "distant" audiences (2001, 141).

12. It should be noted that this is in essence the reverse of the claim that disciplines are too narrow and confining. And if the "problem" with disciplines is that they are too broad and thus lack unifying intellectual principles, then interdisciplinarity can only compound the problem by removing any concerns about intellectual boundaries.

13. Abbott's suggestion that the social sciences all face the same core intellectual dilemmas may be viewed by some as consistent with the need for greater interdisciplinary integration. On this and other points, Abbott's perspective might be mistaken as supporting the interdisciplinary agenda. However, he is quite clear on the need for disciplines on both logical and practical grounds (2001, 134–35).

14. Brint and his colleagues (2012) refer to these as "core fields," which they distinguish from "mass fields" and "niche" fields.

15. Creative writing programs increasingly are staffed by faculty with master of fine arts (MFA) degrees rather than doctoral degrees. This is a source of tension within English departments. In addition to MFA degrees, there are a number of other areas where English departments could seek new faculty members with degrees in other areas to staff various programs: education faculty could serve as instructors in composition classes, in remedial instruction classes, and in meeting the needs of non-English-speaking student; PhDs in film studies and other media could held to direct English-department based programs in these areas, and computer specialists could help to build digital media programs. If English departments were to hire substantial numbers of new faculty from diverse fields outside of English, the disciplinary status of English would begin to blur.

16. Disciplines operate on a national and sometimes on an international basis (see note 1). The emphasis here on department is in recognition of the fact that it is a crucial context for disciplinary authority, autonomy, and control of faculty appointments.

17. Bourdieu (1988) emphasizes the hierarchy of academic fields. Pay, prestige and, most importantly, cultural authority vary markedly across disciplines. In the French context that Bourdieu described, one could even predict the social origins of scholars based on their fields: those from elite families are more likely to be found on the faculties of law and medicine. There are no doubt differences in claims to scholarly status and rank that would complicate efforts to promote interdisciplinarity, yet it should be noted that in the US contexts, enrollments play a part as well. Coveted faculty positions and departmental resources are distributed in part based on student enrollments. As a result, some fields with dominant cultural authority, namely, physics, are hobbled by the expense of their research needs and the scarcity of students. English and history may be more prevalent despite the more contested status of their claims to scholarly authority. There are thus diverse sources of institutional strength that affect the size, power, and influence of different fields on a given university campus.

18. Because smaller schools are typically the ones most likely to combine departments, the representation of these fields looks somewhat better when the data are weighted by the number of students enrolled. As we have seen, less than half of schools offer anthropology degrees, but 77 percent of undergraduates are enrolled in schools with anthropology degrees. French degrees are also accessible to 77 percent of undergraduates, while biochemistry degrees are available in schools that enroll 49 percent of undergraduates. Eighty-four percent of students are enrolled in schools that offer physics degrees, compared with 72 percent for sociology.

19. In her brief historical overview of the development of specialized disciplines, Klein never exactly acknowledges their role in advancing knowledge. In his brief but insightful essay (2010), Weingart unfortunately does not actually credit the remarkable advances in knowledge in the 19th and especially the 20th century to disciplinary specialization. Taylor (2010), to his credit, acknowledges a brief "golden age" but claims that it has dissipated by 1970.

20. Turner (2000) emphasizes both contingency as well as recency in the emergence of disciplines.

21. In this section, data from a series of reports entitled *American Universities and Colleges*, published by the American Council on Education (1928–36), were examined. In the first three editions, published in 1928, 1932, and 1936, data on the number of faculty by department and rank were reported. The tabulations discussed here included data on full, associate, and assistant professors, but not instructors. The 1936 volume included data on 514 colleges and universities (teachers' colleges and normal schools are not included in this analysis of liberal arts departments). Of these, twenty-one, including Harvard and Penn, did not list the number of faculty in individual departments.

22. Weingart (2010) notes the internal differentiation of disciplines, which he attributes principally to the growth in their size and secondarily to external, or political, factors. However, he does not link this to the breadth of fields that have succeeded in becoming disciplines, and he does not consider the possibility that internal differentiation contributes to disciplines' dynamism.

23. This sketch is not meant to offer a comprehensive review of the intellectual history or even the early organizational establishment of sociology. More comprehensive histories can be found in Turner and Turner (1990) and Bernard and Bernard (1965 [1943]).

24. The name changed from American Sociological Society to American Sociological Association during the 1950s. The current name is used throughout for consistency. Department size in 1950 was estimated by tabulating ASA membership by department (American Sociological Society 1950). This technique probably understates department size to some degree, because not all faculty would have been members of the association. The 1950 Membership Directory lists sociology faculty in 438 US colleges and universities.

25. The growth in membership in the American Sociological Association ended suddenly in 1972 after three decades of steady and consistent growth, which illustrates the fact that social trends do not always gracefully follow the trajectory of logistic curves but can come to an end rather abruptly.

26. While some sociologists quietly suspect that fifty-three or more specialties is far too many, it is actually much fewer per capita than was the case at the fiftieth anniversary of *AJS*. If we take Shanas's (1945) list of ten fields as an indicator of the specialties of the field in 1945, then there were roughly 120 sociologists per specialty (the ASA membership in 1945 was 1,242). Today's fifty-three fields translates into roughly 265 members per specialty. As a result, one could argue that if sociology had one hundred specialties, each would still be more fully staffed than was the case in 1945.

27. These figures were culled in 2012 from the websites of the American Political Science Association, the American Chemical Society, the American Mathematics Society, and the American Economic Association. The URLs of these websites are included in the references.

28. The contrast between highly splintered undergraduate offerings for applied fields and broader offerings for liberal arts disciplines is developed in chapter 9, which addresses interdisciplinarity in connection with undergraduate education.

29. Metzger refers to this process "subject parturition." The discussion follows the logic of Metzer's distinctions but not his precise terminology

30. In his book, *The People's Choice* (1944), Lazarsfeld analyzed the factors shaping people's political decision making. Later, in an important book, Lazarsfeld and his coauthor Elihu Katz suggested that information was dissemination via channels including newspapers, radio, and the then new medium of television but was reinforced or confirmed as valid by trusted friends and associates who played the role of opinion leaders (Katz and Lazarsfeld 1955). Because surveys were collected on samples of individuals who did not know each other, public opinion surveys

were better designed for measuring the patterns of opinion than they were at tapping the role of social networks in the opinion formation process.

31. Before 1970, journalism rather than communication was listed as a major by the Department of Education, and sometimes journalism was reported as a branch of English. More detail on the number of degree recipients in various majors is provided in chapter 9.

32. For example, in 1965, the *College Blue Book* listed only a handful of PhD programs in communication; by 2009, sixty-five PhD programs in communications were established at research universities in the United States.

33. Figure 3.1 presents age comparisons at a single point in time. While longitudinal data would be preferable, time trends can be inferred from age differences.

34. Pfau's map of the field is more complex, as it includes nodes related to qualitative and quantitative research, historical and critical perspectives, and rhetorical analyses. The historical and rhetorical segments of communication research may be underrepresented in the Leydesdorff and Probst map because this research tends to appear in books and other outlets not fully captured by the Web of Science database.

Chapter Four

1. An earlier version of this chapter was presented at the August 2012 American Sociological Association meeting held in Denver, Colorado. Rebecca Henderson is a coauthor of this chapter.

2. A major discontinuity in Ulrich's journal counts occurred during 2011. At that time, a journal publishing a print copy and an electronic copy began to be counted as two separate journal entries rather than one. Consequently, the count of academic peer-reviewed journals jumped to fifty-three thousand. The analyses reported here were conducted before this change was introduced.

3. A limited literature has explored role of the Internet in promoting interdisciplinary communication (Weller 2011; Aimeur, Brassard, and Paquet 2005; Barjak 2005), while other studies have tracked journal growth (e.g., Mabe 2003). This analysis, however, represents the first systematic study of new interdisciplinary journals.

4. One solution is collaboration, which potentially brings specialized skills from different domains together to answer questions that rely on more than one set of knowledge. The growing prevalence of teamwork and coauthorship in many fields, documented in chapter 5, has generated interest in understanding what makes such collaborations work. The "Science of Team Science" Conference attempts to explore these issues (Northwestern University Clinical and Translational Sciences Institute [NUCATS] 2012).

5. This study (Nerad, Aanerud, and Cerny 2004) reports that 54 percent of respondents with PhD degrees in English were employed in tenured faculty positions ten to fourteen years later. This indicator in all likelihood overstates employment to some extent because one third of the sample pool did not respond to the questionnaire. If one makes the plausible assumption that those with tenured positions were more likely to respond, then the overall tenure rate is likely to be lower than that observed in the sample of respondents. On the other hand, the survey was based on the cohort that earned degrees during the 1983–85 period, which was a particularly difficult era for faculty hiring in general and hiring in the humanities in particular. See the valuable series of discipline-specific reports on doctoral degree employment produced by the University of Washington Center for Innovation and Research in Graduate Education (2012).

6. Abbott (2011) approaches this issue of information overload in the context of the history of research libraries. He suggests that librarians and research scholars reacted to the overwhelming volume of publications in different ways. Librarians attempted to systematize their holdings by expanding the number of indexes and by centralizing materials in the main university library, while researchers typically relied on less systematic search strategies that emphasized quality over comprehensiveness.

7. An assessment of periodical indices concludes that Ulrich's index is far more comprehensive than the main alternative, the Serials Directory (Bachand and Sawallis 2003).

8. Author's calculations based on the number of new journals included in the Ulrich database by decade. These figures represent net additions; in other words, they reflect newly created journals per decade that are still active. A small number of peer-reviewed journals cease publication in a given year. More analysis can be done on the timing of these terminations. For a long-term study of journal growth rates, see Mabe 2003.

9. The publication of the latest *Times Higher Education World University Rankings* (2012) gave new impetus to debates on how best to compare universities. A growing number of ranking systems compete with the Times rankings, but most place considerable emphasis on the volume of research and the publication rate of faculty.

10. A 50 percent sample of the largest fields was selected in order to make the coding process more manageable. The number of journals coded was four hundred. Results presented are weighted to reflect the sampling design.

11. In 82 percent of the journals classified as interdisciplinary, the journal description or mission statement made explicit reference to some variant of this term. The remainder of the cases mentioned multiple disciplines or clearly straddled disciplinary boundaries.

12. Ulrich's system includes three headings that are likely to include many interdisciplinary journals: Social Sciences Comprehensive, Humanities Comprehensive, and Sciences Comprehensive. Based on these three comprehensive groups, one can infer from Ulrich's classification system that approximately 5 percent of academic journals are interdisciplinary. The present analysis validates these three classifications as indeed interdisciplinary in orientation: twenty-four of the twenty-nine journals founded in 2008 in one of these three subject headings meets the definition of interdisciplinarity employed here. In other words, the Ulrich "comprehensive" classifications are interdisciplinary even if they represent only a subset of journals that cut across fields.

13. The URL for the home page for each of the journals discussed in this chapter is included in the references.

14. In some respects, this typology of interdisciplinarity parallels that developed by Lattuca (2001). "Disciplinary plus" journals resemble Lattuca's "informed disciplinarity." The sixth type of journal listed here, "theoretical interdisciplinarity," resembles her "transdisciplinarity" (she employs this term differently from most in this area). The mapping of her "synthetic" and "conceptual" categories to those employed here is not as clear. This study provides empirical support for some of her distinctions and provides an empirical estimate in one context of the prevalence of each type.

15. Specialists in this area will recall that there is a long history to the notion that some interdisciplinary fields are quite narrow. For example, Klein mentions a number of examples in her first book on this topic (1990, 43, 108). And Frickel's example of genetic toxicology (2004) would fit under the rubric of an area that is clearly interdisciplinary but also focused and specialized in nature. Kelly's (1996) usage of the term "narrow" is much wider than that employed here. Yet a

prominent theme in this literature equates interdisciplinarity with breadth and disciplines with depth a decline (Repko 2008, 322–23).

16. The distinction between theoretical advances and applied problem solving features prominently in Klein's typology of interdisciplinarities (2010b, 24–26).

17. These forty-four comparisons are based on thirty-three journals with eleven double counts, that is, rankings of a single journal in two comparison fields.

Chapter Five

1. The emphasis in this book is on organization forms rather than the goals of interdisciplinary research. In other words, the analysis presented here does not depend on any particular view of the ultimate ends of interdisciplinarity. The data presented below will be pertinent to diverse critiques of disciplines, including those summarized in chapter 2. A discussion of types of transdisciplinarity (drawing from Klein 2010b and other sources) can be found in chapter 7.

2. This emphasis on the degree of interchange or integration will no doubt disappoint aficionados but some simplification is necessary if the book is not going to be given over completely to a review of terminology.

3. Klein (2010b, 24–26) distinguishes among four types of transdisciplinarity. The main distinction is between intellectual synthesis and integrated problem solving. She also includes the category "critical interdisciplinarity" (see also Lattuca 2001). This distinction surfaces in many discussions of interdisciplinarity, as we have seen in the analysis of interdisciplinary journals in chapter 4. Klein also notes that interdisciplinarity is sometimes equated with transgressive or critical inquiry. The disciplines themselves are sometimes the target of critique. However, as Frickel and Gross (2005) show, insurgent intellectual movements most frequently occur within disciplines. Thus, the overlap between transgressive and interdisciplinary ideas is far from complete.

4. Klein acknowledges the movement of ideas between fields in her chapter on "borrowing" (1990, chapter 5). See chapter 2, note 4, for a discussion of Klein's account. When Kellert (2008) examines how the concept of "chaos"·was "borrowed" by disciplines across the university, the implication is that this case of diffusion represents the exception rather than the rule.

5. Menand's was one of eight entries in an online "Room for Debate" symposium addressing the question "Do Colleges Need French Departments?" As we have seen, a number of disciplines have become well ensconced in American universities, while other fields remain optional. The question of whether a college or a university "needs" a certain field of study speaks simultaneously to the legitimacy, centrality, and utility of disciplines and the legitimacy, goals, and values of the university. The threatened closure of a French department threatens to undermine French's claim to be an essential part of the liberal arts core, and thus risks the possibility that other schools will close their French departments as well.

6. Note that fields such as education, management, and business were classified by the NSF under the heading of "health and professional fields."

7. Porter and Rafols note that the "integration score" increased by only about 5 percent (actually increasing in two of the six fields), and most references drew on "neighboring" fields of research. They note that the growth in citations to other fields is mostly due to the increase in citations per paper and only secondarily due to increased diversity in the sources of citations. See also Abt (2007) for further information on the decline in single-authored papers.

8. For other maps of scientific fields, see Leydesdorff and Rafols (2009a); and Börner 2010.

9. Hargens refers to "foundational" papers as an "orienting reference list text," and thus does

not dismiss these citations as merely ceremonial. He documents variation in citation patterns across seven research specialties spanning the natural sciences, social sciences, and humanities.

10. While Rosenberg recommends more interdisciplinarity in a general way (147), his examples undercut the premise that disciplines stifle communication across fields.

11. The obvious exceptions are the high status natural science journals, *Science* and *Nature*.

12. These statistics were culled from the website of these publications and outlets, and their URLs are included in the references.

13. TED (which stands for Technology, Entertainment and Design) holds conferences and makes short presentations available online (TED: Ideas Worth Spreading, 2012). It has been estimated that the TED website cumulatively has generated over 500 million video views (Kessler 2011).

14. Personal communication from John Mark Ockerbloom, University of Pennsylvania Library Information Technology staff.

15. A title search of the Gale Research Centers Directory yielded 11,027 centers in the United States with the word "university" in the title. The list of research centers is likely to be imprecise because the boundary between a lab and other academic organizations and a research center is often not clear. A sample of research centers included in the Gale database used to produce figure 5.3 was checked against university websites, and the vast majority of these units were actually university-based research centers. Even allowing for the possibility of imprecision in these data, it seems safe to conclude that the number of university-based research centers probably exceeds ten thousand.

16. It is noteworthy that half of the faculty members surveyed who were not affiliated with research centers reported engagement in interdisciplinary research (Rhoten 2003, 4). In other words, while participation in centers increased the frequency of interdisciplinary work (from 51 to 60 percent), the background level of such research is remarkably high. This finding itself suggests that the charge of disciplinary isolation is overstated.

17. The data are drawn from the National Survey of Post-Secondary Faculty (NSOFP), which has been fielded periodically from 1988 through 2004. Jacobs (2004) summarizes some of these data.

Chapter Six

1. It might be objected that schools of education are not fully interdisciplinary in that divisions between specialties within the field remain prominent. As we have seen, specialization is ubiquitous, and it is likely that any issue-based interdisciplinary arrangement will yield to divisions that are organized by specialty in one manner or another.

2. Walters and Lareau (2009) represent something of an exception to the downbeat assessment of educational scholarship.

3. Lagemann makes just this point when she suggests that "educationists continued to churn our school surveys long after sociologists and anthropologists had begun to develop more nuanced approaches to community study" (2000, 233–34)."

4. This analysis does not directly test communication between disciplines but rather the flow of ideas into and out of an applied field, namely, education. This represents a good case for analysis since barriers to effective communication have been identified by leading scholars in the field.

5. The time lag associated with interdisciplinary citations is remarkably small, typically less than one year. It is also striking that there are a number of cases in which the pattern was reversed: namely, where interdisciplinary citations actually occurred faster than disciplinary cita-

tions. Out of fifteen disciplines in the natural sciences examined, Rinia and colleagues report eight where internal references appeared faster, usually by about one-half year; in four cases, internal and external references were about as old, and in three cases, external references were faster than internal ones.

6. Only three members of this list were based in schools of education: Herbert W. Marsh, Ann Leslie Brown, and Michael Pressley. Those based outside education were mostly psychologists (Albert Bandura, Jacob Cohen, Jean Piaget, Keith Stanovich, Robert J. Sternberg, and David Wechsler), along with one philosopher (John Dewey) and one sociologist (Pierre Bourdieu). Walters and Lareau also provide a list of the recipients of the American Educational Research Association's Distinguished Contributions to Research in Education Award. While naturally these awards recognize members to a greater degree than do the citation patterns, nonetheless fully fifteen of the forty-four of these awards were bestowed on scholars from fields other than education. Thus even the process of conferring the highest level of scholarly recognition is by no means closed in the area of education research.

7. Some researchers have questioned the accuracy of citations (Nicolaisen 2007), while others suggest that cross-disciplinary "borrowing" tends to result in the misunderstanding of the cited research (Klein 1990). Here the emphasis is on the timing of citations; their accuracy is not assessed. The analysis will emphasize early adopters, and there is reason to believe that early references to research are more informed and more accurate. The question of cross-disciplinary misunderstanding is more likely to be a matter of drawing selectively on the author's ideas, as Kellert's (2008) study of the reception of chaos theory across disciplines suggests.

8. Jacobs (2009) shows that Google Scholar captures a larger volume of citations than does the ISI Web of Knowledge, in part because it covers books as well as articles, and in part because it is more comprehensive with respect to the coverage of journals.

9. There are good reasons to believe that this understates the full extent of Piaget's influence. A longer version of this analysis that includes a larger set of examples is available in an expanded, online version of this chapter (Jacobs 2013b).

10. It should be noted that many newly proposed scientific findings are not immediately noticed or accepted, including some that are later celebrated. Examples of "premature" scholarly advances were compiled by Hook (2002), although the causes of delayed reception are not well understood.

11. A minority of references appear to be "ritualistic" or "symbolic" in nature. This tendency could inflate the number of references to the prominent books and papers discussed here. However, the findings of detailed investigations of bias and strategic behavior in citations are mixed (Nicolaisen 2007). Furthermore, most theories of bias in citations would point to disproportionate citations within disciplines. The evidence on the speed of interdisciplinary adoption is thus even more striking given the reasons to expect a preference for intradisciplinary references.

12. To obtain this result, the doctoral degree field of study for those with current teaching positions in education was calculated. Sarah Winslow was kind enough to provide this tabulation.

13. The early adoption of meta-analysis by educational researchers may be due to the prominent role of educational statisticians including Gene Glass and Larry Hedges. Glass (2000) recalls that he delivered one of the first papers on meta-analysis as a Presidential Address at the American Educational Research Association meetings in 1975.

14. The complaint is sometimes heard that these statistical packages facilitate the misuse of social statistics. Whatever the merits of this charge, the problem is not isolated to the field of

education. The evidence presented here focuses on the diffusion of ideas and techniques and does not attempt to assess the accuracy or appropriateness of their use.

Chapter Seven

1. For example, Moran (2010), quoted in chapter 5; Frodeman (2010), quoted below.

2. In his studies of priority disputes, Merton (1957) has shown that many important scientific discoveries were recorded by two or more scientists at nearly the same time. Disputes over priority may represent egotists doing battle, but the frequency of simultaneous discoveries is itself notable. One interpretation of this pattern is that certain discoveries are "ripe," that is, that the knowledge base and the techniques available at a given point in time make some discoveries likely to occur.

3. While perhaps one day models of complex systems will yield important insights, Silver (2012) suggests that many such models currently promise more than they can deliver. There are many other possible objections: (a) some relatively successful models (for example, in meteorology) do not depend on interdisciplinary measures; (b) formal models require measures of all systems components, which are often difficult to obtain on many social and cultural phenomenon. Newell (2010) seems to be using the notion of a complex system not in terms of formal models with detailed measures and complex equations, but rather in an informal or heuristic sense, especially when he suggests the applicability of this framework to the humanities.

4. Whitley (2000) maintains that the level of consensus in a scientific field depends on the distribution of resources. When there is dependence on a common resource, such as access to an extremely expensive particle accelerator, consensus tends to be higher. In other words, the level of scientific consensus is not a simple barometer of the breakdown of a scientific paradigm but also have field-specific components as well.

5. Turner (2000) makes the point that interdisciplinary programs need access to financial support, either via undergraduate enrollments or from other sources, to sustain themselves. The argument here is similar, but Turner emphasizes the operation of disciplines as employment cartels with relatively little consideration of their internal operations or their dynamic, intellectual value. In other words, Turner's approach suggests that we are stuck with disciplines, whereas the present analysis argues for their usefulness as well as their inevitability.

6. An examination of a sample of sixty of Brint's 383 colleges yielded no instances of separate interdisciplinary studies departments. However, twenty-four of these sixty schools offered some type of interdisciplinary degree.

7. The Interdisciplinary Studies Department at Wayne State University, which closed in 2007, was something on an anomaly. It was unique in having achieved departmental status but also in limiting program listings to the department's faculty members. Specifically, the interdisciplinary program in historical and cultural studies listed only the department's cultural scholars and not those in the English and history departments. The interdisciplinary programs in gerontology and business were more typical in that they borrowed courses and presumably faculty from relevant departments (Wayne State University 2012).

Chapter Eight

1. A longer version of this chapter, available online (Jacobs 2013c), which provides more detail on enrollment trends and the durability of American studies programs, and presents more fully the results of the multivariate analyses that examine the impact of American studies

programs on the creation of other programs such as African American studies and women's studies.

2. Klein (2005a), chapters 7 and 8; and Dubrow (2011), for additional analyses of American studies as an interdisciplinary field.

3. The intellectual profile of the field is based on articles appearing in the *American Quarterly*, a number of review articles (Spiller 1976; Wise 1979; Gleason 1984; Davis 1990; Zenderland 2006), collections (Maddox 1999; Krabbendam and Verheul 1999), essays debating the appropriate direction for the field, presidential addresses delivered to the American Studies Association, and interviews with six prominent American studies scholars. Data on student enrollment and degrees conferred were obtained from the National Center for Education Statistics. Program information was compiled from a number of sources, including published reports that appeared periodically in *American Quarterly* and, in more recent years, program information obtained from the *Directory of Graduate Programs in American Studies*, and the American Studies Association website. Comparative data on American studies, African American studies, and women's studies programs since 1970 were culled from various editions of *The College Blue Book*. Data compiled by Steve Brint on degree programs offered at US colleges and universities spanning the period 1971–2006 were also examined. Data on citations to articles in the *American Quarterly* were drawn from the Thompson ISI Citation indices. Dissertation abstracts were obtained from listings published in the *American Quarterly*. Data on attendance at American studies conferences was obtained from the American Studies Association.

4. I interviewed Richard Beeman, Walter Licht, Bruce Kuklick, Murray Murphey, Amy Kaplan, and Larry Griffin, along with a number of less formal interviews conducted at the 2010 American Studies Association meetings. All were generous with their time and insights. Their insights and knowledge help to provide context for this discussion, but they are typically not quoted to support particular points. These distinguished scholars are not accountable for whatever mistakes and misinterpretations remain.

5. For example, Murray Murphey, who chaired Penn's American Studies Program for many years, told me that in the 1950s, the introductory survey course in English at the University of Pennsylvania department was a two-semester course that only got as far as the fifteenth century by the end of first semester. This approach to English-language literature clearly deemphasized American writers, since American literature had not begun by 1600 American authors would have had to compete for a sliver of attention during the second semester.

6. During the 1970s, *The College Blue Book* reported American civilization and American studies programs separately. The popularity of the American civilization label declined sharply during the 1970s, with the number of programs featuring this title declining from eighty-nine in 1970 to twenty in 1979. By 1985, the *Blue Book* no longer separated American civilization from other American studies programs. With the increasingly critical stance that Americanists were taking to American culture, perhaps the term "studies" seemed more neutral and the term "civilization" seemed too grandiose to fit the times.

7. Program counts compiled by the American Studies Association (ASA) were published annually in the *American Quarterly* from the late 1960s through the late 1980s.

8. All degree and enrollment data were obtained from the Digest of Education Statistics (National Center for Education Statistics). American studies degrees were not reported separately before 1970.

9. The rapid of expansion of higher education during the 1960s and 1970s transformed colleges and universities from an elite into a mass phenomenon. This trend is discussed in chapter 9. The author's analysis of the HERI data from the period 1976–2006 (results not shown)

indicate that the majority of the trend toward a greater preoccupation with financial rather than moral or spiritual issues was due to changing values, and only a modest fraction was due to the changing demographics of undergraduates.

10. The presidents of the ASA during this period had diverse backgrounds, representing a broad range of institutions. The late 1990s and 2000s saw a series of African American, Hispanic, and Asian American scholars elected president (Mary Helen Washington, George Sanchez, and Stephen Sumida), following only the noted African American historian John Hope Franklin, who had served as ASA president in 1967.

11. The growth since the early 1990s has been due to the growing population of college students. In other words, American studies share of all bachelor's degrees received has been declining since the early 1990s and remains substantially below the level seen during the 1970s.

12. The ASA website in 2009 listed 179 programs including a number of African American and ethnic studies programs, while *The College Blue Book* lists 247 schools offering a bachelor's degree in American studies in 2007. Pinpointing program closures with complete precision is not possible with ASA data, since there was not perfect consistency in program counts from year to year. In particular, in some years, those administering the program surveys may have been stricter than in other years in removing nonresponding schools from the list of active programs. The *Blue Book* reports do not capture the decline during the 1980s as fully as do the data from the ASA, in all probability because small, nondegree programs are tracked by the latter data source but not the former. Unfortunately, the ASA annual surveys ended in the late 1980s, just when the sharp decline in programs was underway. Nonetheless, it seems clear from both data sources that the number of American studies programs peaked during the early 1980s, and declined by the early 1990s, followed by a slight rebound during the first decade of this century.

13. Data on departments and programs were obtained from the website of the American Studies Association, *Directory of Graduate Programs in American Studies*, 2008. http://www .theasa.net/publications/grad_programs/page/directory_of_graduate_programs.

14. Of these twenty-five PhD programs, seven are based in departments while the remainder are interdisciplinary programs without a departmental home.

15. These totals focus on American studies per se and do not include African American studies, women's studies, Chicano studies or liberal studies. They also do not include programs that offer a certificate in American studies along with a PhD in English or history, and do not include programs with "minor" concentrations in American studies as part of a PhD in other subject fields.

16. While these data are informative regarding the destinations of American studies PhDs, the ASA surveys are probably not an appropriate resource for estimating the academic employment rate of recent graduates, since some who were not currently employed in academia might go on to secure a position at a later date, not to mention the question of how to handle nonresponses.

17. This list does not include three other journals that focus on transatlantic studies or similar configurations of research in which American studies plays a prominent role.

18. A more detailed discussion of program survivability is available in Jacobs (2012c).

19. Despite great efforts at survey consistency, especially from the late 1960s through the 1980s when the surveys were administered at the University of Pennsylvania, there are notable jumps in the number of programs at some points in time that likely reflect how the survey was administered. For example, in some years, the sample frame was expanded to include new schools, while in other years, only existing programs were surveyed. In some years, the count included nonresponses, i.e., schools that had not responded to the survey, and in some years

nonresponders were jettisoned from the list. The surveys of programs were conducted every year during the 1970s and every other year during the 1980s. *The College Blue Book* data largely avoid these challenges, although they are limited to programs that offer some type of formal degree.

20. These counts do not include schools where there is only an ethnic studies program or an African American studies program. For example, the University of California at Chico has an American studies program as well as a multicultural and gender studies program, while California State University at Fresno offers an Asian studies program but no stand-alone American studies program. My count includes one program at Chico and none at Fresno, while others may consider there to be three programs at these two schools.

21. The data presented in figure 8.4 refer only to degree-granting programs. The number of schools with nondegree special-studies programs is considerably higher. By 1980, nearly three hundred American studies programs were tallied in the survey reported by the ASA. Stimpson (1986, 21) reports that 150 women's studies programs were established between 1970 and 1975, and the number had reached three hundred by 1980. Along these same lines, Rojas reports ninety-one African American studies programs established in the five years between 1968 and 1971 (see also Rojas 2007; Rooks 2006). These figures may not be strictly comparable, given that the defining elements of what constitutes a program may differ, but it is clear that American studies experienced more gradual long-term growth from the late 1930s through the mid-1980s, whereas African American studies and women's studies experienced much more explosive growth in a shorter period of time.

22. Rojas (2007) maintains that student protests played a significant role in the formation of African American studies programs.

23. The conventional measure of association used to measure this type of relationship is the odds ratio. The most attractive property of this measure is that it is marginal independent; that is, it allows us to track the association over time without worrying about the relative growth in the prevalence of different programs.

24. The full results including parameter estimates are available in Jacobs (2012c).

25. The control variables included in the analysis include total student enrollment, the percentage of international students, the percentage of nonwhite students, the per-student operating budget (logged), Baron's Imputed Selectivity Score, and the presence of masters and PhD programs. The analyses discussed in this section were conducted by Steven Brint and Kristopher Proctor.

26. Murphey (1979) and Verheul (1999) note that the early ties to anthropology were weaker than some suppose. Murphey notes that Perry Miller was not conversant with anthropology, and Verheul notes that Henry Nash Smith does not use the word "culture" even once in *Virgin Land*. Nevertheless, the connections to anthropology during the 1950s, especially the direct personal tie via Margaret Mead, are inescapable. See also Spiller 1960; also Janssens 1999.

27. Penn's American Civilization Department peaked in size during the 1980s with nine faculty members in the department, along with five affiliated colleagues from anthropology, history, and folklore. University of Pennsylvania Bulletin, various years, from 1953–94.

28. This analysis is unfortunately restricted to academic journal articles, and ignores books both as a source of scholarship and as a scholarly audience. It also ignores other types of influence, such as the inclusion on course syllabi or reviews appearing in the *New York Times* or the *New York Review of Books*. This is a particular weakness in the humanities because only a modest share of scholarship appears in journal articles. However limited in coverage, the analysis will nonetheless be informative for several reasons. First, this analysis draws on research that can

be clearly identified as representing American studies. If books were included as sources, the appropriateness of particular entries as representative of American studies scholarship could be debated. Second, it draws on the established classification of hundreds of journals by the ISI Citation system. Third, the analysis focuses on the reception of American studies research in journals in order to consider the range of influence rather than extent of influence. In other words, articles appearing in *AQ* may be more influential than the citation scores in journals indicate, but the journal analysis is nonetheless powerful in providing a picture of the fields to which the audience extends.

29. Another source of division is by nationality: American studies scholars based in countries outside the United States complain that US scholars do not pay sufficient attention to their scholarship (Rydell 1999).

30. James McGovern's 1968 paper explored expanding freedom for women in "manners and morals," while Edward M. Steel's 1970 paper on Mother Jones focused at least as much of issues of union organizing as on gender themes.

31. A comparison with Klein's assessment (2005a) is instructive. It is not surprising that Klein would carefully examine American studies, given her background in the humanities and American studies' prominence as an interdisciplinary field. She finds much to praise, but laments the fields' shortcomings, which she attributes to its failure to fully live up to the goals of interdisciplinarity. In her view, the myth and symbol approach is a "premature" synthesis, and the limitations of a more diverse vision of American culture are to be forgiven since the field is only three and a half decades old. Klein focuses her attention on the intellectual currents of the field and pays less attention to its organizational quandaries.

Chapter Nine

1. Klein (2005b) holds that integrative learning and interdisciplinary studies are not coextensive. She views the former as the broader category with the latter as subset.

2. Huber and Hutchings (2004) reach the same conclusion based on opposite reasoning. They suggest that the blurring of disciplinary boundaries in recent years is itself an argument for integrative learning.

3. Other questions in the HERI survey underscore the importance of financial considerations. In the list of reasons noted as very important in deciding to go to college, roughly 70 percent include "to be able to get a better job" and "to be able to make more money."

4. Zajonc emphasizes resonances between interactive views of physics and interactive ideas in humanities. This may be important in speaking to some prospective physics students, but this is likely not an issue for most students. Physics is a very small major at most institutions. Moreover, a fully integrative approach to liberal arts education would have to make substantive, philosophical, methodological, and spiritual connections among all classes, not just physics and the humanities.

5. In both of these cases, the data are based on faculty self-reports. If interdisciplinarity has become equated with good academic citizenship, then these data may be inflated due to "social desirability bias." However, the HERI faculty data reported high levels of interdisciplinary teaching during the 1990s when the social pressure to be interdisciplinary was likely much lower.

6. The placement of the visual and performance arts (placed here under the liberal arts rubric) has a significant effect on the relative size of these categories. These programs are often housed within schools of arts and sciences, but sometimes are grouped with other applied pro-

grams on campus. Without this sizable group of majors, the share of bachelor's degrees awarded to graduates in the liberal arts barely exceeds 30 percent.

7. The growth in preprofessional fields would have been even greater had the field of education not declined. The number of bachelor's degrees in education declined by half from 1970 through 1986, as education's share of these degrees fell from 21 percent in 1970 to 9 percent in 1986

8. This analysis draws on degree completion organized into a data set and generously made available by Steve Brint, Kristopher Proctor, and their colleagues. (See Brint et al. 2010 for more details.)

9. Portfolios that demonstrate a student's accomplishments during college have been suggested as a way to convey the substance of an interdisciplinary degree. The viability of this approach in the contemporary employment context remains to be demonstrated. Employers often receive hundreds of applications for positions, and online screening systems may not be designed to assess portfolios.

10. The assistance of Dr. Richard Pitt in accessing these statistics is greatly appreciated.

11. This analysis was conducted by Arum and Roska, whose generous assistance is greatly appreciated. They readily acknowledge the limits of the tests used in their study, and suggest that other assessment tools might capture more of what students are learning during the college years.

Chapter Ten

1. In an analysis of the search process in sociology, my colleagues and I followed the process through five stages: the initial advertisement; the search conducted (or cancelled); candidates interviewed; offer proffered; and the job being filled (Spalter-Roth, Jacobs, and Scelza 2009). In recent years in the field of sociology, 70 to 80 percent of the advertisements placed yielded a candidate being hired.

2. Some examples of the commitment to "cluster hiring" include Florida State University, which announced a plan to hire two hundred faculty in this manner over a five-year period, and the University of Iowa, which planned two clusters with ten faculty each (Florida State University 2006; Voelz 2011).

3. Pertinent data on enrollment trends were presented in chapter 9.

References

Abbott, Andrew. 1988. *The System of Professions*. Chicago: University of Chicago Press.

———. 2001. *Chaos of Disciplines*. Chicago: University of Chicago Press.

———. 2011. "Library Research Infrastructure for Humanistic and Social Science Scholarship in the Twentieth Century." Pp. 43–88 in Charles Camic, Neil Gross, and Michele Lamont, eds., *Social Knowledge in the Making*. Chicago: University of Chicago Press.

Abray, Jane. 1975. "Feminism in the French Revolution." *American Historical Review* 80(1):43–62.

Abt, Helmut A. 2007. "The Future of Single-Authored Papers." *Scientometrics* 73(3):353–58.

Aimeur, Esma, Gilles Brassard, and Sebastier Paquet. 2005. "Personal Knowledge Publishing: Fostering Interdisciplinary Communication." *Intelligent Systems, IEEE* 20(2):46–53.

Altbach, Philip, ed. 2011. *The Road to Academic Excellence*. Washington, DC: World Bank. http://issuu.com/world.bank.publications; http://issuu.com/world.bank.publications/docs/9780821388051.

Atkinson, Anthony B., Timothy Smeeding, and Lee Rainwater. 1995. *Income Distribution in the OECD Countries: Evidence from the Luxembourg Income Study*. Paris and Washington, DC: Organization for Economic Cooperation and Development.

American Association for the Advancement of Science. 2011. "What Is AAAS?" http://www.aaas/org/aboutaaas/Fkuhn.

American Association of University Professors. 2003. "Contingent Appointments and the Academic Profession." http://www.aaup.org/AAUP/pubsres/policydocs/contents/conting-stmt.htm.

American Chemical Society. 2012. Divisions by Class. http://portal.acs.org/portal/Public WebSite/membership/td/CNBP_022300.

American Council on Education. 1928–36. *American Universities and Colleges*. Washington, DC: American Council on Education.

———. 2007. *The American College President*. Washington, DC: American Council on Education.

American Economic Association. 2012. Journal of Economic Literature (JEL) Classification System. http://www.aeaweb.org/jel/jel_class_system.php.

American Mathematical Society. 2012. Mathematical Specialties. http://www.ams.org/about-us/contact/customers/specialties.

American Political Science Association. 2012. APSA Organized Sections. http://www.apsanet.org/content_4596.cfm?navID=172.

American Sociological Association. 2010. "Report of the ASA Task Force on Sociology and Criminology Programs." Washington, DC American Sociological Association.

———. 2011. Current Sections. http://www.asanet.org/sections/list.cfm. http://www.asanet.org/teaching/ASA%20TF%20%Report%20FINAL.pdf.

American Sociological Society. 1950. *Directory of Members of the American Sociological Society.* New York: New York University.

American Studies Association. ASA Surveys of Doctoral Recipients in American Studies, 1996–97 through 2003–4. http://www/theasa.net/resources/dissertations/doctoral_recipients_employment_and_career_survey/.

Arcidiacono, Peter. 2004. "Ability Sorting and the Returns to College Major." *Journal of Econometrics* 121(1–2):343–75.

Aronowitz, Stanley. 2000. *The Knowledge Factory: Dismantling the Corporate University and Creating the Higher Learning.* Boston: Beacon Press.

Arrow, Kenneth J. 1963. *Social Choice and Individual Values.* New York: Wiley.

Arum, Richard, and Josipa Roksa. 2011. *Academically Adrift: Limited Learning on College Campuses.* Chicago: University of Chicago Press.

Association of American College and Universities. 1998. Statement on Liberal Learning. http://www.aacu.org/about/liberal_learning.cfm.

———. 2002. Greater Expectations: A New Vision for Learning as a Nation Goes to College. National Panel Report. Washington, DC: Association of American Colleges and Universities. http://www.greaterexpectations.org.

Astin, Alexander W. 1977. *Four Critical Years.* San Francisco: Jossey-Bass.

Astin, A. W., K. C. Green, and W. S. Korn. 1985. *The American Freshman: Twenty Year Trends.* Los Angeles: UCLA Higher Education Research Institute.

Astin, Alexander, Lori J. Vogelgesang, Elaine K. Ikeda, and Jennifer A. Yee. 2000. *How Service Learning Affects Students.* Report issued by the Higher Education Research Institute, University of California, Los Angeles.

Attewell, Paul. 1987. "The Deskilling Controversy." *Work and Occupations* 14(3):323–46.

Avison, David, and Steve Elliot. 2006. "Scoping the Discipline of Information Systems." Pp. 3–18 in John Leslie King and Kalle Lyytinen, eds., *Information Systems: State of the Field.* Chichester: John Wiley and Sons.

Babbage, Charles. 1835. *On the Economy of Machinery and Manufacturers.* 4th ed. London: Charles Knight.

Bachand, Robert G., and Pamela P. Sawallis. 2003. "Accuracy in the Identification of Scholarly and Peer-Reviewed Journals and the Peer-Review Process across Disciplines." *Serials Librarian* 45(2):39–59.

Balsiger, Philip W. 2004. "Supradisciplinary Research Practices: History, Objectives and Rationale." *Futures* 36(4):407–21.

Bandura, Albert. 1973. *Aggression: A Social Learning Analysis.* Englewood Cliffs, NJ: Prentice Hall.

———, ed. 1995. *Self Efficacy in Changing Societies.* Cambridge: Cambridge University Press.

Barjak, Franz. 2005. "The Role of the Internet in Informal Scholarly Communication." *Journal of the American Society for Information Science and Technology* 57(10):1350–367.

Becher, Tony, and Paul R. Trowler. 2001. *Academic Tribes and Territories: Intellectual Enquiry and the Culture of Disciplines*. Buckingham: Open University Press.

Becker, Gary. 1964. *Human Capital: A Theoretical and Empirical Analysis, with Special Reference to Education*. New York: National Bureau of Economic Research, distributed by Columbia University Press.

———. 1991. *A Treatise on the Family*. Cambridge, MA: Harvard University Press.

Bell, Daniel. 1966. *The Reforming of General Education*. New York: Columbia University Press.

Benson, Lee. 1972. *Toward the Scientific Study of History: Selected Essays*. Philadelphia: Lippincott.

———.1978. "Changing Social Science to Change the World." *Social Science History* 2:427–41.

Berman, Elizabeth Popp. 2012. *Creating the Market University: How Academic Science Became an Economic Engine*. Princeton, NJ: Princeton University Press.

Bernard, Luther L., and Jessie Bernard. 1965 (1943). *Origins of American Sociology: The Social Science Movement in the United States*. New York: Russell & Russell.

Berrett, Dan. 2012. "Tenure across Borders." Inside Higher Ed, March 21. http://www.inside-highered.com/news/2011/07/22/usc_rewards_collaborative_and_interdisciplinary_work_among_faculty.

Bhaskar, Roy, Cheryl Frank, Karl G. Hoyer, Peter Naess, and Jenneth Parker, eds. 2010. *Interdisciplinarity and Climate Change: Transforming Knowledge and Practice for Our Global Future*. London: Routledge.

Biosemiotics. 2011. http://www.springer.com/life+sciences/evolutionary+%26+developmental+biology/journal/12304.

Bjurstrom, Andreas, and Merritt Polk. 2011. "Climate Change and Interdisciplinarity: A Co-Citation Analysis of IPCC Third Assessment Report." *Scientometrics* 87:525–50.

Boix Mansilla, V., and E. Duraising. 2007. "Targeted Assessment of Students' Interdisciplinary Work: An Empirically Grounded Framework Proposal." *Journal of Higher Education* 78(2):215–237.

Bogue, A. 1987. "Great Expectations and Secular Depreciation: The First Ten Years of the Social Science History Association." *Social Science History* 11:329–42.

Bok, Derek. 2003. *Universities in the Marketplace*. Princeton, NJ: Princeton University Press.

Borlaug, Norman E. 1970. "Nobel Lecture: The Green Revolution, Peace and Humanity." http://www.nobelprize.org/nobel_prizes/peace/laureates/1970/borlaug-lecture.html.

———. 1983. "Contributions of Conventional Plant Breeding to Food Production." *Science* 219(4585):689–93.

———. 2007. "Feeding a Hungry World" (Editorial). *Science* 318, no. 5849 (October 19):359.

Börner, Katy. 2010. *Atlas of Science: Visualizing What We Know*. Cambridge, MA: MIT Press.

Bourdieu, Pierre. 1984. *Distinction: A Social Critique of the Judgment of Taste*. Translated by Richard Nice. Cambridge, MA: Harvard Univesity Press.

———. 1988. *Homo Academicus*. Translated by Peter Collier. Stanford, CA: Stanford University Press.

Bourdieu, Pierre, and Jean-Claude Passeron. 1977. *Reproduction in Education, Culture and Society*. Translated by Richard Nice. London: Sage Publications.

Boxer, Marilyn Jacoby. 1998. *When Women Ask the Questions: Creating Women's Studies in America*. Baltimore, MD: Johns Hopkins University Press.

Bramwell, B., and B. Lane. 2005. "From Niche to General Relevance? Sustainable Tourism, Research and the Role of Tourism Journals." *Journal of Tourism Studies* 16(2):52–62.

Braun, Tibor, and Andras Schubert. 2007. "The Growth of Research on Inter- and Multidisciplinarity in Science and Social Science Papers, 1975–2006." *Scientometrics* 73(3):345–51.

Braverman, Harry. 1975. *Labor and Monopoly Capitalism*. New York: Monthly Review Press.

Brewer, G. D. 1999. "The Challenges of Interdisciplinarity." *Policy Sciences* 32:327–37.

Brint, Steve, Lori Turk-Bicakci, Kristopher Proctor, and Scott Patrick Murphy. 2008. *The College Catalog Study Database*. Riverside: University of California, Riverside.

———. 2009. "Expanding the Social Frame: The Growth and Distribution of Interdisciplinary Degree-Granting Programs in American Colleges and Universities, 1975–2000." *Review of Higher Education* 32:155–83.

Brint, Steven, Kristopher Proctor, Kerry Mulligan, Matthew B. Rotondi, and Robert A. Hanneman. 2012. "Declining Academic Fields in U.S. Four-Year Colleges and Universities, 1970–2006." *Journal of Higher Education* 83(4):582–613.

Brint Steven, Kristopher Proctor, Scott Patrick Murphy, Kerry Mulligan, Matthew B. Rotondi, and Robert A. Hanneman. 2010. "Who Are the Early Adopters? The Institutionalization of Academic Growth Fields in U.S. Four-Year Colleges and Universities, 1975–2005." *Higher Education* 61:563–85. http://www.springerlink.com/content/123x19237073tv14/.

Brouthers, Keith D., Ran Mudambi, and David M. Reed. 2012. "The Blockbuster Hypothesis: Influencing the Boundaries of Knowledge." *Scientometrics* 90:959–82.

Buckler, Julie A. 2004. "Towards a New Model of General Education at Harvard." http://www.lancs.ac.uk/ias/events/genera107/docs/interdisc/Interdisc-Buckler-Harvard.pdf.

Busch, Lawrence. 2008. "Nanotechnologies, Food, and Agriculture: Next Big Thing or Flash in the Pan?" *Agriculture and Human Values* 25(2):215–18.

Bryk, Anthony S., and Stephen W. Raudenbush. 1992. *Hierarchical Linear Models: Applications and Data Analysis Methods*. Newbury Park, CA: Sage

Calhoun, Craig, and Diana Rhoten. 2010. "Integrating the Social Sciences: Theoretical Knowledge, Methodological Tools and Practical Applications." Pp. 103–18 in Robert Frodeman, Robert, Julie Thompson Klein, and Carl Mitcham, eds. *2010 Oxford Handbook of Interdisciplinarity*. Oxford: Oxford University Press.

Callon, M., J. P. Courtial, and F. Laville. 1991. "Co-Word Analysis as a Tool for Describing the Network of Interactions between Basic and Technological Research: The Case of Polymer Chemistry." *Scientometrics* 22(1):155–205.

Campbell, Donald T. 1969. "Ethnocentrism of Disciplines and the Fish-Scale Model of Omniscience." Pp. 328–48 in Muzafer Sherif and Carolyn W. Sherif, eds., *Interdisciplinary Relationships in the Social Sciences*. Chicago: Aldine Press.

Candy, Philip C. 1991. *Self Direction for Lifelong Learning: A Comprehensive Guide to Theory and Practice*. San Francisco: Jossey Bass.

Case, Sue-Ellen. 2001. "Feminism and Performance: A Post-Disciplinary Couple." *Theatre Research International* 26:145–52.

China Academic Journals Full-Text Data. 2011. *Chinese Digital Library*. http://www.global.cnki.net/grid20/index.htm.

Chronicle of Higher Education. 2011. "About the Chronicle." http://chronicle.com/section/About-the-Chronicle/83.

Clay Mathematics Institute. 2012. "Clay Research Awards." http://www.claymath.org/research_award/.

Cohen, Jacob. 1977. *Statistical Power Analysis for the Social Sciences*. New York: Academic Press.

College Board. 2011. *The College Completion Agenda: 2011 Progress Report*. New York: College Board. http://completionagenda.collegeboard.org/reports.

Cole, Jonathan R. 2009. *The Great American University*. New York: Public Affairs.

Cole, S., and R. Cole. 1987. "Testing the Ortega Hypothesis: Milestone or Millstone?" *Scientometrics* 12(5–6):345–53.

Coleman, James. 1966. *Equality of Educational Opportunity*. Washington, DC: US Department of Health, Education, and Welfare, Office of Education.

———. 1988. "Social Capital in the Creation of Human Capital." *American Journal of Sociology* 94 (Supplement):S95–S120.

Collaborative Anthropologies. 2011. Home page. http://www.nebraskapress.unl.edu/product/Collaborative-Anthropologies,673970.aspx.

College Conference on Composition and Communication. 2011. Conference Program. http://www1.ncte.org/cccc/program.

Collins, Randall. 1999. *The Sociology of Philosophies: A Global Theory of Intellectual Change*. Cambridge, MA: Harvard University Press.

Crane, Diana. 1972. *Invisible Colleges: The Diffusion of Knowledge in Scientific Communities*. Chicago: University of Chicago Press.

———. 2010. "Cultural Sociology and Other Disciplines: Interdisciplinarity in the Cultural Sciences." *Sociological Compass* 4(3):169–79.

Cronbach, Lee J. 1951. "Coefficient Alpha and the Internal Structure of Tests." *Psychometrica* 16:297–334.

Cuéllar, Amanda D., and Michael E. Webber. 2010. "Wasted Food, Wasted Energy: The Embedded Energy in Food Waste in the United States." *Environmental Science and Technology* 44(16):6464–69.

Czerniak, Charlene M., William B. Weber Jr., Alexa Sandmann, and John Ahern. 1999. "A Literature Review of Science and Mathematics Integration." *School Science and Mathematics* 99(8):421–30.

Dauphinée, Dale, and Joseph B. Martin. 2000. "Breaking Down the Walls: Thoughts on the Scholarship of Integration." *Academic Medicine* 75(9):881–86.

Davis, Allen F. 1990. "The Politics of American Studies." *American Quarterly* 42(3):353–74.

Derrida Today. 2011. http://www.derridatoday.org/journal/

Desrochers, Donna M., and Jane V. Wellman. 2011. *Trends in College Spending, 1999–2009*. Delta Cost Project. Washington, DC: Lumina Foundation. http://deltacostproject.org/resources/pdf/Trends2011_Final_090711.pdf.

De Wit, Maarten, and Jacek Stankiewicz. 2006. "Changes in Surface Water Supply across Africa with Predicted Climate Change." *Science* 311(5769):1917–21.

Diabetic Hypoglycemia. 2011. Home page. http://hypodiab.com/.

DiMaggio, Paul J., and Walter W. Powell. 1983. "The Iron Cage Revisited: Institutional Isomorphism and Collective Rationality in Organizational Fields." *American Sociological Review* 48:147–60.

DiPrete, Thomas A. 1987. "The Upgrading and Downgrading of Occupations: Status Redefinition vs. Deskilling as Alternative Theories of Change. *Social Forces* 66:725–46.

"Dissertation Abstracts, 1999–2000." 2000. *American Quarterly* 52(4):808–34.

"Doctoral Dissertations in American Studies, 1989–1990." 1990. *American Quarterly* 42(4):692–711.

Dubrow, Joshua K. 2011. "Sociology and American Studies: A Case Study in the Limits of Interdisciplinarity." *American Sociologist*. Published online. http://www.springerlink.com/content/e35q3qr7j75j3802/fulltext.pdf.

Durkheim, Emile. 1984 (1892). *The Division of Labor in Society*. New York: Free Press.

Eastview Information Services. 2011. *China National Knowledge Infrastructure*. http://www
.eastview.com/Online/FAQ/FAQ_CNKI.aspx.

Eigenfactor. 2012. *Ranking and Mapping Scientific Knowledge*. http://www.eigenfactor.org/.

Eigenfactor Project. 2011. Http://www.eigenfactor.org/about.htm.

Epiphany. 2011. Home page. http://www.ius.edu.ba:8080/epiphany/index.php?journal=epipha
ny&page=index.

Ethnicity and Inequalities in Health and Social Care. 2011. http://www.emeraldinsight.com/
products/journals/journals.htm?id=eihsc.

Eyler, Janet, Dwight E. Giles Jr., and Alexander W. Astin. 1999. *Where's the Learning in Service-
Learning*. San Francisco: Jossey-Bass.

Faust, Drew Gilpin. 2011. "Year End Message." http://president.harvard.edu/speeches/index/
php.

Fink, L. Dee. 2003. *Creating Significant Learning Experiences*. San Francisco: Jossey Bass.

Fish, Stanley. 1989. "Being Interdisciplinary Is So Very Hard To Do." *Profession*, 15–22.

Florida, Richard. 2004. *The Rise of the Creative Class: And How It's Transforming Work, Leisure,
Community and Everyday Life*. New York: Basic Books.

Florida State University. 2006; "FSU to Hire 200 Academic Stars in Cluster Initiative." http://
www.fsu.edu/news/2006/09/01/cluster.hiring/.

Forman, Paul. 2012. "On the Historical Forms of Knowledge Production and Curation: Modernity Entailed Disciplinarity, Postmodernity Entails Antidisciplinarity." *Osiris* 27:56–97.

Frank, Roberta. 1988. "'Interdisciplinary': The First Half-Century." Pp. 91–101 in E. G. Stanley
and T. F. Hoad, eds., *Words: For Robert Burchfield's Sixty-Fifth Birthday*. Cambridge: D. S.
Brewer.

Franzoni, Chiara, Giuseppe Scellato, and Paula Stephan. 2012. "Foreign Born Scientists: Mobility Patterns for Sixteen Countries." National Bureau of Economic Research Working Paper 18067. Cambridge, MA: National Bureau of Economic Research. http://www.nber.org/
papers/w18067.

Freeman, Richard. 1976. *The Overeducated American*. New York: Academic Press.

Frickel, Scott. 2004. *Chemical Consequences: Environmental Mutagens, Scientist Activism, and the
Rise of Genetic Toxicology*. Piscataway, NJ: Rutgers University Press.

Frickel, Scott, and Neil Gross. 2005. "A General Theory of Scientific/Intellectual Movements."
American Sociological Review 70:204–24.

Friedman, R. S., and R. C. Friedman. 1982. *The Role of University Organized Research Units in
Academic Science*. Springfield, VA: National Technical Information Service.

Frodeman, Robert. 2010. "Introduction." Pp. xxix–xxxix in Robert Frodeman, Julie Thompson Klein, and Carl Mitcham, eds. *Oxford Handbook of Interdisciplinarity*. Oxford: Oxford
University Press .

Frodeman, Robert, Julie Thompson Klein, and Carl Mitcham, eds., 2010. *Oxford Handbook of
Interdisciplinarity*. Oxford: Oxford University Press.

Funtowicz, S. O., and Jerome R. Ravetz. 1993. "Science for the Post-Normal Age." *Futures*
25(7):739–55.

Gale Cengage Learning. 2008. *Research Centers Directory*. 23rd Edition. http://www.gale
.cengage.com/.

———. 2009. *The College Blue Book, 1970–2009*. www.gale.cengage.com.

———. 2012. *Research Centers Directory*. 42nd ed. www.gale.cengage.com.

Geiger, Robert. 2006. "Demography and the Curriculum: The Humanities in American Higher
Education from the 1950s through the 1980s." Pp. 50–83 in David A. Hollinger, ed., *The*

Humanities and the Dynamics of Inclusion since World War II. Baltimore: Johns Hopkins University Press.

Geiger, Roger L., and Creso M. Sa. 2009. *Tapping the Riches of Science.* Cambridge, MA: Harvard University Press.

Gibbons, Michael, Camille Limoges, Helga Nowotny, Simon Schwartzman, Peter Scott, and Martin Trow. 1994. *The New Production of Knowledge: The Dynamics of Science and Research in Contemporary Societies.* London: Sage.

Gieryn, Thomas F. 1983. "Boundary-Work and the Demarcation of Science from Non-Science: Strains and Interests in Professional Ideology of Scientists." *American Sociological Review* 48:781–95.

———. 1999. *Cultural Boundaries of Science: Credibility on the Line.* Chicago: University of Chicago Press.

Gilbert, Juan E. 2008. "Silos of Academe Thwart Diversity on Campuses." *Chronicle of Higher Education* 55, no. 5 (September 26):B45.

Ginsberg, Alice, ed. 2008. *The Evolution of American Women's Studies.* New York: Palgrave MacMillan.

Glass, Gene V. 2000. "Meta-Analysis at 25." Online working paper, College of Education, Arizona State University. http://www.gvglass.info/papers/meta25.html.

Gleason, Philip. 1984. "World War II and the Development of American Studies." *American Quarterly* 36(3):343–58.

Gmur, Markus. 2003. "Co-Citation Analysis and the Search for Invisible Colleges: A Methodological Evaluation." *Scientometrics* 57(1):27–57.

Goffman, Erving. 1961. *Asylums: Essays on the Social Situation of Mental Patients and Other Inmates.* New York: Doubleday Anchor.

Golding, Clinton. 2009. Integrating the Disciplines: Successful Interdisciplinary Subjects. Melbourne: Centre for the Study of Higher Education. http://www.cshe.unimelb.edu.au/.

Graff, Gerald. 1987. *Professing Literature: An Institutional History.* Chicago: University of Chicago Press.

Graff, Harvey J. 2001. "The Shock of the 'New Histories': Social Science Histories and Historical Literacies." *Social Science History* 25:483–534.

Griffin, Larry J., and Maria Tempenis. 2002. "Class Multiculturalism and the American Quarterly." *American Quarterly* 54(1):67–99.

Griffin, Larry J., and Robert A. Gross. 1999. "American Studies' Two Cultures: Social Science, Humanities, and the Study of America." Pp. 116–32 in Hans Krabbendam and Jaap Verheul, eds., *Through the Cultural Looking Glass: American Studies in Transcultural Perspective.* Amsterdam: VU Uitgeveri.

Greenwood, Ernest. 1957. "Attributes of a Profession." *Social Work* 2:45–55.

Gross, Neil, and Solon Simmons. 2008. Personal communication.

Gurin, Patricia, Eric L. Dey, Sylvia Hurtado, and Gerald Gurin. 2002. "Diversity and Higher Education: Theory and Impact on Educational Outcomes." *Harvard Educational Review* 72(3):330–67.

Guston, David H. 2000. *Between Science and Politics: Assuring the Integrity and Productivity of Research.* New York: Cambridge University Press.

Guy-Sheftall, Beverly. 2009. "Forty Years of Women's Studies." *Ms. Magazine Online.* Spring edition. http://www.msmagazine.com/womensstudies/fourtyyears.asp.

Hagstrom, Warren O. 1975. *The Scientific Community.* Carbondale and Edwardsville: Southern Illinois University Press.

Hargens, Lowell L. 2000. "Using the Literature: Reference Networks, Reference Contexts, and the Social Structure of Scholarship." *American Sociological Review* 65(6):846–65.

Harrison, K. David. 2007. *When Languages Die.* New York: Oxford University Press.

Hedges, Larry V., and Ingram Olkin. 1992. *Statistical Methods for Meta-Analysis.* Orlando, FL: Academic Press.

Herbst, Susan. 2008. "Disciplines, Intersections and the Future of Communications Research." *Journal of Communication* 58:603–14.

Heritage & Society. http://www.lcoastpress.com/journal.php?id=7.

Higher Education Research Institute (HERI). 1967–2009. *College Freshman: National Norms.* Los Angeles: Higher Education Research Institute (UCLA).

Holmes, Richard. 2011. "Despite Ranking Changes, Questions Persist." World University News. Number 193, October 15. http://www.universityworldnews.com/article.php?story=2011101420085967

Hook, Ernest B., ed. 2002. *Prematurity in Scientific Discovery.* Berkeley: University of California Press.

Hubenthal, Ursula. 1994. "Interdisciplinary Thought." *Issues in Integrative Studies* 12:55–75.

Huber, Mary Taylor, and Pat Hutchings. 2004. "Integrative Learning: Mapping the Terrain." Washington, DC: Association of American Colleges and Universities. http://ctl.laguardia.edu/conference05/pdf/Mapping_Terrain.pdf.

Ikenberry, Stanley O., and Recee C. Friedman. 1972. *Beyond Academic Departments: The Story of Institutes and Centers.* San Francisco, CA: Jossey-Bass.

Inside Higher Education. 2010. "As the Crow Flies: Arizona State University Has Serious Problems, and That's Just the Way That Michael Crow Wants It." July 15. http://www.insidehighered.com/news/2010/07/16/crow.

Institute for Translational Medicine and Therapeutics, University of Pennsylvania. 2011. http://www.itmat.upenn.edu/about.shtml.

International Journal of Research and Review. 2011. Home page. http://journalofresearchandreview.books.officelive.com/default.aspx.

International Journal of Society Systems Science. 2011. Home page. http://www.inderscience.com/browse/index.php?journalCODE=ijsss.

Jacobs, Jerry A. 2004. "The Faculty Time Divide: 2003 Presidential Address, Eastern Sociological Society." *Sociological Forum* 19(1):1–27.

———. 2009. "Where Credit Is Due: Assessing the Visibility of Articles Published in *Gender and Society* with Google Scholar." *Gender and Society* 26(3):817–32.

———. 2011. "Journal Rankings in Sociology: Using the H Index with Google Scholar." Population Studies Center, University of Pennsylvania, PSC Working Paper Series, PSC 11–05. Accessible via Penn Scholarly Commons. http://repository.upenn.edu/psc_working_papers/29.

———. 2013a. "The Contribution of Sociology to the Emergence of Applied and Pre-Professional College Majors." Population Studies Center, University of Pennsylvania, PSC Working Paper Series. Accessible via Penn Scholarly Commons.

———. 2013b. "Receptivity Curves: Educational Research and the Flow of Ideas; Expanded Version." Population Studies Center, University of Pennsylvania, PSC Working Paper Series. Accessible via Penn Scholarly Commons.

———. 2013c. "American Studies: A Case Study of an Interdisciplinary Field." Population Studies Center, University of Pennsylvania, PSC Working Paper Series. Accessible via Penn Scholarly Commons.

Jacobs, Jerry A., and Scott Frickel. 2009. "Interdisciplinarity: A Critical Assessment." *Annual Review of Sociology* 35:43–66. http://arjournals.annualreviews.org/eprint/yyThexc9vmVNN4 DkFjKC/full/10.1146/annurev-soc-070308-115954.

Jacobs, Jerry A., and Sarah Winslow. 2004. "The Academic Life Course, Time Pressures and Gender Inequality." *Community, Work and Family* 7(2):143–61.

Janssens, Ruud. 1999. "American Studies as Exceptionalism: Comparing the Early Years of American Studies, Japanese Studies and Area Studies." Pp. 104–15 in Hans Krabbendam and Jaap Verheul, eds., *Through the Cultural Looking Glass: American Studies in Transcultural Perspective*. Amsterdam: Vu University Press.

Jonsson, Jan O. 1998. "Class and the Changing Nature of Work: Testing Hypotheses of Deskilling and Convergence among Swedish Employees." *Work, Employment and Society* 12(4):603–33.

Journal of Cultural Economy. 2011. http://www.tandf.co.uk/journals/RJCE.

Journal of Innate Immunity. 2011. http://content.karger.com/ProdukteDB/produkte.asp?Aktion =JournalHome&ProduktNr=234234.

Journal of the North Atlantic (JONA). 2011. http://www.eaglehill.us/programs/journals/jona/ JONAflyer.pdf

Kaplan, Amy. 2004. "Violent Belongings and the Question of Empire Today." Presidential Address to the American Studies Association, Hartford, Connecticut, October 17, 2003. *American Quarterly* 56(1):1–18.

Kantrowitz, Mark. 2010. "What Is Gainful Employment? What Is Affordable Debt?" http:// www.americasfocus.com/articles/03012010finaidgainfulemployment.pdf.

Kardashian, Kirk. 2011. "Four More Years." *Tuck at Dartmouth News*. http://www.tuck.dart mouth.edu/news/articles/four-more-years/.

Katz, Elihu, and Paul F. Lazarsfeld. 1955. *Personal Influence: The Part Played by People in the Flow of Mass Communications*. New York: Free Press.

Kellert, Stephen H. 2008. *Borrowed Knowledge: Chaos Theory and the Challenge of Learning across Disciplines*. Chicago: University of Chicago Press.

Kelley, Mary. 1999. "Commentary on Barbara Welter, the Cult of True Womanhood: 1820–1860." Pp. 67–70 in Lucy Maddox, ed., *Locating American Studies: The Evolution of a Discipline*. Baltimore: Johns Hopkins University Press.

Kelly, James S. 1996. "Wide and Narrow Interdisciplinarity." *Journal of Education* 45(2):95–113.

Kerber, Linda K. 1989. "Diversity and the Transformation of American Studies." *American Quarterly* 41(3):415–31.

Kessler, Sarah. 2011. "With 500 Million Views, TED Talks Provides Hope for Intelligent Videos." *Mashable Social Media*. http://www.mashable.com/2011/06/27/ted-anniversary.

Klein, Julie Thompson. 1990. *Interdisciplinarity: History, Theory, and Practice*. Detroit: Wayne University Press.

———. 1996. *Crossing Boundaries: Knowledge, Disciplinarities, and Interdisciplinarities*. Charlottesville: University of Virginia Press.

———. 2005a. *Humanities, Culture and Interdisciplinarity: The Changing American Academy*. Albany: State University of New York Press.

———. 2005b. "Interdisciplinary Learning and Integrative Studies." *Peer Review* (Summer/ Fall):8–10.

———. 2010a. *Creating Interdisciplinary Campus Cultures: A Model for Strength and Sustainability*. San Francisco: Jossey-Bass.

————. 2010b. "A Taxonomy of Interdisciplinarity." Pp. 15–30 in Robert Frodeman, Julie Thompson Klein, and Carl Mitcham, eds., *Oxford Handbook of Interdisciplinarity*. Oxford: Oxford University Press.

Knorr-Cetina, Karin. 1999. *Epistemic Cultures: How the Sciences Make Knowledge*. Cambridge, MA: Harvard University Press.

Krabbendam, Hans, and Jaap Verheul, eds. 1999. *Through the Cultural Looking Glass: American Studies in Transcultural Perspective*. Amsterdam: Vu University Press.

Krishnan, Armin. 2009. *What Are Academic Disciplines? Some Observations on the Disciplinarity vs. Interdisciplinarity Debate*. University of Southampton. National Centre for Research Methods Working Paper Series 3/09.

Krohn, Wolfgang. 2010. "Interdisciplinary Cases and Disciplinary Knowledge." Pp. 31–58 in Robert Frodeman, Julie Thompson Klein, and Carl Mitcham, eds. *2010 Oxford Handbook of Interdisciplinarity*. Oxford: Oxford University Press.

Kuhn, Thomas. 1996 (1962). *The Structure of Scientific Revolutions*. Chicago: University of Chicago Press.

Kuklick, Bruce. 1972. "Myth and Symbol in American Studies." *American Quarterly* 24(4): 435–50.

Labaree, David F. 2004. *The Trouble with Ed Schools*. New Haven, CT: Yale University Press.

Lagemann, Ellen C. 2000. *An Elusive Science: The Troubling History of Education Research*. Chicago: University of Chicago Press.

Lamont, Michele. 2009. *How Professors Think: Inside the Curious World of Academic Judgment*. Cambridge, MA: Harvard University Press.

Lamont, Michele, and Virag Molnar. 2002. "The Study of Boundaries in the Social Sciences." *Annual Review of Sociology* 28:167–95.

Larson, Magali Sarfatti. 1977. *The Rise of Professionalism: A Sociological Analysis*. Berkeley: University of California Press.

————. 1993. *Behind the Postmodern Facade: Architectural Change in Late Twentieth-Century America*. Berkeley: University of California Press.

Latour, Bruno. 1987. *Science in Action: How to Follow Scientists and Engineers through Society*. Cambridge, MA: Harvard University Press.

Latour, Bruno, and Steven Woolgar. 1986 (1979). *Laboratory Life: The Construction of Scientific Facts*. Princeton, NJ: Princeton University Press.

Lattuca, Lisa R. 2001. *Creating Interdisciplinarity: Interdisciplinary Research and Teaching among College and University Faculty*. Nashville, TN: Vanderbilt University.

Lazarsfeld, Paul F. 1944. *The People's Choice: How the Voter Makes Up His Mind in a Presidential Campaign*. New York: Duell, Sloan and Pearce.

Levitt, Jonathan M., and Mike Thelwall. 2008. "Is Multi-Disciplinary Research More Cited? A Macro-Level Study." http://cba.scit.wlv.ac.uk/~cm1993/papers/multidisciplinary_pre print.doc

Leydesdorff, Loet, and Carole Probst. 2009. "The Delineation of an Interdisciplinary Specialty in Terms of a Journal Set: The Case of Communication Studies." *Journal of the American Society for Information Science and Technology* 60(8):1709–18.

Leydesdorff, Loet, and Ismael Rafols. 2009. "A Global Map of Science Based on ISI Subject Categories." *Journal of the American Society for Information Science and Technology* 60(2):348–62.

Liu, Alan. 2008. *Local Transcendence: Essays on Postmodern Historicism and the Database*. Chicago: University of Chicago Press.

Lohmann, Larry. 2006. "Carbon Trading: A Critical Conversation on Climate Change, Privatisation and Power." Pp. 4–359 in *Development Dialogue*. Vol. 48. Dorset: Corner House.

Mabe, Michael A. 2003. "The Growth and Number of Journals." *Serials* 16(2):191–97.

———. 2009. "Scholarly Publishing." *European Review* 17(1):3–22.

Mack, Raymond W. 1969. "Theoretical and Substantive Biases in Sociological Research." Pp. 52–64 in Muzafer Sherif and Carolyn Sherif, eds., *Interdisciplinary Relationships in the Social Sciences*. Chicago: Aldine Press.

Maddox, Lucy, ed. 1999. *Locating American Studies: The Evolution of a Discipline*. Baltimore: Johns Hopkins University Press.

Marine Genomics. 2011. Home page. http://www.elsevier.com/wps/find/journaldescription .cws_home/713752/description.

Martin, Robert E. 2011. *The College Cost Disease: Higher Cost and Lower Quality*. Northampton, MA: Edward Elgar.

Marx, Leo. 1964. *The Machine in the Garden*. New York: Oxford University Press.

Massachusetts Institute of Technology. 2011. *The Third Revolution: The Convergence of the Life Sciences, Physical Sciences and Engineering*. Washington, DC: Massachusetts Institute of Technology. http://web.mit.edu/dc/Policy/MIT%20White%20Paper%20on%20Convergence .pdf.

McDowell, Tremaine. 1948. *American Studies*. Minneapolis: University of Minnesota Press.

McGovern, James R. 1968. "The American Woman's Pre–World War I Freedom in Manners and Morals." *Journal of American History* 55(1):315–33.

McKeown, Thomas. 1976. *The Modern Rise of Population*. New York: Academic Press.

Menand, Louis. 2001. "Undisciplined." *Wilson Quarterly* 25(4):51–59.

———. 2010a. *The Marketplace of Ideas: Reform and Resistance in the American University*. New York: W. W. Norton.

———. 2010b. New York Times Online (Room for Debate). October 18. http://www.nytimes .com/roomfordebate/2010/10/17/do-colleges-need-french-departments/the-point-of -education.

Merton, Robert K. 1957. "Priorities in Scientific Discovery." *American Sociological Review* 22(6):635–59.

———. 1973. *The Sociology of Science: Theoretical and Empirical Investigations*. Chicago: University of Chicago Press.

Metzger, Walter P. 1987. "The Academic Profession in the United States." Pp. 123–208 in Burton Clark, ed., *The Academic Profession: National Disciplinary and Institutional Settings*. Berkeley: University of California Press.

Meyer, M., and O. Persson. 1998. "Nanotechnology—Interdisciplinarity, Patterns of Collaboration and Differences in Application." *Scientometrics* 42(2):195–205.

Milgram, Stanley. 1969. "Interdisciplinary Thinking and the Small World Problem." Pp. 103–20 in Muzafer Sherif and Carolyn W. Sherif, eds., *Interdisciplinary Relationships in the Social Sciences*. Chicago: Aldine Press.

Miller, Perry. 1939. *The New England Mind (Volume I): The Seventeenth Century*. New York: MacMillan.

———. 1953. *The New England Mind (Volume 2): From Colony to Province*. Cambridge, MA: Harvard University Press.

Misra, Joya, Abby Templer, and Jennifer Lundquist. 2012. "Gender, Work Time, and Care Responsibilities among Faculty." *Sociological Forum* 29(2):300–323.

Mommsen, Wolfgang J. 1987. "The Academic Profession in the Federal Republic of Germany."

Pp. 60–92 in Burton R. Clark, ed., *The Academic Profession: National, Disciplinary, and Institutional Settings.* Berkeley: University of California Press.

Moody, James, and Ryan Light. 2006. "A View from Above: The Evolving Sociological Landscape." *American Sociologist* 37(2):67–86.

Moody, James, Ryan Light, Jon Coleman, and Erin Leahy. 2012. "Scientific Integration in Sociology." Paper presented at the American Sociological Association Meetings, August, Denver, CO.

Moran, Joe. 2010. *Interdisciplinarity (The New Critical Idiom).* 2nd ed. New York: Routledge.

Murphey, Murray G. 1979. "American Civilization in Retrospect." *American Quarterly* 31(3):402–6.

Myles, John. 1988. "The Expanding Middle: Some Canadian Evidence on the Deskilling Debate." *Canadian Review of Sociology* 25(3):335–64.

National Academy of Sciences. 2004. *Facilitating Interdisciplinary Research.* Washington, DC: US Government Printing Office.

National Center for Education Statistics. 1972–2009. *Digest of Education Statistics.* Washington: US Government Printing Office.

———. 2011. *National Study of Postsecondary Faculty: Overview.* http://nces.ed.gov/surveys/nsopf/.

National Opinion Research Center. 2011. "General Social Survey." http://www.norc.uchicago.edu/GSS+Website/.

National Public Radio. 2011. "About Science Friday." http://www.sciencefriday.com/about/sponsor.

National Science Foundation. National Center for Science and Engineering Statistics. 2008. *Data Tables 2008.* http://www.ns.gov/statistics/bsf10309/content.cfm?pub=3996id-8.

National Service Learning Clearinghouse. 2012. http://www.servicelearning.org/.

Nature. 2011. Home page. http://www.nature.com/nature/index.html.

Neal, Anamary. 2011. "NSF Graduate Fellowship Tips." http://people.cs.vt.edu/leal/wordpress/articles/nsf-graduate-fellowship-tips.

Nerad, Maresi, Rebecca Aanerud, and Joseph Cerny. 2004. "So You Want to Become a Professor! Lessons from the *PhDs—Ten Years Later* Study." Pp. 137–58 in Donald H. Wulff, Ann Austin, and associates, eds., *Paths to the Professoriate: Strategies for Enriching the Preparation of Future Faculty.* San Francisco: Jossey-Bass. http://depts.washington.edu/cirgeweb/c/publications/351/.

Network of Transdisciplinary Research. 2011. "About." http://www.transdisciplinarity.ch/e/Transdisciplinarity/.

New York Review of Books. 2001. "About." http://www.nybooks,com/about/.

New York Times. 2010. *"Did You Know."* http://www.nytco.com/pdf/DidYouKnow_March2010_Final.pdf.

Newell, William H. 2001. "A Theory of Integrative Studies." *Issues in Integrative Studies* 19:1–25.

———. 2010. "Educating for a Complex World: Integrative Learning and Interdisciplinary Studies." *Liberal Education* 96:4.

Nicolaisen, Jeppe. 2007. "Citation Analysis." *Annual Review of Information Science and Technology* 41:609–41.

North, Stephen M. 1984. "The Idea of a Writing Center." *College English* 46(5):433–46.

Northwestern University Clinical and Translational Sciences Institute (NUCATS). 2012. "Annual International Science of Team Science Conference." http://www.scienceofteamscience.org/.

Nussbaum, Martha C. 1997. *Cultivating Humanity: A Classical Defense of Reform in Liberal Education*. Cambridge, MA: Harvard University Press.

Olson, Eric M., Orville C. Walker Jr., Robert W. Ruekerf, and Joseph M. Bonnerd. 2001. "Patterns of Cooperation during New Product Development among Marketing, Operations and R&D: Implications for Project Performance." *Journal of Product Innovation* 18(4):258–71.

Open Enzyme Inhibition Journal. 2011. http://www.benthamscience.com/open/toeij/.

Open Sociology Journal. 2011. Home page. http://www.benthamscience.com/open/tosocij/.

Oxidative Medicine and Cellular Longevity. 2011. http://www.hindawi.com/journals/oximed/.

Palmer, Parker J., and Arthur Zajonc. 2010. *The Heart of Higher Education: A Call to Renewal*. San Francisco: Jossey Bass.

Parrington, Vernon Louis. 1927. *Main Currents in American Thought*. New York: Harcourt, Brace and World.

Pennsylvania State University. 2011. "Homeland Security Initiative: Research Centers, Institutes and Labs." http://homelandsecurity.psu.edu/discovery/centers/index.html.

Petit, J. R., J. Jouzel, D. Raynaud, N. I. Barkov, J. M. Barnola et al. 1999. "Climate and Atmospheric History of the Past 420,000 Years from the Vostok Ice Core, Antarctica." *Nature* 399(3):429–36.

Pfau, Michael. 2008. "Epistemological and Disciplinary Intersections." *Journal of Communication* 58(4):597–602.

Philadelphia Business Journal. 2011. "Penn's $370 Million Research Center." May 3. http://assets.bizjournals.com/philadelphia/blog/john-george/2011/05/penn-healths-370m-research-center.html.

Piaget, Jean. 1952a. *The Origins of Intelligence in Children*. New York: International Universities Press.

———. 1952b. *Play, Dreams and Imitation in Childhood*. Translated by C. Gattegno and F. M. Hodgson. New York: Norton.

———. 1954. *The Construction of Reality in the Child*. Translated by Margaret Cook. New York: Basic Books.

Pieters, Rik, and Hans Baumgartner. 2002. "Who Talks to Whom? Intra- and Interdisciplinary Communication of Economics Journals." *Journal of Economic Literature* 40:483–509.

Pooley, Jefferson, and Elihi Katz. 2008. "Further Notes on Why American Sociology Abandoned Mass Communication Research." *Journal of Communication* 58(4):767–86.

Popp, Trey. 2008. "Proof of Concept." *Pennsylvania Gazette*, September/October. http://www.upenn.edu/gazette/0908/feature1.html.

Porter, Alan, and Ismael Rafols. 2009. "Is Science Becoming More Interdisciplinary? Measuring and Mapping Six Research Fields over Time." *Scientometrics* 81(3):719–45.

Posner, Richard. 1972. *Economic Analysis of Law*. Boston: Little, Brown.

Preston, Samuel H. 1975. "The Changing Relationship between Mortality and Economic Development." *Population Studies* 29:231–48.

Price, Derek J. De Solla. 1963. *Little Science, Big Science*. New York: Columbia University Press.

Prosser, D. C. 2004. "The Next Information Revolution: How Open Access Repositories and Journals Will Transform Scholarly Communications." *Liber* Quarterly 14(1):23–36. http://hdl.handle.net/10760/4732.

Radway, Janice. 1999. "What's in a Name? Presidential Address to the American Studies Association, November 20, 1998." *American Quarterly* 51(1):1–32.

Rahmstorf, S. 2002. "Ocean Circulation and Climate during the Past 120,000 Years." *Nature* 419:207–14.

Rationality and Society. 2011. http://rss.sagepub.com/

Raudenbush, Stephen W., and Anthony S. Bryk. 1986. "A Hierarchical Model for Studying School Effects." *Sociology of Education* 59:1–17.

Registry of Open Access Repositories (ROAR). 2012. http://roar.eprints.org/.

Repko, Allen F. 2008. *Interdisciplinary Research: Process and Theory.* Los Angeles: Sage.

Repko, Allen F., William H. Newell, and Rick Szostak. 2012. *Case Studies in Interdisciplinary Research.* Thousand Oaks, CA: Sage Publications.

Rhoten, Diana. 2003. *A Multi-Method Analysis of the Social and Technical Conditions for Intellectual Collaboration.* San Francisco: Hybrid Vigor Institute.

Rinia, E. J., T. N. Van Leeuwen, E. W. Bruins, H. G. Van Vuren, A. F. J. Van Raan, et al. 2001. "Citation Delay in Interdisciplinary Knowledge Exchange." *Scientometrics* 51(1):293–309.

———. 2002. "Impact Measures of Interdisciplinary Research in Physics." *Scientometrics* 53(2): 241–48.

Robst, John. 2007. "Education and Job Match: The Relatedness of College Major and Work." *Economics of Education Review* 26(4):397–407.

Rogers, Everett M. 1999. "Anatomy of the Two Subdisciplines of Communication Study." *Human Communications Research* 25(4):618–31.

Rojas, Fabio. 2007. *From Black Power to Black Studies.* Baltimore: Johns Hopkins University Press.

Rooks, Noliwe M. 2006. *White Money/Black Power: The Surprising History of African American Studies and the Crisis of Race in Higher Education.* Boston: Beacon Press.

Rosenberg, Carroll-Smith, and Charles Rosenberg. 1973. "The Female Animal: Medical and Biological Views of Woman and Her Role in Nineteenth-Century America." *Journal of American History* 60(20):332–56.

Rosenberg, Nathan. 1994. *Exploring the Black Box Technology, Economics and History.* Cambridge: Cambridge University Press .

Rosich, Katherine. 2005. *A History of the American Sociological Association.* Washington, DC: American Sociological Society. http://www/asanet.org/images/asa/docs/pdf/Rosich%20 Appendices.pdf.

Rowe, John Carlos. 2002. *The New American Studies.* Minneapolis: University of Minnesota Press.

Rupp, Jam C. C. 1999. "American Studies and the Fulbright Program: A Plea for Repoliticizing." Pp. 32–52 in Hans Krabbendam and Jaap Verheul, eds., *Through the Cultural Looking Glass: American Studies in Transcultural Perspective.* Amsterdam: Vu University Press.

Rydell, Robert. 1999. "Re-Entry: NASA and the American Studies Orbit." Pp. 23–31 in Hans Krabbendam and Jaap Verheul, eds., *Through the Cultural Looking Glass: American Studies in Transcultural Perspective.* Amsterdam: Vu University Press.

Sabatier, Paul A. 1986. "Top Down and Bottom Up Approaches to Implementation Research: A Critical Analysis and Suggested Synthesis." *Journal of Public Policy* 6(1):21–48.

Sahlins, Marshall. 1999. "What Is Anthropological Enlightenment? Some Lessons from the 20th Century." *Annual Review of Anthropology* 28:i–xxii.

Saltiel, Alan. 2011. "Big Science, Small World." University of Michigan Life Science Institute. http://www.lsi.umich.edu/about/administration/saltiel-columns/bigscience.

Sampson, Robert, and W. Byron Groves. 1989. "Community Structure and Crime: Testing Social Disorganization Theory." *American Journal of Sociology* 94(4):774–802.

Schmidt, Jan C. 2010. "Prospects for a Philosophy of Interdisciplinarity." Pp. 39–41 in Robert Frodeman, Julie Thompson Klein, and Carl Mitchem, eds., *Oxford Handbook of Interdisciplinarity*. Oxford: Oxford University Press.

Schmitz, Betty. 1985. *Integrating Women's Studies into the Curriculum: A Guide and Bibliography*. Old Westbury, NY: Feminist Press.

Schofer, Evan, and Jown W. Meyer. 2005. "The World Wide Expansion of Higher Education in the Twentieth Century." *American Sociological Review* 70(6):898–920.

Scholarly Research Exchange. 2012. Home page. http://gulib.georgetown.edu/newjour/s/msg03504.html

Schummer, J. 2004. "Multidisciplinarity, Interdisciplinarity, and Patterns of Research Collaboration in Nanoscience and Nanotechnology." *Scientometrics* 59(3):425–65.

Science. 2011. Home page. http://www.sciencemag.org/.

Sewell, William H. 2005. *Logics of History: Social Theory and Social Transformation*. Chicago: University of Chicago Press.

Shank, Barry. 1992. "A Reply to Steven Watt's 'Idiocy.'" *American Quarterly* 44(3):439–48.

Shanas, Ethel. 1945. "The American Journal of Sociology through Fifty Years." *American Journal of Sociology* 50(6):522–33.

Sherif, Muzafer, and Carolyn W. Sherif. 1969. "Interdisciplinary Coordination as a Validity Check: Retrospect and Prospects." Pp. 1–20 in Muzafer Sherif and Carolyn W. Sherif, eds., *Interdisciplinary Relationships in the Social Sciences*. Chicago: Aldine Press.

Shorter, Edward. 1973. "Female Emancipation, Birth Control and Fertility in European History." *American Historical Review* 78(3):605–40.

Sibal, Kapil. 2011. "Preface." Pp. xiii–xv in Philip Altbach, ed., *The Road to Academic Excellence*. Washington, DC: World Bank. http://issuu.com/world.bank.publications; http://issuu.com/world.bank.publications/docs/9780821388051.

Silver, Nate. 2012. *The Signal and the Noise: The Art and Science of Prediction*. New York: Penguin Press.

Sklar, Robert. 1970. "American Studies and the Realities of America." *American Quarterly* 22, no. 2 (Part 1, Summer):597–605.

Slaughter, Sheila. 2004. *Academic Capitalism and the New Economy*. Baltimore: Johns Hopkins University Press.

Smith, Adam. 2007. *An Inquiry into the Nature and Causes of the Wealth Nations*. Introduction and notes by Jonathan B. Wight. Petersfield, Hampshire: Harriman House, Ltd.

Smith, Henry Nash. 1950. *Virgin Land*. Cambridge, MA: Harvard University Press.

———.1957. "Can American Studies Develop a Method?" *American Quarterly* 9, no. 2 (Part 2, Summer):197–208.

Social Science Research Network. 2012. SSRN eLibrary Statistics. http://papers.ssrn.com/s013/DisplayAbstractSearch.cfm.

Society for Clinical and Translational Medicine. 2011. "Background and Mission." http://www.ctssociety.org/?page=Background.

Soloveichik, G. L. 2011. "Battery Technologies for Large-Scale Stationary Energy Storage." *Annual Review of Chemical and Biomolecular Engineering* 2:503–27

Spalter-Roth, Roberta, Jerry A. Jacobs, and Janene Scelza. 2009. "Down Market? Findings from the 2008 ASA Job Bank Survey." Washington, DC: American Sociological Association. http://www.asanet.org/research/ASAJobBankStudy09.pdf.

Spiller, Robert E. 1960. "American Studies, Past, Present and Future." Pp. 207–20 in Joseph H.

Kwiat and Mary C. Turpie, eds., *Studies in American Culture: Dominant Ideas and Images.* Minneapolis: University of Minnesota Press.

———.1973. "Unity and Diversity in the Study of American Culture." *American Quarterly* 25(5):611–18.

———.1976. "The Fulbright-Hays Program in American Studies." Pp. 3–9 in Robert H. Walker, ed., *American Studies Abroad.* Westport, CT: Greenwood Press.

Stavins, Robert N. 2003. "Experience with Market-Based Environmental Policy Instruments." *Handbook of Environmental Economics* 1:355–435.

Steel, Edward M. 1970. "Mother Jones in the Fairmont Field, 1902." *Journal of American History* 57(2):290–307.

Stevens, Mitchell L., and Cynthia Miller-Idriss. 2009. *Academic Internationalism: U.S. Universities in Transition.* New York: Social Science Research Council.

Stimpson, Catherine R. 1986. *Women's Studies in the Untied States.* New York: Ford Foundation.

Stirling, I., et al. 2011. "Polar Bear Population Status in the Northern Beaufort Sea, Canada, 1971–2006." *Ecological Applications* 21(3):859–76.

Strober, Myra. 2011. *Interdisciplinary Conversations: Challenging Habits of Thought.* Stanford, CA: Stanford University Press.

Sullivan, Kathleen. 2011. "From Human Trafficking to Endangered Coral Reefs: Graduate Fellows Take Interdisciplinary Approach to Solving Social and Environmental Issues." *Stanford News*, March 21, 2011. http://news.stanford.edu/news/2011/march/fellows -interdisciplinary-studies-03211.html.

Sun, Guang-Shen, ed. 2005. *Readings in the Economics of the Division of Labor: The Classical Tradition.* Hackensack, NJ: World Publishing.

Swaminathan, Monkombu S. 2006. "An Evergreen Revolution." *Crop Science* 46(5):2293–2303.

Swiss Academy of Arts and Sciences (2011). "Transdisciplinary Research." http://www.trans disciplinarity.ch/e/Transdisciplinarity/.

Tate, Cecil. 1973. *The Search for a Method in American Studies.* Minneapolis: University of Minnesota Press.

Taylor, Mark. 2009. "The End of the University As We Know It." *New York Times*, April 26, A-23.

———. 2010. *Crisis on Campus: A Bold Plan for Reforming Our Colleges and Universities.* New York: Knopf.

TED: Ideas Worth Spreading. 2012. http://www.ted.com.

Theory in Action. 2011. Home page. http://www.transformativestudies.org/publications/theory -in-action-the-journal-of-tsi/.

Thomson Reuters. 2011. Journal Citation Reports. http://thomsonreuters.com/products_services/ science/science_products/a-z/journal_citation_reports.

Tierney, William, and Linda Serra Hagedorn, eds. 2011. *Increasing Access to College: Extending Possibilities to All Students.* Albany: State University of New York Press.

Times Higher Education World University Rankings 2012–13. 2012. http://www.timeshigher- education.co.uk/world-university-rankings/.

Tinto, Vincent. 1975. "Dropout from Higher Education: A Theoretical Synthesis of Recent Research." *Review of Educational Research* 45:89–125.

Trachtenberg, Alan. 1965. *Brooklyn Bridge.* Chicago: University of Chicago Press.

Trowler, Paul. 2011. University World News. "Rethinking Academic Tribes and Territories."

University World New November 20. http://www.universityworldnews.com/article.php ?story=2011111819340377.

Tuchman, Gaye. 2009. *Wannabe U: Inside the Corporate University.* Chicago: University of Chicago Press.

Turner, Stephen P. 2000. "What Are Disciplines? And How Is Interdisciplinarity Different?" Pp. 46–65 in P. Weingart and N. Stehr, eds., *Practicing Interdisciplinarity.* Toronto: University of Toronto Press.

Turner, Stephen P., and Jonathan H. Turner. 1990. *The Impossible Science: An Institutional Analysis of American Sociology.* Newbury Park, CA: Sage Publications.

Ulrich's Periodical Directory. 2011. http://ulrichsweb.serialssolutions.com/.

United Nations, Food and Agriculture Organization. 2011. "The State of Food and Agriculture 2010–2011: Women in Agriculture; Closing the Gender Gap for Development." Rome. http://www.fao.org/docrep/013/i2050e/i2050e00.htm.

University of California Commission on General Education in the 21st Century. 2007. *General Education in the 21st Century.* Berkeley, CA: Center for Studies in Higher Education. http://cshe.berkeley.edu/research/gec/.

University of Missouri, Kansas City. 2011. http://unews.com/2011/06/01/new-leadership-for -college-of-arts-sciences/.

University of Washington Center for Innovation and Research in Graduate Education. 2012. CIRGE Publications. http://depts.washington.edu/cirgeweb/c/resources-2/publications -presentations/.

US Department of Education. National Center for Education Statistics. 1970–2012. *Digest of Education Statistics: Tables on Earned Degrees Conferred.* http://nces.ed.gov/programs/digest/.

———. 1988. *National Education Longitudinal Study of 1988.* (NELS:88). http://nces.ed.gov/ surveys/nels88/.

———. 2011. National Survey of Postsecondary Faculty: Overview. http://nces.ed.gov/surveys/ nsopf/.

Vaill, Peter B. 1996. *Learning as a Way of Being.* San Francisco: Jossey Bass.

Van Leeuwen, Thed, and Robert Tijssen. 2000. "Interdisciplinary Dynamics of Modern Science: Analysis of Cross-Disciplinary Citation Flows." *Evaluation Research* 9(3):183–87.

Van Raan, A. F. J. 2005. "Fatal Attraction: Conceptual and Methodological Problems in the Ranking of Universities by Bibliometric Methods." *Scientometrics* 62(1):133–43.

Verheul, Jaap. 1999. "The Ideological Origins of American Studies." Pp. 91–103 in Hans Krabbendam and Jaap Verheul, eds., *Through the Cultural Looking Glass: American Studies in Transcultural Perspective.* Amsterdam: Vu University Press.

Vissers, Geert, and Ben Dankbaar. 2002. "Creativity in Multidisciplinary New Product Development Teams." *Creativity and Innovation Management* 11(1):31–42.

Voelz, Luke. 2011. "UI to Hire 20 Faculty for Newest 'Cluster Hires.'" *Daily Iowan*, July 8. http:// www.dailyiowan.com/2011/07/08/Metro/24059.html.

Walker, Robert. 1958. *American Studies in the United States: A Survey of College Programs.* Baton Rouge: Louisiana State University Press.

———. 1976. *American Studies Abroad.* Westport, CT: Greenwood Press.

Walters, Pamela B., and Annette Lareau. 2009. "Education Research That Matters: Influence, Scientific Rigor and Policymaking." Pp. 197–220 in Pamela B. Walters, Annette Lareau, and Sheri H. Ranis, eds., *Education Research on Trial: Policy Reform and the Call for Scientific Rigor.* New York: Routledge.

Washington, Mary Helen. 1998. "Disturbing the Peace: What Happens to American Studies if You Put African American Studies at the Center?" Presidential Address to the American Studies Association, October 29, 1997. *American Quarterly* 50(1):1–23.

Watts, Steven. 1991. "The Idiocy of American Studies: Poststructuralism, Language and Politics in the Age of Self-Fulfillment." *American Quarterly* 43(4):625–60.

Wayne State University. Interdisciplinary Studies Program. 2012. http://www.clas.wayne .edu/is/.

Wechsler, David. 1991. *WISC-III: Wechsler intelligence scale for children*. San Antonio, TX: Psychological Corporation, Harcourt Brace Jovanovich.

Weinberg, Stephen. 1994. *Dreams of a Final Theory: The Scientist's Search for the Ultimate Laws of Nature*. New York: Vintage.

Weingart, Peter. 2005. "The Impact of Bibliometrics on the Science System: Inadvertent consequences?" *Scientometrics* 62(2):117–31.

———. 2010. "A Short History of Knowledge Formations." Pp. 3–14 in Robert Frodeman, Julie Thompson Klein, and Carl Mitchem, eds., *Oxford Handbook of Interdisciplinarity*. Oxford: Oxford University Press.

Weiss, Helen A., Maria A. Quigley, and Richard J. Hayes, 2000. "Male Circumcision and Risk of HIV Infection in Sub-Saharan Africa: A Systematic Review and Meta-Analysis." *AIDS* 14(15):2361–70.

Weller, Martin. 2011. *Digital Scholar: How Technology Is Changing Scholarly Practice*. London: Bloomsbury.

Welter, Barbara. 1966. "The Cult of True Womanhood: 1820–1860." *American Quarterly* 19, no. 2 (Part 1):151–74.

Whitley, Richard. 2000 (1984). *The Intellectual and Social Organization of the Sciences*. Oxford: Clarendon Press.

Wickson, F., A. L. Carew, and A. W. Russell. 2006. "Transdisciplinary Research: Characteristics, Quandaries and Quality." *Futures* 38(9):1046–59.

Wilensky, Harold. 1964. "The Professionalization of Everyone?" *American Journal of Sociology* 70(2):137–58.

Wise, Gene. 1979. "Paradigm Dramas in American Studies: A Cultural and Institutional History of Movement." *American Quarterly* 31(3):293–337.

Zenderland, Leila. 2006. "Constructing American Studies: Culture, Identity and the Expansion of the Humanities." Pp. 273–313 in David A. Hollinger, ed., *The Humanities and the Dynamics of Inclusion since World War II*. Baltimore: Johns Hopkins University Press.

Index